Breadfruit or Chestnut?

Breadfruit or Chestnut?

Gender Construction in the French Caribbean Novel

Bonnie Thomas

LEXINGTON BOOKS

A division of
ROWMAN & LITTLEFIELD PUBLISHERS, INC.
Lanham • *Boulder* • *New York* • *Toronto* • *Oxford*

LEXINGTON BOOKS

A division of Rowman & Littlefield Publishers, Inc.
A wholly owned subsidary of The Rowman & Littlefield Publishing Group, Inc.
4501 Forbes Boulevard, Suite 200
Lanham, MD 20706

PO Box 317
Oxford
OX2 9RU, UK

Copyright © 2006 by Lexington Books

British Library Cataloguing in Publication Information Available

Library of Congress Cataloging-in-Publication Data

Thomas, Bonnie, 1975–
  Breadfruit or chestnut? : gender construction in the French Caribbean novel /
by Bonnie Thomas.
      p. cm. — (After the empire)
  Includes bibliographical references and index.
  ISBN-13: 978-0-7391-1583-1 (cloth : alk. paper)
  ISBN-10: 0-7391-1583-9 (cloth : alk. paper)
  1. Caribbean fiction (French)—History and criticism. 2. Gender identity in
literature. I. Title. II. Series.
PQ3944.T46 2006
843.009'9729—dc22   2006008349

Printed in the United States of America

⊗ ™ The paper used in this publication meets the minimum requirements of
American National Standard for Information Sciences—Permanence of Paper
for Printed Library Materials, ANSI/NISO Z39.48-1992.

Contents

Acknowledgments

This book would not have come together without the help and support of many people. First of all I would like to thank Beverley Noakes, Rob Stuart and Hélène Jaccomard for their outstanding vision, knowledge and encouragement. Working with Beverley was an honor and a privilege and I am indebted to her for her wise insights into the Caribbean, her unwavering optimism and her generous spirit. Rob's commitment to my career has long been an inspiration to me and I am very grateful to him for his attention to detail, his innovative ideas and his constructive criticism. His considered commentary and generous gift of his time were instrumental in bringing this book to life. Hélène has consistently provided challenging commentaries of my work and is a fount of knowledge and ideas. I would also like to make a special mention of Professor A. James Arnold who has been most generous in supporting my work. Katie Funk and Rebekka Istrail at Lexington Books have been efficient, enthusiastic and a dream to work with. I consider myself extremely lucky to have been the recipient of such dedication and professionalism.

I was extremely fortunate to be able to travel to Martinique, Guadeloupe and Paris as part of my research and I would like to acknowledge the generosity of Patrick Chamoiseau, Maryse Condé, Raphaël Confiant and Gisèle Pineau in allowing me to interview them. I am particularly grateful to Raphaël Confiant for the many opportunities he has offered me since that time to continue my connection with the French Caribbean. Maryse Condé and Richard Philcox's visit to Perth, Australia, in 2005 added further inspiration to my love of French Caribbean literature.

I would like to acknowledge with thanks the generous financial support I received from the University of Western Australia during my doctoral research and without which I would not have been able to pursue my dream: the Australian Postgraduate Award, the Jean Rogerson postgraduate scholarship, the UWA Graduates Association postgraduate research travel award, the Jackson scholarship for postgraduate research travel, the postgraduate research student travel award, and the Faculty of Arts postgraduate research travel grant.

Finally, I would like to thank my family and friends for their unwavering support and enthusiasm for my work over so many years. I would particularly like to thank Clare Ozich and Nicole Crawford for their intellectual insights and stimulating ideas and Gill Hallett and David Smart for their positive energy, warmth and friendship. I would like to thank Alex Thomas for his calm, intelligence and humor and Rod Lillywhite and Russell Leith for their generous support and caring. John Thomas and David Leith have also provided valuable feedback and encouragement. I would like to make a special mention of Donald, Daisy and Sally Thomas who are a constant inspiration. Most importantly, I would like to thank Margaret Thomas and Richard Barna who are my two rocks. Without their unconditional love and infinite patience I would not be where I am today.

Preface

An appreciation of the past forms a necessary backdrop to any inquiry into the present-day French Caribbean. France's introduction of slavery into Martinique and Guadeloupe during the sixteenth century permanently altered French Caribbean life and continues to haunt contemporary reality. A. James Arnold has rightly pointed out that it is essential to consider the regional sociocultural aspects of the French Caribbean when applying the principles of postcolonial theory. He reminds us that France's policy of cultural assimilation toward Martinique and Guadeloupe as well as the social and economic complexities of the plantation system mark the French Caribbean islands quite differently from former colonies found in Africa, India and the Near East.[1] With the exception of Maryse Condé who prefers to look toward the future, all the authors I interviewed in the French Caribbean emphasized the persistent effects of slavery on present-day relationships. The way in which each of these authors has appropriated the past for their own literary purposes provides a fascinating insight into this society.

When examining the French Caribbean through a gendered framework, I have found the insights of a number of feminist thinkers to be useful. Gayle Rubin's radical and innovative distinction between "sex" and "gender" in the mid-1970s has since been retheorized, problematized and made more complex by writers such as Judith Butler who, in *Gender Trouble* and later works, examines the way in which sex, as well as gender, may be read as socially constructed rather than biological.[2] By insisting on gender as a process or "a doing" without origin or end, rather than as an essentialist given, feminists such as Butler have sought to exceed the limitations of binary thinking. In the context of French Caribbean gender identity, this insistence on the socially constructed nature of sexuality and gender allows values typically identified with the masculine and the feminine to be applied to both sexes. Contemporary French Caribbean literature embodies this project, thus affirming gender as a cultural experience.

Alongside this fluid conception of gender, there also exists a more general trend of contrasting strong women with weak men. The observations of object-relations theorists such as Nancy Chodorow and Dorothy Dinnerstein provide a useful conceptual tool for explaining this gender model found in so many cultures.[3] Drawing on neo-Freudian analytical techniques and focusing on the fundamental role of the mother, these thinkers construct a novel framework for understanding why patterns of gender emerge in society. Their advances in theorizing mothering and its importance in creating femininity and dysfunctional masculinity are particularly relevant in the matrifocal context of the French Caribbean.

This study brings together both historical and theoretical sources to analyze gender identity in contemporary French Caribbean literature. A significant component of the analysis is the relationship between text and context, and the way in which historical memory constitutes a haunting backdrop for many of the novels examined. French Caribbean gender identity remains problematical and recurrent literary stereotypes reveal this society's difficulty in liberating itself from the oppressive bonds of the past.

NOTES

1. A. James Arnold, "Francophone Postcolonial Studies: The Field: Regional vs. Global Models," *Francophone Postcolonial Studies* 1, no. 2 (2003): 7.

2. Judith Butler, *Gender Trouble: Feminism and the Subversion of Identity* (New York: Routledge, Chapman & Hall, 1990). See also Eudine Barriteau-Foster, "The Construction of a Postmodernist Feminist Theory," *Social and Economic Studies* 41, no. 2 (1992).

3. Nancy Chodorow, *The Reproduction of Mothering: Psychoanalysis and the Sociology of Gender* (Berkeley: University of California Press, 1978), and Dorothy Dinnerstein, *The Mermaid and the Minotaur: Sexual Arrangements and Human Malaise* (New York: Harper & Row, 1976).

1

~~

Gender Identity and the French Caribbean

Maryse Condé cites a famous Creole proverb in the opening pages of her influential book on French Caribbean women writers, *La Parole des femmes*, "'Fem-n cé chataign, n'hom-n cé fouyapin,' c'est-à-dire: 'La femme, c'est une châtaigne, l'homme c'est un fruit à pain.'"[1] Translated into English as "woman is a chestnut and man is a breadfruit," this evocative expression underlines the resilient and tough nature of women and the tendency of men to fall apart in the face of adversity—spattering on the ground like a breadfruit as it falls from the tree. While Condé has commented that this book now appears somewhat dated,[2] many of its gendered claims continue to ring true today. Dramatically influenced by the experience of colonization and slavery, the French Caribbean islands of Martinique and Guadeloupe remain past saturated societies, as is evident in their continuing preoccupation with identity issues. Condé's work underlines the link between these damaging historical experiences and gender roles, locating gendered behavior as the result of the particular circumstances, hardships and obligations of a Caribbean slave existence. This notion runs like a thread through many of the novels studied in this volume.

In order to understand the heavily gendered nature of French Caribbean society, it is important first to consider the region's preoccupation with cultural identity. As a result of their shared history of colonization, slavery and, finally, departmentalization by France in 1946, the inhabitants of Martinique and Guadeloupe have long had a sense of "otherness" in their personal and cultural identities. By the time the

French colonizers arrived in the sixteenth century, almost all of the original Carib population had been exterminated. The majority of today's inhabitants are the descendents of slaves imported to the Caribbean in the
seventeenth century to work on the sugar plantations. There are also a
considerable number of mixed blood Caribbean people and a smaller
number of white people, both Europeans and the Caribbean-born *békés*.
Because they have had their entire existence defined for them by the
Other, the culturally dominant France, Caribbean people have long suffered from a lack of "authentic" history and tangible roots. The situation
is exacerbated by the fact that France operates both as the Other (the islands are possessions of France) and the Same (the people of Martinique
and Guadeloupe have interiorized the language and values of France).[3]
This fragmented sense of self has left French Caribbean people with a
powerful desire to belong to their own history and culture.

For the French Caribbean population, constructing a cultural identity
clearly distinct from that of France has become increasingly elusive. The
difficulty of pinpointing one's origins in a hybrid community has led
many of the region's intellectuals to reconstruct French Caribbean identity through storytelling and dialogue. For this reason the figure of the
conteur, or Caribbean storyteller, plays a vital role in the French Caribbean
historical imaginary. First arising in the context of plantation life, the *conteur* spun tales, riddles and proverbs that subverted the master's authority and instilled hope in the slaves. It is not surprising then that many contemporary *créoliste* writers such as Patrick Chamoiseau and Raphaël
Confiant attribute the role of modern-day storyteller to themselves.
Chamoiseau in particular refers to himself as a *marqueur de parole*, or
"word scratcher," in many of his novels.

The role of literature in creating a postcolonial subjectivity is pivotal in
this context, given that it was through writing that French Caribbean intellectuals first began the process of reclaiming their identity and reversing centuries of almost uninterrupted French domination. From the early
twentieth century writers and intellectuals began the process of reassess-
ing their islands' heritage as a way of counteracting their fragmented
selves. The sense of alterity experienced by French Caribbean people who
have been consistently forced to perceive themselves through the eyes of
the Other is reflected in the literary history of the region. This tradition
first saw island life defined by European outsiders, then by black writers
who wrote within a Western and often exoticized paradigm, and finally
by authors searching to define an authentic postcolonial subjectivity
through their books. The works of these more recent writers represent a
complex interplay of adaptation and appropriation of European norms.
They often feature linguistic game-playing and literary techniques in
which irony and magic realism are paramount. These works also feed into

the postmodern challenge to long-established givens such as the all-knowing, autonomous subject and therefore privilege individual, localized histories over the master discourses of the past. This postmodern element is further evident in the undisguised presence of the author, who, in a writer such as Chamoiseau, frequently intrudes into the text in the form of footnotes, glossaries and explanations. All of these techniques serve to shake the universalist ideals of traditional European literary paradigms. This reconstruction of the role of literature can perhaps best be summed up in Chamoiseau's ideal of *diversalité* in which difference and diversity are to be celebrated and are set against the monolithic tendencies of universalism.

As significant inroads were made into this reorientation of the past throughout the twentieth century, a new agenda has emerged which has broadened the definition of identity to include not only cultural identity but also personal identity. Consistent with the postmodern refusal to categorize people into homogeneous groups, this renewed quest for individual self-definition demonstrates the difficulty of cloaking all French Caribbean people with the garb of one particular racial group or social class. The current populations of Martinique and Guadeloupe attest to the diversity of their origins. with the basic categories of black, white and *métis* that dominated island life after French colonization more recently supplemented by Chinese, Syrians, Lebanese and Indians who arrived to fill the spaces left in the workforce by the abolition of slavery in 1848. It has therefore become imperative to work from a hybrid theoretical model that thrives on the vast cultural, racial and gendered differences of the French Caribbean people.

While personal identity encompasses a huge range of factors such as race, colour, class, religion, family background and personal experience, the present study focuses on the issue of gender identity which has developed as an intellectual field along a similar timeframe to the French Caribbean search for a cultural identity. Some early theorists in the realm of gender studies have been criticized for minimizing the differences between women and between men in order to theorize about groups as a whole, yet more recent thinkers have pointed to the importance of diversity and difference. These early challenges began with African-American and Asian women who could not see themselves reflected in the so-called universal category of womanhood. They have now become an entrenched part of current theory, especially in the area of postcolonial studies. As gender theory has grown to embrace men as well as women, it is now possible to paint a more nuanced picture of the constructed nature of gender in different societies.

Postcolonial feminist writers such as Gayatri Spivak and Chandra Mohanty have warned against the uncritical application of "first world" theories, developed out of a model of predominantly white, middle-class female experience, to the vastly different context of the "third world." They argue that some "first world" feminists have constructed a monolithic "third world" which fails to take into account the diversity of these societies, thereby falling into what Spivak terms the essentialist trap.[4] Nonetheless, contemporary theories of gender developed in Europe, North America and Australia provide theoretical frameworks that are useful for examining the question of gender identity in the French Caribbean. While these insights must always be placed within the context of the specificities of the Caribbean experience, they make an important contribution to understanding the operation of gender in Martinican and Guadeloupean society.

The process of harnessing theories formulated outside the Caribbean for use within the region remains a problematic undertaking as the fertility of debates on black and "third world" feminism attests. Black American feminist bell hooks writes that contemporary feminist thinkers cite sexual politics as the primary origin of our global problems. In hooks' view, white preoccupations have obscured the more specific experiences of other races, classes and cultures, thereby setting up the white worldview as the only valid approach.[5] Chandra Talpade Mohanty also alludes to the tendency of the West to conceive all alternative points of view as the Other, arguing that "third world" feminisms thereby run the risk of marginalization or ghettoization.[6] Patricia Hill Collins has developed an alternative path to female liberation with her insistence on the fundamental difference between white Western feminists and black feminists which is found in the latter's ability to express their standpoint through their own concrete experiences.[7] Hill's insistence on personal experience and situated knowledge mirrors the thoughts of some French Caribbean women writers who do not align themselves with Western ways of seeing. It is important also to realize that black women do not constitute a single, homogenous group in the same way as white women do not. Any attempt to impose a monolithic, universal approach on a study of different cultures comes fraught with danger, highlighting the need for an appreciation of cultural diversity and specificity.

Henry Louis Gates Jr. suggests a way out of this theoretical and ideological impasse by insisting on the transformative powers of applying theories to new situations: "I have found that, in the 'application' of a mode of reading to black texts, the critic, by definition, transforms the theory and . . . transforms received readings of the text into something different, a construct neither exactly 'like' its antecedents, nor entirely new."[8] The creative capacity of theory can greatly enrich an understanding of a topic or a region, particularly if it embraces both new and already existing perspectives. An appreciation of gender identity in the French

Caribbean can thus be enhanced with theories of gender not typically applied to the area.

In an essentialist approach to gender, theorists argue for an inbuilt, "essential" nature in men and women while deconstructionists refuse to categorize people according to a fixed nature. In essentialist thought, gender is aligned to sex and men are shown to have specific characteristics (for instance, rationality, insensitivity to nature) and women to have other characteristics (being intuitive, closely linked to nature). Deconstructionist theories, by contrast, argue that gender is a fluid category and that both men and women can display its variations. This study tests the deconstructionist model in a French Caribbean context and explores the notion that men and women are not constructed in a particular way because of their sex, but rather, that the cultural overlay of gender moves between the two.

A noteworthy feature of gender theory in a French Caribbean setting is the reluctance of many Caribbean women to be associated with the term "feminism," generally considered to be equivalent to radical feminism. Indeed, one might argue that French Caribbean women have constructed a monolithic "feminism" that denies the multiple strands that exist within the field. Although writing within an African-American tradition, Alice Walker's coining of the word "womanist" offers a way for nonwhite women to represent themselves, rather than adopting a label they perceive as inappropriate to their experience.[9] Walker's term has found resonance among anglophone women from Africa who also shy away from an association with the (radical) feminist label in a phenomenon similar to that in the Caribbean. As African woman writer Buchi Emecheta writes, "I will not be called a feminist here, because it is European. It is as simple as that. I just resent that . . . I don't like being defined by them . . . It is just that it comes from outside and I don't like people dictating to me."[10] Emecheta's words mirror the sentiments of many French Caribbean women. There are a number of points of connection between female writers in Africa and those in Martinique and Guadeloupe, not the least being their fear of radical feminism.

Maryse Condé, Simone Schwarz-Bart and Gisèle Pineau have all offered their opinions on the question of feminism and French Caribbean society. They each stress the particularities of their situation, distancing themselves from the perceived dominant views of "Western" feminism, which again they regard as equivalent to radical feminism. As the most prolific writer of the three and the one whose words have been most widely represented in books, interviews and conferences, Condé has spoken in detail about this topic. When asked whether she would consider herself a feminist, Condé offers her vision of what constitutes feminism.

I was never somebody fighting for what they call the woman's cause. I was just expressing my own feelings, and I happen to be a woman. So I was speaking of me, and of people similar to me, i.e., women. But I am not building a wall against the male part of society. Am I feminist? I am not sure. I do believe in that old West Indian and West African tradition: if a woman is not associated with a man in a harmonious way, her life is not complete. I do believe that a man has to be somewhere in your life. Of course, he has to be an equal partner. He mustn't be in your life to debilitate you, to suppress your voice, or to prevent you from expressing yourself. But I do believe that without him life is not fulfilled. I do believe also that having children is much more important than writing books. I have written books, okay, I'm happy about that. But, I'm so much happier about my daughters, about their achievements, about my granddaughter and grandson. I'm just a woman speaking for myself and for human beings like me who happen sometimes to be afraid of expressing their own selves. As I am not afraid of anything, I speak for them. But, I'm not a woman warrior, so to speak.[11]

As Condé makes patently clear in this passage, she is not so much interested in blaming men for the exploitation that exists in Caribbean society as understanding and explaining why a situation of inequality has arisen. In *La Parole des femmes* Condé attributes the structure of male-female relationships in the French Caribbean to the experience of slavery, which broke all previous family structures and denied slaves the right to autonomy over their own lives. Thus, she does not agree with the radical feminist agenda of asserting women's rights *against* men. "The kind of world that the radical feminists are dreaming of frightens me. Petrifies me."[12] Her approach to women's liberation is one of living in harmony with men, where equality forms an integral part of the relationship. While this gendered arrangement constitutes a part of many feminist hopes, Condé does not feel comfortable labelling this approach "feminist." Her words highlight above all her disinclination to associate herself with the ideals of radical feminism and her belief in the necessity of grounding the Caribbean female experience in the region's history.

Simone Schwarz-Bart has spoken less about her feelings on gender than Condé, but she also conveys a vision of Caribbean life that she has seen and experienced. For example, Schwarz-Bart takes up the common image of the drifting and irresponsible man in *Pluie et vent sur Télumée Miracle*, but the portrait, while unflattering, is not laced with radical feminist judgment. She acknowledges that the absence of the father figure is a constant thread in her narrative, reflecting the reality of many French Caribbean women. "C'est ce que j'ai vécu. Pas moi, mais mon entourage, cette défection des pères; de l'homme" [That is what I lived. Not me, but the people around me, this defection of fathers, of men].[13] Schwarz-Bart's words are simple and matter-of-fact, further attesting to the idea that these women are interested in portraying their own worldview and not creating generalizations applicable to all.

Schwarz-Bart also sheds light on the gender imbalance experienced by so many in the French Caribbean, drawing attention to the stability of women as men pass fluidly through their lives: "Mes amis parlaient de plusieurs pères . . . On parlait de beau-père, pas de père, d'un homme de passage, dans la maison. Les femmes, les mères, recherchaient un père, un poteau-mitan, mais se retrouvaient chaque fois toutes seules" [My friends always used to talk about several fathers . . . We would talk about a stepfather, but not a father, about a man passing through the house. Women, mothers, used to look for a father, a central support, but each time they would find themselves alone].[14] This statement is a powerful illustration of the way in which women have had to assume the role of provider and carer in many families in the French Caribbean.

For Gisèle Pineau, feminism does have a role to play in French Caribbean society, but "c'est un féminisme qui s'exprime pour les femmes et pas contre les hommes. Nous avons une histoire, une histoire aux Antilles, je ne peux pas la mettre de côté et dire qu'elle n'a pas d'importance, qu'elle n'a pas de conséquences sur les relations entre les hommes et les femmes d'aujourd'hui" [it is a feminism which expresses itself for women and not against men. We have a history, a history in the Caribbean that I cannot put aside and say that it is not important, that it does not have consequences for the relationships between men and women today].[15] Placing her conception of gender relations firmly in its historical context, Pineau echoes Condé's and Schwarz-Bart's emphasis on the situated nature of French Caribbean gender identity.

Pineau discusses the stereotypical images of men and women in the Caribbean, shedding light on the image of the strong women likened to the all-powerful *femme matador* and the irresponsible men who flit from woman to woman like a butterfly. Speaking of women she interviewed for *Femmes des Antilles*, Pineau remarks that "presque toutes ont cette façon de valoriser l'homme, de le rassurer, de le considérer comme leur enfant. Je crois que cela vient directement de la période esclavagiste" [almost all of them have this manner of valorizing men, of reassuring them, of considering them as their child. I believe this comes directly from the time of slavery].[16] Like Condé, Pineau situates the origin of these inequalities back in that "time of slavery." According to Pineau, black men under slavery did not have the same status as other men who could assert their ownership over their family; rather, partners, wives and children remained the property of the master. Against this backdrop, Pineau records the extraordinary ability of women to survive and sustain life.

An exploration of this historically determined approach to French Caribbean gender roles makes an important starting point when exploring gender within the region's literature. While the role of slavery in moulding contemporary relationships between men and women may be contested in favour of the argument that men have always oppressed women, it nonetheless represents one key to unlocking the way in which men and women relate today. A prominent legacy of slavery was the creation of a phenomenon of "strong women" and "weak men," which, although certainly representing a simplified version of gendered relationships, finds resonance in much contemporary literature. By treating slaves as little more than animals, the white masters effectively denied their charges sovereignty over their own lives. Black male slaves were further denied rights to any children they fathered and were therefore subject to a symbolic castration by their masters. The profound psychological scars of this period continue to reverberate in contemporary relationships with family responsibilities frequently left to women and their extended families. This enduring gender arrangement is exemplified in the dominance of the French Caribbean matrifocal family where the all-powerful mother reigns supreme and the father is noteworthy for his frequent absence and unreliability.

The plantation system was a complex social and economic network dependent upon a rigidly controlled hierarchy of power and submission. While black field slaves were firmly relegated to the bottom of the plantation's social hierarchy, black female slaves suffered additional oppression because of their sex. Male slaves were valued only for the economic contribution they made to the plantation, yet women were expected to perform both sexual and economic tasks. These duties included sexual favours for white masters and more importantly, childbearing, which was considered an economic event that signalled the arrival of a new slave. However, some female slaves were able to transform their oppression into a means of autonomy by using their body as a bartering asset. By bearing a child to a white master or any other white person in authority, black female slaves could sometimes find themselves in easier working conditions than if they had only black children. These relationships with white men could also be advantageous given that they could lead to a lighter workload and preferential treatment for their children.

A nineteenth-century Haitian proverb encapsulates the importance of colour in this region where a vicious system of exploitation pivots on the shade of one's skin: "Every rich man is a mulatto; every poor man is a black."[17] Within the plantation system, social status was inextricably linked to skin color and therefore mixed blood slaves enjoyed certain privileges not available to their black counterparts. For example, they often worked as artisans or house servants rather than doing the backbreaking work in the fields. Before emancipation, "brown" men and women were freed as individuals more often than dark-skinned blacks and skin color was clearly associated with the distribution of labor.

Given the pervasive repercussions of skin color that continue to characterize Caribbean societies, it is significant that female slaves had the opportunity of exceeding the limitations of this system through their reproductive capacity while male slaves did not. As Olive Senior asserts, "it is the Caribbean female who has in the past carried the burden of moving the family to higher status."[18] Women were also able to gain a degree of autonomy with the opportunity to retain power over their children, a power denied to black slave fathers. Although reproduction did not favour black slave women with black children, as social and material improvement required the lightening of the skin and a relationship with the master, maternity continued to be valued for its capacity to provide a steady and free source of labor. It can therefore be argued that women were in fact more valuable than men under slavery because they could offer both sexual and economic advantages for their masters while male slaves could only ever be work machines.

Edouard Glissant argues that an enduring product of this period was the creation of the Martinican "anti-family."[19] In *Le Discours antillais* he draws attention to the fact that the slave family amounted to little more than the coupling of a man and a woman for the profit of the master. Glissant also acknowledges the presence of certain African traditions in the newly created Martinican "anti-family," including the powerful role occupied by the mother, the importance of the female-dominated extended family and the significance of women in relation to work. Yet even within this more positive conception of the family, Glissant emphasizes the negative legacy of slavery. He argues that even as the Martinican "anti-family" grew beyond the simple delineation of woman as dam and man as sire, it remained a place of psychic unrest, a *"perversion de la filiation originelle"* [*perversion of the original filiation*][20]. The gendered familial roles that developed under slavery contribute to an understanding of gender positions adopted within the modern-day family.

Through a study of Glissant's fictional characters in novels such as *Le Quatrième Siècle*, *La Case du commandeur* and *Tout-monde*, Valérie Loichot examines the role occupied by the symbolic father within the French Caribbean family and its consequences for the development of gender roles. Loichot situates her work in a postcolonial context, arguing that the varied manifestations of the father figure in Glissant's work "rejects the Western idea of an omnipresent, omnipotent single father" and highlights instead that fatherhood is constantly being renamed, reconstructed and redefined.[21] In Loichot's view, the origins of the Caribbean father can be traced either to the white master, a violent wielder of power, or to the black male slave who is notable for his absence, neither of whom adequately fill the fatherly role. The father function appears fraught from the beginning and partially explains the reluctance and apparent inability of Caribbean men to act responsibly in this position within the family.

Loichot also brings to attention the conflicting familial models that arise between the extended slave family, usually dominated by women, and the patriarchal nuclear family that characterizes the master's family unit.[22] These two kinships systems intermingled, however, and the master came to dominate as father in the frequent absence of the slave father who could be sold without his family or killed in the fields. The organization of the plantation system meant that the slave family was a constantly changing phenomenon, "a permeable and open structure,"[23] that was able to accept the incorporation of new elements and the disappearance of old through frequent adaptation. The central authority of the master, however, appears as "a violently imposed, grafted element,"[24] reinforcing Glissant's conception of the Caribbean "anti-family."

In the face of frequent paternal absence, the role of the Caribbean mother needed to expand and she became the one who provided strength and stability for her family. The Creole proverb made famous in Simone Schwarz-Bart's *Pluie et vent sur Télumée Miracle* encapsulates the specifically female capacity to resist and triumph over adversity: "les seins ne sont jamais trop lourds pour la poitrine" [one's breasts are never too heavy for one's chest]. Sociologists such as Raymond Smith and Diane Austin have demonstrated that a range of households exist in the Caribbean, including some with male heads, but that the majority remain matrifocal. Francesca Velayoudom Faithful affirms that women are traditionally the strongholds of the family and that the mother passes on the flame of responsibility to her daughter.[25] Raymond Smith has shown that the "theme of male 'irresponsibility' in marriage and fatherhood is insistent and recurrent in modern West Indian social life."[26] This behavioral pattern contrasts dramatically with the connected and involved conduct of women within the family.

An examination of male and female attitudes to parenting reveals an important divergence that further contributes to the reduced function of the father figure. While bearing and bringing up children is considered a natural and desirable part of being a Caribbean woman, for men, the importance lies more in the making of babies than in bringing them up: "'fathering' a child—as opposed to parenting—[is seen] as the true sign of manhood."[27] It is significant that children generally are perceived not as a joint responsibility in a family situation, but as ultimately the responsibility of their mothers.[28] Livia Lesel suggests that this dominant maternal role has served as a self-fulfilling prophecy in which women actually exclude their partners from involvement with their children to the point where: "L'enfant, c'est l'affaire de la femme antillaise" [children are the business of Caribbean women].[29] Caribbean women's experience of mothering, however, comes across as a process of struggle, hardship and sacrifice. In the absence of reliable male support, whether financial or emotional, women have been required to assume the role of sole parent and provider for the family.

A further contributor to the low rate of male participation in the family is the lack of positive definition of the male gender role. While potential female role models surround girls as they are growing up, the frequent absence of men in the family denies young boys this formative influence. "Boys are . . . growing up in situations where female gender identity is strong, and, where a father or other older male is absent, he might not be able to absorb notions of male status and identity through role modelling in the home. On whom does such a boy model himself?"[30] While some sociologists have demonstrated that male role modelling may occur in peer group "crews,"[31] the lack of direction in how to become a male in Caribbean society means that many young boys unconsciously absorb the notion that a man's role is not within the family. Rather, they are free to drift through life evading responsibility.

Barry Chevannes observes that "achieving and maintaining one's masculinity may be less secure in cultures where women also appropriate the same symbols that men use as signifiers of male identity."[32] While the dominant cultural expectation is for men to take up the leadership role in the home, the overwhelming pattern of female-headed households provides an additional challenge to the Caribbean man's sense of masculinity. The frequent unavailability of positive male role models creates a vicious circle where men perpetuate patterns of unreliability by passing them onto their children through lack of involvement in their offspring's lives. Young girls also model their expectations of men on those of their mothers. The parental models that children absorb as they are growing up perpetuate a situation of unequal power in both sexes.

Valérie Loichot offers a damning analysis of the lack of male role models within the family, arguing:

> There is . . . no possible identification with the father, the Name of the Father—no Oedipus complex where the son projects himself in the position of the father—rather only a constant subordination, a constant immaturity. In Martinique, the name father, *père*, is reserved for God, the captain of a soccer team, or other authorities; the father is *papa*. The Caribbean man cannot be father, and cannot have a father.[33]

Male infidelity, a common feature of French Caribbean life, is an additional contributing factor to the weak paternal role in the family. Maryse Condé states in *La Parole des femmes* that such behavior is an example of Caribbean men reacting to their feelings of frustration and dispossession by retreating into attitudes of irresponsibility that have survived the political evolution of the islands.[34] The tendency to indulge in adulterous affairs is considered part of the privilege of becoming an African Caribbean man and is a way to prove his virility. The fear of being labelled a homosexual in an island that resolutely refuses to acknowledge a gay culture is another reason for the prevalence of male infidelity in the French Caribbean. Infidelity is linked to virility and in popular mythology a true French Caribbean man should be able to take any woman at any time.

It is interesting to observe that no writers make a comment on female infidelity, revealing the potency of textual absence. While male characters are valorized or cursed for their butterfly-like ways, female characters are exempt from judgment. In no way taking away from the image of the courageous Caribbean women who battle to provide for their families, it is curious that the partners of these promiscuous men are completely silenced. One wonders then what each sex is gaining from this sharply contrasting image of gender identity. Perhaps it allows men to retain the social validation offered by sexual virility and women to reinforce the picture of their long-suffering life. Either way, it is a striking absence that is evident in all the books studied in this volume, despite the markedly different approaches of their authors.

David Murray suggests that a stereotypical "hypermasculine" image of men "is supported by men and women across racial, class, and educational lines and acts as a central symbol in combating the historical, racialized imagery of the weak and powerless colonized male subject."[35] As we have seen, black female slaves were arguably able to gain some sense of sovereignty over their lives while male slaves suffered complete emasculation under the plantation system. The creation of an exaggerated masculinity characterized by promiscuity and sometimes violence toward women appears as a partial redress to this state of historical oppression. The psychological uncertainty that underpins this gendered stance is evident in the development of attitudes of ambivalence toward women: on the one hand, Caribbean men are permanently attached to their mothers and, on the other, they are promiscuous in relation to their partners.[36]

Within this negative familial framework, the need to reconstruct the father figure becomes a way of combating constricting and oppressive gender roles. Loichot suggests that Glissant's fictional work provides a model of success in this challenging task, asserting that "his texts offer the testimony of a long and painful work of reconstruction of the father, who emerges not as a centralized, authoritarian, dominating locus but as a conglomerate figure, patched up with the thread of fragmented voices that compose the community."[37] Loichot's comments expose a possible way forward for the positive definition of male gender identity, one in which men and women come together as a group rather than remaining as isolated individuals who must battle against the painful legacies of the past.

While Loichot specifically mentions the reconstruction of the father, it is also possible to see the reconstructive powers of female community in writers such as Simone Schwarz-Bart and Maryse Condé. These supportive groups of women serve to bolster other women in times of intense suffering. We see this, for example, when Télumée's marriage to Elie ends and she falls into a deep depression. When two of her female neighbors declare their faith in her, they ultimately help to revive the heartbroken young woman. These supportive female communities are a particular feature of the texts of French Caribbean women writers, although Schwarz-Bart and others also demonstrate the patterns of conflict that exist between women. In the same example of *Pluie et vent sur Télumée Miracle*, both Télumée and Reine Sans Nom suffer from the jealousy of their female neighbours. These women undermine their sisters' happiness and prosperity, inflicting their jealous rages on Télumée and Reine Sans Nom.

The patterns of conflict and community that exist in the novels attest to the complexities of a society struggling to find a place for itself in the ambiguities of its history. Edouard Glissant in *Le Discours antillais* gives one of the most impassioned accounts of the effects of French colonial policy on Martinique and Guadeloupe. In his chapter entitled "Histoire, histoires" he delineates the opposition between history with a capital "H" that is synonymous with Western history and the myriad histories that exist among the creolized peoples of the French Caribbean. The imposition of the Western historical model is symbolized in the brutal uprooting of slaves from Africa and their transplantation onto Caribbean soil without regard for their language, culture or family bonds. This violent period marks the beginning of what Glissant terms a "non-history," a historical imaginary that is characterized by rupture rather than continuity and which dominates French Caribbean culture until the twenty-first century.[38] The unequal relationship that has developed between France and its Caribbean colonies has resulted in the near erasure of Creole culture and the unquestioning embrace of all things French. The continuing dominance of French culture, economics and politics places Martinique and Guadeloupe in a unique situation that influences any discussion of identity issues. These historical considerations also condition personal identity and are particularly potent when examining the nature of gender in French Caribbean society.

The contrast between historical determinism and gender as construct remains a hotly contested debate in contemporary scholarship and is mirrored in Caribbean authors' own approach to this subject. Chamoiseau, Confiant and Pineau, for example, continue to look toward the past to explain present-day behavior. Maryse Condé, by contrast, declares in a 2001 interview that French Caribbean people need to come to terms with the fact that slavery was abolished more than 150 years ago and that it is now time to look toward the future. She also comments that her own ground-breaking work, *La Parole des femmes*, was published a long time ago and needs to be supplemented by more forward-looking texts. It is therefore insightful to observe the ways in which contemporary French Caribbean writers appropriate the past for their own purposes. They create a textualized memory in their novels, revealing their valuation of the legacies of the past and their opinion of its relevance to the future. The novels chosen for this study particularly underline the heavily gendered nature of these historical legacies.

Each book has been chosen for its insight into the construction and perception of gender identity in the French Caribbean and therefore are not confined to the most recent publications of each author. In a writer such as Edouard Glissant who rarely discusses gender overtly, an earlier and a later text appear most attuned to the theme of gender identity. The comparison between older fictional works and those produced by a younger generation of writers focuses new light on the nature of gender relations in the region. In the first generation of these writers, a generation including Edouard Glissant and Simone Schwarz-Bart, there was a tendency to stereotype notions of the "strong" woman and the "weak" man. Among more recent authors such as Gisèle Pineau, however, this rigid view is changing and her work depicts a number of characters that refuse to conform to gendered norms.

The present work examines the construction of gender identity in the light of these major twentieth-century preoccupations and highlights the trends that are emerging as these writers make the transition to the twenty-first century. An analysis of the presentations of gender in ten contemporary works of fiction reveals the extent to which the authors conform to or challenge dominant cultural paradigms. The progression of novels demonstrates the authors' engagement with gendered stereotypes and their gradual movement toward a more fluid conception of contemporary gender roles.

In Simone Schwarz-Bart's *Pluie et vent sur Télumée Miracle* and Maryse Condé's *Moi, Tituba, sorcière . . . noire de Salem* the theme of the "strong woman" and the "weak man" emerges with clarity. This trend is most evident in the stoic vision of the Lougandor women versus disempowered male characters such as Elie and l'ange Médard [Angel Medard], and in the contrast between Tituba and her conniving husband John Indien. While these novels depict clearly delineated figures of female strength and male weakness, they also portray characters who highlight the fluidity of gender. One finds, therefore, examples of "feminine" men and "masculine" women in the books. Their authors, in contrast to certain male *créoliste* writers who privilege the male *conteur*, draw attention to the role women play in the transmission of oral culture with their depiction of female storytellers. They also explore gendered themes such as female solidarity, the positive feminine qualities associated with nature, healing and spirituality, non-traditional definitions of motherhood, and the irresponsibility of men.

Edouard Glissant's books tend not to focus specifically on gender, concentrating instead on the psychological and cultural effects of the French Caribbean's historical lack. Gendered preoccupations nonetheless emerge as an important theme in *Le Quatrième Siècle* and *La Case du commandeur*. Glissant's work underlines the way in which the scars of the past continue to condition male-female relationships in the Caribbean. He portrays, for example, a debilitating sexual alienation that plagues many of his characters. *La Case du commandeur* represents a rare insight into Glissant's conception of the female psyche and his protagonist demonstrates some of the contradictions of Caribbean womanhood. His large cast of characters includes gendered stereotypes such as the *femme matador* who courageously resists life's trials and the *nègre marron*, the hero of male philosophical thought. He also acknowledges the capacity of men to exhibit feminine qualities and women to display masculine traits.

A comparison between Patrick Chamoiseau's *Texaco* and Maryse Condé's *Les Derniers Rois mages* reveals two different faces of the *femme matador*. While both texts' protagonists demonstrate the characteristics of this celebrated figure of female resistance, Chamoiseau's and Condé's characters form a striking contrast to each other. Despite her human failings, Chamoiseau's Marie-Sophie emerges as an overwhelmingly positive character with her tenacious fight for Texaco. *Les Derniers Rois mages'* Debbie, however, appears as a victim of her surroundings, her obsessive need for "political correctness" manifesting itself through the constant subjugation of her husband. Both books highlight the enduring presence of history as well as portraying the themes of the unreliability of male behavior, the fluidity of gender and alternative understandings of maternity.

The depiction of gender identity in the works of *créoliste* writers is somewhat problematic given the tendency of these writers to privilege the male voice and to portray their characters through stereotypes. Patrick Chamoiseau's *Solibo Magnifique* and Raphaël Confiant's *Eau de café* draw heavily on satirical humor, employing exaggerated depictions of Caribbean men and women which provide a fresh perspective on gendered norms. While both books are humorous and entertaining, they also reveal some of the more serious undercurrents of gender inequalities in French Caribbean society. In contrast to novels such as *Pluie et vent sur Télumée Miracle* and *Moi, Tituba, sorcière . . . noire de Salem*, these novels feature a male narrator who links with the mythology surrounding the *conteur* in French Caribbean history, highlighting the masculinist bias of this literary movement. Their authors also explore issues such as the role of maternity, the categorization of women into prostitute or angel, and the positive valuation of qualities such as connection with nature.

Gisèle Pineau is the youngest writer discussed in this work and her approach forms a striking contrast to the *créolistes* in her refusal to conform to stereotypes. Initially finding a space for herself within the *créoliste* movement, Pineau has since drifted away from its narrow confines, preferring to explore a wide range of themes, characters and contexts. Pineau's first novel, *La Grande Drive des esprits*, portrays familiar gender stereotypes, but the author rarely accepts them at face value. Rather, Pineau nuances her characters, demonstrating the fluid nature of gendered characteristics and the impossibility of confining her fictional creations to narrow categories. Like Chamoiseau and Confiant, she employs satirical humor to convey the poignant realities of the French Caribbean in an entertaining manner. *L'Espérance-macadam* further extends this theme, depicting a constellation of characters who reject categorization into simple stereotypes. The characters in this novel appear deeply conditioned by history and the culture of violence that surrounds them results in a disturbing presentation of male-female relationships.

Together these works provide a compelling picture of the evolution of gender identity in French Caribbean literature. They also highlight the importance of history in engaging with past, present and future stereotypes. The complex interplay of text and context underlines the need to bring together sociology, history and literature to provide a fuller vision of the construction of French Caribbean gender identity at the dawn of a new century.

Clearly the experiences of slavery and colonization had a dramatic impact on the development of French Caribbean society. The continuing preoccupation with the past among the region's intellectuals and novelists emphasizes the importance of these historical events in shaping French Caribbean identity. However, there are also universal aspects to French Caribbean gender identity that respond well to a combined Caribbean and non-Caribbean theoretical approach. An enduring by-product of these past events was the emergence of a predominantly matrifocal society where the role of the Caribbean mother became central in the raising of her children, further reinforced by the frequent absence of the father. The insights of object-relations theorists such as Nancy Chodorow and Dorothy Dinnerstein therefore become a particularly useful tool for analyzing the assumption of gender identity under these conditions of maternal dominance. Furthermore, as gender relations continue to evolve in the Caribbean with men and women resisting simple gender categorization, the feminist understanding of the constructed nature of gender provides a helpful means of explaining the phenomena of "feminine" men and "masculine" women. An exploration of gender identity in contemporary French Caribbean literature thereby benefits from a multipronged theoretical approach, while the Caribbean experience nuances today's theoretical abstractions.

NOTES

1. Maryse Condé, *La Parole des femmes: Essai sur des romancières des Antilles de langue française* (Paris: L'Harmattan, 1979), 4.

2. Maryse Condé, interview by Bonnie Thomas, Montebello, Guadeloupe, 27 June 2001.

3. For further discussion of this issue, see Richard D. E. Burton, "The French West Indies *à l'heure de l'Europe*: An Overview," in Richard D. E. Burton and Fred Reno (eds.), *French and West Indian: Martinique, Guadeloupe and French Guiana Today* (London: Macmillan, 1995), 1–19.

4. Donna Landry and Gerald MacLean (eds.), *The Spivak Reader* (New York: Routledge, 1996), 68.

5. bell hooks, *Talking Back: Thinking Feminist, Thinking Black* (Boston: South End Press, 1989), 19.

6. Chandra Talpade Mohanty, "Under Western Eyes: Feminist Scholarship and Colonial Discourses," in Chandra Talpade Mohanty, Ann Russo and Lourdes Torres (eds.), *Third World Women and the Politics of Feminism* (Bloomington: Indiana University Press, 1991), 51.

7. Patricia Hill Collins, *Black Feminist Thought: Knowledge, Consciousness and the Politics of Empowerment* (New York: Routledge, 1991), 17.

8. Henry Louis Gates Jr., *Black Literature and Literary Theory* (New York: Methuen, 1984), 4.

9. Alice Walker, *In Search of Our Mothers' Gardens: Womanist Prose* (London: The Women's Press, 1987), xi.

10. Buchi Emecheta in a 1989 interview. Cited in Juliana Makuchi Nfah-Abbenyi, *Gender in African Women's Writing: Identity, Sexuality, and Difference* (Bloomington: Indiana University Press, 1997), 7.

11. Mohamed B. Taleb-Khyar, "An Interview with Maryse Condé and Rita Dove," *Callaloo* 14, no. 2 (1991): 358.

12. Taleb-Khyar, "An Interview with Maryse Condé and Rita Dove," 359.

13. Roger Toumson (ed.), "Interview avec Simone et André Schwarz-Bart: Sur les pas de Fanotte," *Textes, études et documents* 2 (1979): 17.

14. Toumson, "Interview avec Simone et André Schwarz-Bart," 17.

15. Gisèle Pineau, unpublished interview by Bonnie Thomas, Paris, 12 July 2001.

16. M.-J. DuFour, "Gisèle Pineau: La fin des tabous," *Le Figaro*, 20 mai 1998.

17. Michel Leiris, *Contacts de civilisations en Martinique et en Guadeloupe* (Paris: Unesco, 1985), 31.

18. Olive Senior, *Working Miracles: Women's Lives in the English-Speaking Caribbean* (Cave Hill, Barbados: Institute of Social and Economic Research, University of the West Indies; London: James Currey; Bloomington: Indiana University Press, 1991), 27.

19. Edouard Glissant, *Le Discours antillais* (Paris: Seuil, 1981), 97. Original italics.

20. Glissant, *Le Discours antillais*, 148. Original italics.

21. Valérie Loichot, "Negations and Subversions of Paternal Authority in Glissant's Fictional Works: (*Le Quatrième Siècle, La Case du commandeur, Tout-monde*)," in Eva Paulino Bueno, Terry Caesar and William Hummel (eds.), *Naming the Father: Legacies, Genealogies and Explorations of Fatherhood in Modern and Contemporary Literature* (Lanham, Md.: Lexington Books, 2000), 97.

22. Loichot, "Negations and Subversions of Paternal Authority," 99.

23. Loichot, "Negations and Subversions of Paternal Authority," 100.

24. Loichot, "Negations and Subversions of Paternal Authority," 101.

25. Francesca Velayoudom Faithful, "La Femme antillaise," *Présence Africaine* 153 (1996): 112.

26. Raymond T. Smith, *Kinship and Class in the West Indies: A Genealogical Study of Jamaica and Guyana* (Cambridge: Cambridge University Press, 1988), 117.

27. Senior, *Working Miracles*, 66.

28. Senior, *Working Miracles*, 116.

29. Livia Lesel, *Le Père oblitéré: Chronique antillaise d'une illusion* (Paris: L'Harmattan, 1995), 7.

30. Senior, *Working Miracles*, 38.

31. Peter J. Wilson, "Caribbean Crews: Peer Groups and Male Society," *Caribbean Studies* 10, no. 4 (1970): 1.

32. Barry Chevannes, *Learning to Be a Man: Culture, Socialization and Gender Identity in Five Caribbean Communities* (Kingston: University of the West Indies Press, 2001), 219.

33. Loichot, "Negations and Subversions of Paternal Authority," 101.

34. Condé, *La Parole des femmes*, 36.

35. David A. B. Murray, "Homosexuality, Society, and the State: An Ethnography of Sublime Resistance in Martinique," *Identities* 2, no. 3 (1996): 252.

36. Chevannes, *Learning to Be a Man*, 2.

37. Loichot, "Negations and Subversions of Paternal Authority," 97.

38. Glissant, *Le Discours antillais*, 131–32.

2

*

Literary Background
and Gender Bias

J. Michael Dash states that French Caribbean literature grew essentially
from the experience of slavery and its aftermath, arguing that there are
"less than two centuries of writing that could properly be called
Caribbean."[1] He asserts, moreover, that it was the milieu of a post-
plantation society that allowed a literature to emerge in Martinique and
Guadeloupe because of the colonizers' policy of cultural assimilation. Jack
Corzani, the author of a six-volume study of French Caribbean literature,
attests to the importance of these beginnings in slavery as well as to the
subsequent struggle over colonial status, noting that slavery, freedom, independence and loyalty are common obsessions in Caribbean writing.[2]
Créoliste writers Patrick Chamoiseau and Raphaël Confiant affirm that it
is from the plantation system that one can trace the birth of the *conteur
créole*, or Caribbean storyteller. Enduring figures in Caribbean mythology,
these storytellers embody a cleverly disguised resistance to the colonial
order in the passing of their multilayered stories and histories from one
generation to the next.[3] Although the *conteurs* form part of an oral tradition, their importance in the written domain is evident in the proliferation
of contemporary literature centred on their role in the construction of a
French Caribbean identity. The experience of slavery and the subsequent
development of post-plantation society after 1848 thus provide vital seeds
of germination for the creation of French Caribbean literature.

In opposition to critics such as Dash who trace a French Caribbean literary history of approximately two hundred years, certain leading intellectuals from Martinique have cast doubt on the whole notion of
"Caribbean literature." A prominent example is Aimé Césaire, the

groundbreaking poet and politician from Martinique, who began writing in the 1930s when there was no Caribbean literary framework available to him. In the face of this paradigmatic absence, Césaire placed himself within the traditions of European modernism, rather than in the Caribbean context from which he originated. While the focus of Césaire's work is on distinctly Caribbean issues of identity, his writing nonetheless reflects the dramatic collision of his theoretical grounding in classical humanism and the daily realities he observes in a culturally dominated Martinique.[4] In his perception of the lack of a tangible Caribbean literary framework and his consequent association with European artistic trends such as surrealism, Césaire casts doubt on the concept of a literature that has flourished in Martinique and Guadeloupe since the aftermath of slavery.

In a subsequent generation, Martinican intellectual Edouard Glissant, who began his writing career in the 1950s, situates himself more firmly within a Caribbean context than Césaire. However, he argues that although there may be individual Martinican writers, there is no Martinican literature and no literary audience in Martinique.[5] In his book, *Soleil de la conscience*, published in 1956, Glissant alludes to a nation "becoming" and therefore to a country incapable of producing a distinct national literature. "Or aux Antilles, d'où je viens, on peut dire qu'un peuple positivement se construit" [In the Antilles, where I come from, it is possible to say that a people is actually constructing itself].[6] Novelist Simone Schwarz-Bart has stated in an interview that Caribbean literature is "une littérature en marche" [a literature on the move],[7] while Jean Bernabé, Patrick Chamoiseau and Raphaël Confiant have written that Caribbean literature does not exist and that it is still in a state of pre-literature.[8] With these varied responses to the notion of a French Caribbean literature, a discussion of Martinique and Guadeloupe's literary heritage thus becomes a highly contested theoretical domain.

Martinique and Guadeloupe remain economically, politically and culturally dependent upon France and therefore there is an intimate link between the literature produced in the French Caribbean and literary fashions in France. Roger Toumson, for example, outlines three distinct phases in French Caribbean literature, all of which were dictated by the French market. The first was a literature of exoticism which dominated until the 1930s; the second arose as a result of *négritude* and the French interest in black literature; and the third was sparked by Frantz Fanon's *Peau noire, masques blancs* and developed into the literary movement of *antillanité*.[9] From this schematization it is clear that French Caribbean literature does not exist independently and for itself. Rather, it is heavily reliant on France not only for the publication of Caribbean works of literature but also for providing a large part of the literary audience for these books.

A number of factors help to explain this curious situation of a French Caribbean literature which exists primarily as a result of French subsidization. Maryse Condé, for example, remarks that Caribbean people tend not to read and that they access ideas more through newspapers and television than books. She also comments that Caribbean people only have a vague idea that the novels and anthologies by Caribbean writers are published in Paris.[10] Largely for economic reasons, the population in the French Caribbean islands are traditionally not buyers or readers of books. Moreover, the language dichotomy of French and Creole in Martinique and Guadeloupe also conditions the lack of reader interest with the emphasis on Creole as a verbal art form rather than a written one. Consequently, there are very few Caribbean publishers and the ones that do exist are reluctant to take on serious fiction. Patrick Chamoiseau, for example, presented his novel *Chronique des sept misères* to local publishing houses in the Caribbean and was rejected by all of them for fear of commercial failure.[11] Finally, French publishers aim at a French market and not a local Caribbean one, which further alienates Martinican and Guadeloupean writers from potential readers in their home islands.

While exoticism and European literary models dominated Caribbean literature prior to 1930, writers since then have increasingly focused on developing their own literary style. The turning point for this new way of interpreting reality was the publication of Aimé Césaire's *Cahier d'un retour au pays natal* in 1939. For the first time, French Caribbean writers began to turn away from a Cartesian dualism which orders the world into the Self (France) and the Other (Martinique and Guadeloupe), moving instead toward a new conception of the self in relation to others. This decisive ideological shift from accepting the alienating gaze of the Other to exploring the uniqueness of the Caribbean experience found expression in the political, philosophical and literary theory of *négritude*.

First appearing in 1935, the journal *L'Etudiant noir* provided the vehicle for the development of this revolutionary intellectual movement, featuring the work of writers from Africa and the Caribbean. The most notable of its contributors were Aimé Césaire, Léopold Sédar Senghor and Léon Damas who are considered the founders of *négritude*. The principal aims of this movement were to valorize black identity and to affirm Africa as the source of Caribbean identity. The implication of this new philosophy was that for the first time Caribbean and African people were seen to resist colonialism and its collective and personal alienation.

Césaire's literary and political priority was to reclaim "blackness" and he looked to Africa to give contemporary Caribbean society a tangible history and motherland. Césaire's *Cahier* was the most influential text of this time and the one that best encapsulates the search for and celebration of a black identity. This epic poem depicts in symbolic imagery the degradation of black people in the Caribbean and describes in exalted terms the rediscovery of an African identity—seen as a path to healing and pride. Equally importantly, Césaire drew attention to the shameful and oppressive past of the Caribbean and the huge physical and emotional cost for its people. In his *Cahier*, Césaire "considers the psychological make-up of his fellow West Indians to be still influenced by the memory of slavery, and still affected by an unacknowledged rancor against Africa—'Africa which is reproached for not having protected her children, or for having handed them over, but which, at the same time, still has the secret savour of a lost paradise.'"[12] *Négritude* provided the all-important starting point to the claiming of a black Caribbean identity.

A useful way to conceptualize *négritude* is to liken it to the image of a tree which evokes the idea of taking root in one's land and growing up into strong branches that reach out to the world. The choice of the tree as a symbol to encapsulate Césaire's project gives the idea of a single root, Africa, which produces the abundant blossoms that are the Caribbean islands. For Césaire, the origins of the Caribbean are clearly located in mother Africa and only from there can the specificity of the islands grow and expand. Césaire draws a distinctive and continuous link between Africa and the Caribbean and Caribbean identity appears as a single branch.[13]

In relation to gender, it is clear that a masculine figure emerges as the champion of *négritude* even if Césaire's stance is symbolic rather than prescriptive for what should unfold. The images he employs emphasize the prominence of the phallus and reify qualities traditionally linked to masculinity. Written in a style deeply permeated with symbolism, the following section from the *Cahier* highlights the masculine imagery and certain values typically associated with each gender:

et toi veuille astre de ton lumineux fondement tirer
lémurien du sperme insondable de l'homme la forme non osée
que le ventre tremblant de la femme porte tel un minerai!

[and you star please from your luminous foundation draw lemurian being
of man's unfathomable sperm the yet undared form
carried like an ore in woman's trembling belly!][14]

The linking of the man with the heavenly powers of the star and more importantly, with life-giving, "sperme insondable," underlines the indispensable role of the man in the establishment of a new social order. This male figure is seen to provide the spark for the foundation of a new world and a new acceptance of black values. The woman, by contrast, features only as a physical being with no other role than her reproductive capacity. Rather than depicting man and woman as equal partners in bringing about this new world, she is instead reduced to her womb. Furthermore, this womb is described as "trembling" which highlights her weakness in relation to man and reinforces the fearful, passive role she occupies. Conforming to traditional gender roles, Césaire's man in this extract is the one endowed with activity while the woman is passive, valued only for her maternal role.

A second extract draws on images of fertility and the vibrant, masculine force of the phallus.

[Ma négritude] plonge dans la chair rouge du sol
elle plonge dans la chair ardente du ciel
elle troue l'accablement opaque de sa droite patience (47).

[[My négritude] plunges into the red flesh of the earth
it plunges into the burning flesh of the sky
it pierces the opaque despondency of its rightful patience].

The language in these lines is graphic and evocative, powerfully mirroring the action of a man penetrating a woman in the act of love. Césaire introduces the images of redness, linked to female menstruation, and of yielding, in the woman's readiness to be penetrated by the man. Both of these images link women to their biological function. Although no specific woman is described here, Césaire is drawing on traditional binary oppositions that align men with strength and action and women with weakness and passivity. Césaire emphasizes this notion of masculine activity in his call for his fellow blacks to be upright in the fight against injustice. In this passage he mentions the word "debout" [upright] seventeen times (61–62), leaving no ambiguity as to the masculine connotations of the word. The black person standing erect is endowed with the strength, force and ability to overturn the current social order in contrast to the traditionally passive nature linked to femininity.

While Césaire's language and imagery are undoubtedly masculine throughout the *Cahier*, there are several instances when the image he presents of women is more positive. One example is the description of his mother working day and night at her sewing machine in order to provide food for her family.

[E]t ma mère dont les jambes pour notre faim inlassable pédalent, pédalent de jour, de nuit, je suis même réveillé la nuit par ces jambes inlassables qui pédalent la nuit et la morsure âpre dans la chair molle de la nuit d'une Singer que ma mère pédale, pédale pour notre faim et de jour et de nuit. (18)

[And my mother whose legs pedal for our tireless hunger, pedals day and night, I am even woken in the night by these tireless legs which pedal at night and the harsh bite of the soft flesh of night with the Singer that my mother pedals, pedals for our hunger both day and night.]

The picture Césaire paints of his mother is a woman endowed with strength and devotion to her family. She is willing to sacrifice herself in order to provide for her loved ones and she thus becomes part of the greater project of *négritude*. Her commitment to her family embodies the commitment required by all black people to transcend the limitations placed upon them by whites. In contrast to some of Césaire's other descriptions, the woman in this depiction is life-giving and nurturing, essential characteristics in the creation of a valued black identity.

In subsequent currents of intellectual thought, critics of *négritude* have drawn attention to the simplicity of Césaire's method which replaces the essence of metropolitan France with that of Africa. However, Césaire remains one of the most influential literary and political figures despite the fact that his theories have been developed, disputed or disregarded in recent years. As Beverley Ormerod asserts, from the time of the *Cahier*'s publication in 1939, "the major literary works to emerge from the French Caribbean have all accepted Césaire's basic premise of a historic loss and of the need to devise present strategies to overcome the consequences of this loss."[15] Césaire's insights provoked the first major break with the alienating gaze of colonialism and he occupies a place of extraordinary importance in French Caribbean literature.

Césaire's *négritude* was followed by the concept of *antillanité*, exemplified in the work of Edouard Glissant, which shifts the focus from Africa back to the Caribbean. Glissant published a major theoretical text, *Le Discours antillais*, in 1981 and this work remains the central theoretical reference point of *antillanité*, enhanced by his 1990 publication, *Poétique de la relation*. In *Le Discours antillais* Glissant depicts the French Caribbean as a place of missed opportunities for self-definition and autonomy. It is therefore necessary to consolidate all that is uniquely Caribbean in defiance of the alienating gaze of metropolitan France. Glissant perceives the role of the writer as instrumental in bringing a consciousness to the people and his work has come to be regarded as "the militant foundation of a specifically *situated* literature."[16]

While the tree is an effective symbol to conceptualize *négritude*, Glissant employs the image of a rhizome,[17] borrowed from Gilles Deleuze and Felix Guattari's *Mille plateaux*, as a useful way to consider *antillanité*. "Submarine roots: that is floating free, not fixed in one position in some primordial spot, but extending in all directions in our world through its network of branches" (67). In Glissant's view of Caribbean identity, French Caribbean people are not a simple derivation from Africa, but, rather, a complex cultural creation. While the nucleus of the Caribbean identity is African, there are important graftings of European, Indian and Caribbean influences which result in a distinct cultural entity. Importantly, moreover, within this system of "multiple interrelated cultures, the

Caribbean represents not a closed space but one that is open, both internally, within the archipelago, and externally, exposed to the continental mass of the Americas and the Atlantic Ocean."[18]

Glissant calls attention to the process of *métissage* and creolization in Martinique and Guadeloupe and argues that the mixing of colour, country and culture produces an identity that is uniquely Caribbean. Literary works aligned to *antillanité* are generally written in French although there is often a concealed subtext of Creole.

Glissant's use of gendered imagery is more subtle than Césaire's and indeed it appears at first glance that *antillanité* is more inclusive of women than *négritude* had been. A closer examination of his text, however, reveals that it is not immune to gender stereotyping. A central theme in Glissant's *Le Discours antillais* is the role of history in shaping French Caribbean identity, particularly the collision between the History imposed by metropolitan France and the nonhistories left unrecorded in official accounts of the region. Glissant explains the official history of Martinique as

> conceived in terms of the list of discoverers and governors of this country, without taking into account the sovereign beauties—since there were no male sovereigns—that it has produced . . . The Martinican elite can see "power" only in the shape of the female thigh. Empress, queen, courtesan: History is for them nothing but a submission to pleasure, where the male is dominant; the male is the Other. This notion of history as pleasure is about making oneself available. (73)

In this provocative passage, Glissant makes reference to Joséphine, a white Creole who later married Napoleon, and who was set forth as the ideal of beauty in the region. Glissant reinvents a standard stereotype and likens Martinique to a prostitute who has allowed herself to be exploited in order to profit from the glittering riches put before her. In one sense, he has invested a historical situation—that of some black female slaves using their bodies as a way to gain privileges—with new meaning. Throughout his book, Glissant severely chastises his fellow Martinicans for permitting France to dominate them economically and culturally through departmentalization and for allowing themselves to be seduced by consumerism instead of fighting for a national identity.

There are two images at play in this passage—first, the woman who submits to pleasure and aspires to nothing higher than instant gratification. This portrait of women conforms to gender stereotyping in which women are in a position of powerlessness in relation to men. At a deeper level, however, this woman also represents Martinique, equally content to submit to domination by the French. In a thought-provoking reversal of the traditional dichotomy of men representing the Self and women the Other, Glissant invokes the male as the Other. For this scenario, Glissant attributes otherness to the metropolitan French as they are foreigners in the French Caribbean. By contrast, the Martinicans represent selfhood although significantly this categorization does not align them with power. Glissant thus draws on evocative images of gender in order to convey some of the central tenets of his philosophy of *antillanité*.

In Glissant's 1990 publication, *Poétique de la relation*, he resorts again to feminine imagery to convey his complex ideas on Caribbean cultural identity. Glissant begins by sketching the tragic historical event of the importation of slaves from Africa. Bringing this experience alive in the most graphic language, he writes of the horrors of the Middle Passage in which boats housed hundreds of slaves in appalling conditions:

> This boat is a womb, a womb abyss . . . This boat is your womb, a matrix, and yet it expels you. This boat: pregnant with as many dead as living under the sentence of death. (6)

Glissant's choice of maternal imagery creates a haunting evocation of the torment of this journey from Africa to the Caribbean. Not only does he point to the suffering and shared fate of the slaves, but he also highlights the discrepancy between what should be a safe and comfortable environment and what turns out to be the most horrific fate imaginable. Glissant describes the boat as pregnant, but again reverses conventional expectations, transforming this biological event heralding new life into something that announces death, suffering and eternal hardship. Glissant's images align women closely to their bodies, particularly their reproductive capacity, and thereby reinforce the standard biological associations of the female. Glissant's descriptions exemplify the fact that no text is free of gender bias and that, consciously or unconsciously, writers reveal something of the way gender is constructed in their society.

In the 1990s, *antillanité* was further developed into the concept of *créolité*. Encapsulated in the work of Jean Bernabé, Patrick Chamoiseau and Raphaël Confiant who published *Eloge de la Créolité* in 1989, *créolité* shifted the focus of Caribbean identity yet again, this time to the Creole nature of Martinique and Guadeloupe. "Neither Europeans, nor Africans, nor Asians, we proclaim ourselves Creoles."[19] This movement emphasizes the embracing of *all* races present in the Caribbean—including Chinese, Indians, Syrians, Lebanese, black and white people as well as the various *métis* groups. *Créolité* emphasizes the need to look to other islands in the Caribbean which are both linguistically and culturally related to Martinique and Guadeloupe as well as to Guyane and other Creole-speaking places such as Réunion. Far from being closed and complete, *créolité* advocates a place that is open, forward-looking and constantly in flux.

Drawing on the environment for an appropriate natural image, *créolité* identifies itself as a mangrove,[20] thereby highlighting the impossibility of a single, all-encompassing origin. In a mangrove it is difficult to pinpoint a beginning or an end and it sustains an ecological life of extraordinary richness. Emphasizing the fluidity and interconnection of identity in all its facets, *créolité* comes to embody a kind of harmonious chaos in which exist both order and disorder, unity and multiplicity.[21] Patrick Chamoiseau likens Creole identity to a mosaic which has no core and in which multiple cultures are placed together to create something uniquely Caribbean. "[I]l faut comprendre que l'Antillais n'est pas un Africain, ni un Européen, ni un Indien, ni un descendant d'Amérindiens, mais *qu'il est tout cela en même temps*" [It is necessary to understand that a Caribbean person is neither an African nor a European, neither an Indian nor a descendant of the Amerindians, but *is all of that at the same time*].[22] For the *créolistes*, Caribbean identity flourishes above all in the Creole culture. The writers of this movement have attempted to create an intermediate space between French and Creole, often called *français créolisé* or *français régional*. Following its emphasis on the shifting nature of identity and the fact that meaning is always dependent on the cultural and historical context, *créolité* could be characterized as postmodern.

Like its intellectual predecessors *négritude* and *antillanité*, *créolité* displays a gendered nature. A. James Arnold states that *créolité* is the latest example of the strongly masculinist culture of the French Caribbean. However, it is gradually being challenged by the more recent emergence of women writers.[23] While its major text, *Eloge de la Créolité*, does not express its aims in overtly gendered terms, the outcome nonetheless is that women have tended to be excluded from the movement. The ultimate *créoliste* project appears to be the promotion and production of a male literary culture.

Arnold calls attention to the work of Patrick Chamoiseau and Raphaël Confiant who, he argues, are guilty of keeping gender divisions in place in their writing as well as reifying certain ethnoclasses in their fiction and autobiography.[24] In Arnold's eyes, Confiant is particularly at fault for his uncritical acceptance of gender and ethnic roles and for his promotion of these divisions in his literature. Citing a passage from Confiant's 1993 autobiography, *Ravines du devant-jour*, Arnold reveals a graphic example of Confiant's perceived denigration of women, particularly East Indian women:

Quant à leurs femelles, malgré leur maigreur-jusqu'à-l'os et leur odeur fauve, elles peuvent te charrier le coeur de l'homme le plus prévenu en moins de temps que la culbute d'une puce. Ce sont des briseuses d'épousailles, des détourneuses de concubins, des voleuses de fiancés, des vicieuses de première catégorie, bien que les poils de leur coucoune soient effilés comme la lame du rasoir.

[As for their women, despite their extreme skinniness and their musky
smell, they can carry away the most prejudiced man's heart in less time than
it takes to crush a flea.[25] They are marriage-breakers, seducers of live-in
lovers, stealers of fiancés, and first-class kinky women, although their cunt
hairs are as fine as razor blades].[26]

Drawing on stereotypical notions of gender, Confiant's narrative voice
appears to denigrate sexual relations between black Creole men and East
Indian women. While the intolerance of racial and sexual differences may
seem in poor taste in this extract, it is important to remember that the
adult Confiant does not present these views as direct speech. Rather, it is
his aunt Emérante who is speaking, reflecting the rural prejudices of her
class, colour and sex. All of these views are heavily exaggerated in the text
and can be compared with his mulatto grandparents' opinions of blacks.
His grandmother, for example, says: "'*Nègrès-la, ay pwòpté kò'w, non, ton-
nan di sò! Ou ka pit chawony kouman!*' (Hé, négresse, va te laver, bon sang!
Tu pues la charogne!)" [Hey, negress, go and wash, good God! You stink
like a corpse!] (14).

Thomas Spear underlines Confiant's tendency to stereotype his male
characters in a similar fashion, noting that most of them "restent, comme
des coqs de basse-cour, suprêmes dans leur force sexuelle dominatrice"
[remain, like farmyard cocks, supreme in their dominating sexual
strength].[27] While it is clear that Confiant's characters often draw heavily
on stereotypes and reinforce traditional divisions, there is an element of
exaggeration in his work which can be considered part of his status as
professional *enfant terrible* of contemporary French Caribbean literature.

As an alternative to the masculinist bias of many works of *créolité*,
Arnold suggests a reading of Dany Bébel-Gisler's novel *Léonora: l'histoire
enfouie de la Guadeloupe*. This story of one woman's quest to survive illustrates a new possibility for gender relations in French Caribbean society,
representing a powerful example of "a woman-centred vision of creole
language and culture in Guadeloupe in the interests of national independence."[28] In contrast to the glorified philanderers presented in Confiant's
books, for example, Bébel-Gisler focuses on the daily consequences of this
behavior for women. Despite the humiliation and shame of her husband's
infidelities, Léonora's greatest concern remains providing for her family
while her husband's resources support his mistress. While Arnold considers Bébel-Gisler's novel "a more creolized text—at the level of language and style—than anything yet produced by the male *créolistes*," he
has found that there is little critical acceptance of it among these writers.

While women may be excluded as significant characters in the works of
some *créoliste* writers and while women authors may not be studied in
depth by certain *créoliste texts*, Arnold's statement is not borne out by the

work of literary criticism *Lettres créoles*. In this study, Chamoiseau and Confiant include an examination of selected novels by Simone Schwarz-Bart and Maryse Condé which are considered just as important as books by male writers. Indeed, it is female writers such as Condé and Schwarz-Bart who have far outsold their male counterparts and enjoy a wider readership than many of the male writers. Furthermore, many women writers, including Schwarz-Bart and Condé, were writing before the development of *créolité* and thus cannot be enclosed within the confines of this movement. Arnold's criticisms effectively demonstrate, however, the gendered bias that bubbles under the surface of many *créoliste* texts.

Alongside the predominantly masculine literary movements of *négritude*, *antillanité* and *créolité*, an alternative vision of Caribbean identity has emerged in literature by women. From a gendered perspective, the most notable characteristic of Caribbean literature prior to 1930 is the sparseness of women writers. Carole Boyce Davies and Elaine Savory Fido in their influential book *Out of the Kumbla: Caribbean Women and Literature* consider the concept of female voicelessness as inextricably linked to any discussion of Caribbean literature.[29] While a number of female writers did produce literary works in the early part of the twentieth century, their books tended to reflect the values of the dominant patriarchal society in which they lived and wrote. In a strange irony, however, one of the first books to be celebrated as an example of early women's writing, Mayotte Capécia's *Je suis martiniquaise*, published in 1948, was recently revealed as a hoax.[30]

Women's writing as a distinct entity has taken on a higher profile in recent years. Beginning from a time when female writers were almost absent in a male-dominated literary domain, scholars have uncovered since the 1970s a small, but ever-growing, body of talented women novelists, poets and playwrights. In contrast to the male writers of the same region, these female writers have resisted theory and have centered their work on the portrayal of both everyday life and fantasy in the French Caribbean. Like their male counterparts, they have used fiction as a way to examine issues of identity, but have also included questions of gender and sexual difference.

A study of Simone Schwarz-Bart, Maryse Condé and Gisèle Pineau's views of writing reveals their dislike of categorization. While they may share certain preoccupations and portray similar situations, their work does not conform to a particular theory or ideology. Gerise Herndon, for example, asserts that female authors such as Maryse Condé "are simply making the reading public aware of the conditions of their lives, of their gender, and their sexuality, including the contradictions inherent in their identity constructions."[31] Although they acknowledge the way their work can shape others, women writers in general conceive of their literature as one woman's view and not as the collective expression of a whole society.

Maryse Condé has articulated in a variety of books and interviews her personal view of what constitutes the role of the writer. In an interview with Alexyna Mekel, Condé speaks about her return to Guadeloupe after a long period living overseas, stating that she had finally identified herself as a Caribbean person and that she needed to be directly involved with her society. Condé felt her action could best be expressed in literature as "the only form of combat for a writer is writing."[32] In contrast to a writer like Raphaël Confiant who is deeply involved with political issues, Condé does not attribute a political role to herself, dissociating herself from the independence movement in Guadeloupe and seeing her role instead as helping to elucidate the unique experience of being French Caribbean. "I do not write political pamphlets. What seems important to me is Marcus Garvey's statement: '*I shall teach the black man to see into himself.*' That, in my opinion, is a writer's function."[33]

Simone Schwarz-Bart also attests to the lack of a political agenda in her writing and her commitment to portraying inclusive social histories. Speaking of her novel, *Pluie et vent sur Télumée Miracle*, Schwarz-Bart cites the inspiration for her story as "le besoin de ne pas laisser échapper, une fois de plus, un pan de notre histoire. J'ai essayé de mettre, dans une espèce de forme—le roman—tout un univers antillais que je voyais dilapider, une partie de notre capital, de notre somme" [the need not to let escape once more a piece of our history. I tried to put into a kind of form—the novel—an entire Caribbean universe that I saw being wasted, a part of our capital, of our whole being].[34] The motivation for this novel is a personal one, which, like Condé's work, also has ramifications on a social level with the desire to claim a cultural identity.[35] A parallel could be made with the work of Schwarz-Bart and Glissant who also examines the link between society and identity. However, when asked to reflect further on her work, Schwarz-Bart refuses to be locked into a highly analytical view of the novel. "Je ne suis pas une universitaire, je n'analyse pas ce que je fais. Je travaille . . ." [I am not a university type, I don't analyze what I do. I work . . .][36] Her approach to literature appears more instinctual, drawing on her own experiences and personal vision of life.

Schwarz-Bart avoids seeing her work as an overtly political act, stressing instead her choice not to be aggressively theoretical. "Je n'ai pas la prétention d'adresser un message. J'écris ce que j'aurais voulu lire . . . Message, c'est un grand mot. J'aimerais transmettre tout ce que je connais de notre réalité, tout ce que je ressens, mais sans prétention" [I am not so pretentious as to deliver a message. I write what I would have wanted to read . . . Message is a big word. I would like to convey everything I know about our reality, everything I feel, but without pretentiousness].[37] The unspoken pretentious Other in this scenario is intriguing and it is clear that Schwarz-Bart is drawing a clear boundary between herself and some of the male writers who have chosen highly intellectual theories with which to convey their thoughts. She, by contrast, prefers to allow her novels alone to articulate her perceptions of society.

While Condé and Schwarz-Bart both began writing in the 1970s, Gisèle Pineau is a more recent female writer from Guadeloupe who began writing in the 1990s. As a member of a younger generation of women writers, Pineau represents both continuity with the reflections of her literary predecessors and an evolution toward a more self-consciously committed act of writing literature. In Pineau's words, "[s]eule la parole peut libérer les êtres humiliés. Il faut parler si on veut s'en sortir" [only the word can liberate humiliated people. We must speak if we want to get out of it].[38] However, even while her writing is committed and actively exposes the injustices she sees in the world, Pineau remains firm that she is not a theoretician. "Je ne suis pas une théoricienne et je revendique le droit d'être différente. Grâce à mon 'exil' en France, je ne suis pas tentée, comme certain Créoles, par le repli sur soi. Moi, je ne veux pas être enfermée par mon île" [I am not a theoretician and I claim the right to be different. Thanks to my "exile" in France, I am not tempted, like certain Creoles, to withdraw into myself. I don't want to be imprisoned by my island].[39] Once again it is possible to discern the presence of the Other in this declaration which one can identify as the theoretical male writers of Martinique.

It is evident from this brief survey of the origins and evolution of French Caribbean literature that this domain holds the key to unlocking many of the issues relating to subjectivity. While the early stages of its development attest to the overwhelming quest for a cultural identity above and beyond that imposed by the French, more recent preoccupations highlight the growing importance of gender identity. Literature remains one of the most effective means to write oneself from absence to presence in the French Caribbean and as women have come to populate this previously male-dominated arena it effectively illustrates the changing status of men and women in that society. As Joan Anim-Addo asserts, "it is undeniably and overwhelmingly a literature shaped by experiences of gender in interaction with the socio-cultural historical period of the latter twentieth century."[40]

NOTES

1. J. Michael Dash, "Introduction," in A. James Arnold (ed.), *A History of Literature in the Caribbean*, Volume One: *Hispanic and Francophone Regions* (Philadelphia: John Benjamins, 1994), 309.

2. Jack Corzani, *La Littérature des Antilles-Guyane françaises*, tome 1: *Exotisme et régionalisme* (Fort-de-France: Emile Désormeaux, 1978), 25.

3. Patrick Chamoiseau and Raphaël Confiant, *Lettres créoles: Tracées antillaises et continentales de la littérature 1635–1975* (Paris: Hatier, 1991), 35–41.

4. M. a M. Ngal, *Aimé Césaire: Un homme à la recherche d'une patrie* (Dakar: Les Nouvelles Editions Africaines, 1975), 12.

5. Dash, "Introduction," 310.

6. Edouard Glissant, *Soleil de la conscience* (Paris: Seuil, 1956), 15.

7. Héliane Toumson and Roger Toumson, "Interview avec Simone et André Schwarz-Bart: Sur les pas de Fanotte," in Roger Toumson (ed.), *Textes, études et documents* (No. 2) (Paris: Editions Caribéennes, 1979), 22.

8. Jean Bernabé, Patrick Chamoiseau and Raphaël Confiant, *Eloge de la Créolité* (Paris: Gallimard, 1993), 76.

9. Roger Toumson, "La Littérature antillaise d'expression française," *Présence Africaine* 121–22 (1982): 130–34.

10. Françoise Pfaff, *Entretiens avec Maryse Condé* (Paris: Karthala, 1993), 61.

11. Patrick Chamoiseau, "Interview avec Odile Broussillon et Michèle Desbordes," *Notes Bibliographiques* Caraïbes 48 (1988): 19.

12. Beverley Ormerod, *An Introduction to the French Caribbean Novel* (London: Heinemann, 1985), 4. Aimé Césaire cited from the introduction to Daniel Guérin's *Les Antilles décolonisées*, trans. Beverley Ormerod (Paris: Présence Africaine, 1956), 15–16.

13. For the idea that Africa is the root and the Caribbean a branch that has broken off and grown again see Simone Schwarz-Bart, *Ti-Jean l'horizon* (Paris: Seuil, 1979), 248.

14. Aimé Césaire, *The Collected Poetry*, trans. Clayton Eshleman and Annette Smith (Berkeley: University of California Press, 1983), 67.

15. Ormerod, *French Caribbean Novel*, 3.

16. Peter Hallward, "Edouard Glissant between the Singular and the Specific," *Yale Journal of Criticism* 11, no. 2 (1998): 441.

17. The *Collins English Dictionary* defines a rhizome as a "thick horizontal underground stem of plants such as the iris or mint whose buds develop into new plants." See J. M. Sinclair (ed.), *Collins English Dictionary* (Sydney: HarperCollins, 2001), 1328.

18. J. Michael Dash, *Edouard Glissant* (Cambridge: Cambridge University Press, 1995), 146.

19. Bernabé, Chamoiseau and Confiant, *Eloge*, 75.

20. Tropical evergreen trees or shrubs that have intertwining roots and that form dense thickets along coasts.

21. Christine Chivallon, "Texaco ou l'éloge de la 'spatialité,'" *Notre Librairie* 127 (1996): 103.

22. Ottmar Ette and Ralph Ludwig, "En guise d'introduction: Points de vue sur l'évolution de la littérature antillaise: Entretien avec les écrivains martiniquais Patrick Chamoiseau et Raphaël Confiant," *Lendemains* 67 (1992): 10. Original italics.

23. A. James Arnold, "The Erotics of Colonialism in Contemporary French West Indian Literature," *New West Indian Guide/Nieuwe West-Indische Gids* 68, nos. 1 and 2 (1994): 5.

24. A. James Arnold, "From the Problematic Maroon to a Woman-Centred Creole Project in the Literature of the French West Indies," in Doris Y. Kadish (ed.), *Slavery in the Caribbean Francophone World: Distant Voices, Forgotten Acts, Forged Identities* (Athens: University of Georgia Press, 2000), 167.

25. The phrase suggests, through a pun, "la culbute d'une pucelle" (screwing a virgin).

26. Raphaël Confiant, *Ravines du devant-jour* (Paris: Gallimard, 1993), 80. Translations from this text are my own.

27. Thomas C. Spear, "Jouissances carnavalesques: Représentation de la sexualité," in Maryse Condé and Madeleine Cottenet-Hage (eds.), *Penser la créolité* (Paris: Karthala, 1995), 138.

28. Arnold, "Problematic Maroon," 171.

29. Carole Boyce Davies and Elaine Savory Fido, "Introduction: Women and Literature in the Caribbean: An Overview," in Carole Boyce Davies and Elaine Savory Fido (eds.), *Out of the Kumbla: Caribbean Women and Literature* (Trenton, N.J.: Africa World Press, 1990), 1.

30. See A. James Arnold, "Frantz Fanon, Lafcadio Hearn et la supercherie de 'Mayotte Capécia,'" *Revue de Littérature Comparée* 76 (2002): 148–66.

31. Gerise Herndon, "Gender Construction and Neocolonialism," *World Literature Today* 67, no. 4 (1993): 736.

32. Alexyna Mekel, "Interview with Maryse Condé," *Caribbean Contact* (1989).

33. Mekel, "Interview with Maryse Condé."

34. Toumson and Toumson, "Interview avec Simone et André Schwarz-Bart," 18.

35 Although Schwarz-Bart may not have a highly formulated political program, she shares a certain social agenda with Edouard Glissant. See his ideas on cultural identity and memory in *Caribbean Discourse: Selected Essays*, trans. J. Michael Dash (Charlottesville University of Virginia Press, 1989): 231–32.

36. Toumson and Toumson, "Interview avec Simone et André Schwarz-Bart," 18.

37. Toumson and Toumson. "Interview avec Simone et André Schwarz-Bart," 21.

38. Sébastien Le Fol, "Gisèle Pineau: La fin des tabous," *Le Figaro*, 20 mai 1998.

39. M.-J. DuFour, "Gisèle Pineau: Infirmière et romancière," *Le Progrès*, 26 octobre, 1998.

40. Joan Anim-Addo, "Introduction," in Joan Anim-Addo (ed.), *Framing the Word: Gender and Genre in Caribbean Women's Writing* (London: Whiting & Birch, 1996), xii.

3

$\sim$

"Man is a Breadfruit and Woman is a Chestnut"

Man is a Breadfruit and Woman is a Chestnut.

Creole proverb

Two novels which clearly demonstrate the image of the French Caribbean woman as a chestnut and the French Caribbean man as a breadfruit are Simone Schwarz-Bart's *Pluie et vent sur Télumée Miracle*, published in 1972, and Maryse Condé's *Moi, Tituba, sorcière . . . noire de Salem*, published in 1986. Both of these books have achieved outstanding critical success and continue to attract attention and admiration in the form of books, articles and theses Each story is a "hybrid blend of fact and fiction,"[1] drawing on real-life events to convey the authors' passionate view of women's lives during slavery and beyond. Schwarz-Bart took her inspiration for Télumée from an old woman she knew as a child in rural Guadeloupe while Condé came across Tituba's story during a research trip to the UCLA library in the United States.

This merging of history and storytelling, encapsulated in the French word *histoire*, is an effective postcolonial literary technique that allows the author to subvert categorization into a single genre. Condé's writing contains further subversive powers with her ironic tone. While her novels contain many themes concerning postcolonial identity, history and feminism, her use of irony consistently overturns facile ideological generalizations. Together these two novels provide an important voice for the historically marginalized black woman whilst also demonstrating the way in which the gender roles established at the time of slavery have filtered down to subsequent generations of French Caribbean people.

A remarkable aspect of both Schwarz-Bart's and Condé's portrayal of men in their novels is their lack of judgment toward their characters' treatment of women. Patricia Mohammed asserts that this nonconfrontational approach to gender issues is a product of Caribbean "colonization and continuing imperialism in which both masculinity and femininity have had to be defined in relation to the other, feminism has largely been . . . a nurturing one, a recognition of a shared condition, despite sexual difference and despite obvious inequalities."[2] The predominant image of men to emerge in these novels is comparable to the breadfruit that spatters onto the ground where it quickly turns rotten, while the female characters display the strength of character and physical toughness that is characteristic of the chestnut.

Schwarz-Bart draws attention to "the madness of the West Indies" (23) in *Pluie et vent sur Télumée Miracle*, a psychological state bequeathed by slavery, which she perceives as continually influencing the behavioural patterns of Caribbean people, particularly men. This chapter shows that Caribbean men have tended to remain bound to the personal and cultural alienation that began with slavery while Caribbean women have demonstrated a superior capacity to overcome these obstacles. The presence of female community in both novels is one of the vital elements in allowing women to maintain their capacity to resist oppression in a hostile colonial environment.

In *Pluie et vent sur Télumée Miracle*, Schwarz-Bart employs the narrative technique of storytelling to convey the lives of four generations of women. Her literary style mirrors the Caribbean tradition of oral history, focusing particular attention on the role women have played in the transmission of folk traditions. While this important cultural role is not traditionally attributed to women, particularly in *créoliste* literature, which paints it as very much a male occupation, Schwarz-Bart insists on the active role of women in making history. She also draws attention to the importance of the grandmother in preserving these traditions, reinstating a figure frequently left in the margins of history.

Pluie et vent sur Télumée Miracle consistently places a female viewpoint at the forefront of the story, offering a distinct perspective on slavery, poverty, love, relationships, work and death. The primacy of the female speaking-position in the novel allows Toussine and Télumée, the two central characters, to confidently assume their subjectivity and to portray their experiences unfettered by the patriarchal point of view. This proactive stance reinforces the theme of the French Caribbean woman as a tough and resilient chestnut.

The French Caribbean's historical past plays a determining role in *Pluie et vent sur Télumée Miracle* with its portrayal of the Caribbean matrifocal family and the relative strength women embody when compared to men.

The families described in the book are marked by the absence of a coherent father figure, either through death or the choice to remain unconstrained by familial responsibility. Schwarz-Bart states in a 1979 interview that her editor wanted to remove the first section of her book detailing the central narrator's ancestors because it lacked interest and took away from the story of Télumée. However, Schwarz-Bart insisted that the historical progression of the Lougandor women is essential to her narrative.[3] The emphasis on the genealogy of the Lougandor women and the accompanying agency they derive from this sense of historical roots forms a vital component of Schwarz-Bart's depiction of strong female identity. By offering these women a tangible link with the past, Schwarz-Bart helps to oppose the scattering of the Caribbean family imposed by slavery.

The Lougandor women develop into characters who display strength and a resolve to survive that is not shared by the majority of men around them. Schwarz-Bart describes a number of male characters who appear detached from the evolution of history and remain permanently associated with the erasure of male identity suffered under slavery. Schwarz-Bart has effectively appropriated the Caribbean historical experience, portraying it as a conditioning factor in her presentation of gender identity.

The first woman described in the Lougandor line is Télumée's great-grandmother, Minerve [Minerva], who is linked to the Roman goddess of wisdom through her mythical name. Despite her direct experience of the injustices of the plantation system, Minerve displays the quality that comes to characterize all the Lougandor women with her "unshakable faith in life" (3). This courageous attitude toward the trials of existence represents the defining philosophy of Minerve and her descendants as they encounter times of great prosperity and others of deep suffering. What distinguishes the Lougandor women from those around them is their ability to maintain this approach to life in both the good times and the bad. Their refusal to idealize life or minimize the pain that periodically encompasses them highlights a no-nonsense approach to existence that is directed above all by the will to survive. These women view both positive and negative experiences as the defining facets of life and believe, therefore, that both must be lived fully. These realistic expectations become empowering elements for the Lougandor women, contributing to Schwarz-Bart's portrayal of them as women of great strength.

As a young woman Minerve becomes pregnant to a wandering black man from Dominica who rapidly abandons her when he learns of their approaching child. Living in the ironically named village, L'Abandonnée, Minerve refuses to submit to the shame of her desertion, choosing instead to maintain her unwavering faith in life. By contrast, the Dominican man demonstrates a state of personal alienation, appearing as morally weak in his inability to maintain family ties. Perhaps because of her proud comportment and integrity, Minerve soon finds herself in a relationship with an exemplary man named Xango. When Minerve's child, Toussine, is born, "Xango loved her as if she were his own" (3), helping to raise a child with a secure sense of herself. Unlike the familial irresponsibility that characterizes the man from Dominica, Xango embodies the nurturing qualities often linked to femininity. He displays openness to relationships and he engages fully with his new family. Schwarz-Bart emphasizes the empowering value of parenting by pointing to the love and fulfilment it creates in the parents. She also reveals the precious legacy it bequeaths to the child. Xango's preference of relationships over separation allows him to embrace his nurturing role fully and, in this way, he appears in tune with his "feminine" side.

Through the novel's positive weighting of feminine qualities such as caring for others, fostering a connection with nature and adopting a humanitarian approach to life, men associated with femininity are linked to strength rather than to weakness. Schwarz-Bart includes a number of men who project these positive feminine traits including Toussine's husband, Jérémie, who supports her through her deepest sorrows and never falters in his love and devotion to her; Télumée's father, Angebert, who saves Victoire [Victory] from self-destruction and provides his daughter with a model for compassion and selflessness; and Télumée's second husband, Amboise, who is a quiet man full of gentleness and wisdom.

Toussine forms one of the central narrative interests in the novel and, together with Télumée, she emerges as a woman of great courage. Deeply loved and growing up in the secure domestic environment provided by Minerve and Xango, Toussine dominates the story with her mythical presence. However, Schwarz-Bart's portrayal of her moral strength and resilience is always grounded in the highs and lows of everyday life. Schwarz-Bart reveals that it is principally as a result of her suffering that Toussine assumes the voice of wisdom throughout the novel.

Happily married to Jérémie, Toussine begins her life as a woman in profound happiness. However, her world falls to pieces when one of her daughters dies in a devastating house fire. Toussine falls into a deep depression lasting three years, which leads to her and her family's ruin. Symbolically, the house they live in becomes overrun by weeds and flimsy pieces of cardboard cover the windows. Shocking the people around her, Toussine languishes in sorrow until one day a man "announced that Toussine, the little stranded boat, the woman thought to be lost forever, had come out of her cardboard tower and was taking a little walk in the sun" (14).

Beverley Ormerod draws attention to the metaphorical qualities of Toussine's transformation, emphasizing the way in which boats are able to withstand the forces of nature due to their sturdy construction of wood.

Ormerod's stress on the changeable nature of life reinforces the idea that strength is born of both hardship and joy. Schwarz-Bart announces Toussine's readiness to embrace the full experience of life and therefore to adopt her role as a strong woman by describing her renewed faith in nature. Toussine plants the pip of a hummingbird orange tree, the same tree that provided food for her daughters' afternoon tea before Méranée's premature death. Communion with nature thus becomes an empowering element and allows Toussine to face her tragedy from a position of strength rather than from one of overwhelming sorrow.

The profound ramifications of this metamorphosis in consciousness surface in Schwarz-Bart's description of Toussine as "a bit of the world, a whole country, a plume of a Negress, the ship, sail, and wind, for she had not made a habit of sorrow" (14). The ultimate recognition of Toussine's courageous nature and reinvigorated zest for life occurs in the birth of her new daughter called Victoire and her crowning as "Reine Sans Nom" [Queen without a Name] by the villagers around her. Reine Sans Nom represents a shining example of the image of the French Caribbean woman as a chestnut in her remarkable capacity to weave together the positive and negative threads of existence.

Like Minerve, Toussine's daughter, Victoire, is not discussed in great detail in the novel, but she too carries the Lougandor legacy of faith in life. Closely linked to the power of song, Victoire uses this skill as a strategy of resistance against the pain, drudgery or injustice of her existence. Singing becomes a Lougandor family trait linking mothers to daughters and creating a reserve of feminine strength that can be drawn upon in times of hardship. Télumée, for example, gains considerable fortitude when she sings to overcome the racist treatment she receives whilst working for the white Desaragne family: "when I sang I diluted my pain, chopped it into pieces, and it flowed into the song, and I rode my horse" (60). In this passage bubbling with courage and determination, Télumée is linked twice to the power of women, first to her mother with her recourse to the empowering nature of song and second to her grandmother with reference to her wisdom. Télumée becomes aware of a further inheritance bequeathed from mother to daughter when she is forced to work in the canefields: the steely strength of her laundress' wrists. Schwarz-Bart thus highlights the way in which qualities of resistance passed down the female family line can act as a powerful rallying point in challenging moments, perpetuating a tradition of strong Caribbean women.

Apart from these admirable facets of her personality, Schwarz-Bart depicts Victoire as the most flawed of the Lougandor women. She frequently chooses unreliable partners and has a penchant for alcohol in times of trial. When she falls passionately in love with a Carib called Haut-Colbi, Victoire alters the course of her life and privileges her relationship with him over her role as a mother. As Télumée remembers, "my mother found her god that day, and that god was a great connoisseur of feminine flesh. The first thing my mother did was send me away, remove my little ten-year-old flesh to save herself the trouble, a few years later, of trampling on the womb that betrayed her" (26). In a sinister suggestion of future incest, Schwarz-Bart highlights a male behavioral pattern that has persisted since the time of slavery. Gisèle Pineau argues that such sexual abuse is commonplace in the Caribbean, but that it is frequently swept under the carpet and left undiscussed or unacknowledged: "on préfère nier la souffrance d'un enfant plutôt que d'aller exploser une histoire familiale sur la place publique."[4] One perception of incest is that it allows perpetrators to establish power over their victims precisely because the former suffer from low self-esteem and a lack of sovereignty over their lives. While Schwarz-Bart provides little biographical information about Haut-Colbi, it is possible to interpret his actions as demonstrative of an unstable identity and pervasive sense of personal alienation.

In a reversal of traditional expectations that would ally a mother with her child over anything else, Victoire's conduct challenges the stereotype of the omnipresent Caribbean mother. While Victoire undoubtedly loves her children, her personal needs overshadow her sense of parental responsibility, bringing to light a character largely neglected in French Caribbean literature: the nonmaternal woman. Despite the strong mother figure she had in Reine Sans Nom, Victoire behaves in a similar way to a Caribbean man by refusing a responsible role in relation to her children. Wendy Goolcharan-Kumeta argues that the "failure to bond with the mother or any other surrogate mother figure often results in extreme difficulty and generally failure to connect to the network of associations with the mother which can nurture and sustain the female self,"[5] suggesting the possibility that Victoire did not share a close relationship with Reine Sans Nom. Perhaps the fact that she was born after the death of her sister Méranée meant that she was never able to overcome the ghosts of the past and compensate for her mother's loss. The relationship between Reine Sans Nom and Victoire is left unexplored in the novel and it is in relation to Télumée that Reine Sans Nom's mothering capacities come to fruition.

Clarisse Zimra observes that it is often "the chosen Mother (rather than the inherited genitrix) through whom ancestral wisdom is transmitted."[6] In *Pluie et vent sur Télumée Miracle* Reine Sans Nom is clearly the one who guides and initiates Télumée into the joys and pains of life. Schwarz-Bart depicts a powerful bond between Télumée and her grandmother and in many ways this relationship forms the basis of Télumée's identity, "precisely because grandmother is not other, but rather same."[7] With her female-dominated upbringing, Télumée learns openness to relationships and she develops a sturdy sense of identity as a result of her deep connection with her grandmother. Goolcharan-Kumeta asserts that "Schwarz-Bart has reworked and replaced the Name-of-the-Father with the Queen with no Name,"[8] highlighting the importance of women in forming a child's identity. The fact that the powerful impact of the mother is not necessarily found in biology, but may also be located in the female extended family, is particularly relevant in the French Caribbean context. The relationship between Télumée and Reine Sans Nom suggests that sometimes the nonbiological mother who has chosen motherhood may be more effective than a woman who has found herself unexpectedly in this role.

A dominant characteristic of the Lougandor women is their ability to survive in the face of adversity. Reine Sans Nom's triumph over tragedy represents an inspiring example of the human survival instinct, a trait particularly associated with women in the novel. Télumée assimilates Reine Sans Nom's sturdy example and she transposes her grandmother's actions into an image drawn from nature, which enables her own quest for survival to sustain her in difficult times. Imagining herself as "a pebble in a river just resting on the bottom" (60), Télumée wills herself to let the trials of life wash over her in order to retain a strong sense of identity. Yolande Helm asserts that Télumée's chosen of image of water is a natural element linked more closely to women than to men and that it offers liberation from rational thought in its fluid, open appearance.[9] Water also represents the source of life and is a means of purification, embodying the feminine principle in cultures such as China.[10] Télumée thus adopts a strategy of distinctly feminine opposition by calling upon her attachment to nature. This attitude of survival is characteristic of the Lougandor female line.

Mireille Rosello remarks upon Télumée's capacity for resistance in her encounters with Madame Desaragne, her white employer at Belle-Feuille. In contrast to the women who foster community in the novel, such as Reine Sans Nom's neighbors who rally around her during her depression, Madame Desaragne tries to separate Télumée from her compatriots and to re-create the state of personal and cultural alienation initiated by slavery.

> But do you even know what you've escaped? You might be wild savages now, running through the bush dancing naked, and eating people stewed in pots. But you're brought here, and how do you live? In squalor and vice and orgies. How often does your husband hit you? And all those women with their bellies on credit? Personally I'd rather die, but you people, you like it. Some taste! You wallow in the mire, and laugh. (61)

Rosello asserts that Madame Desaragne's words constitute a particularly sly weapon against Télumée, emphasizing her employee's solitude and suggesting that suicide is the only worthy solution to her situation.[11] However, Télumée connects to an inner resilience and dismisses these destructive words by visualizing herself gliding through the water, unaffected by Madame Desaragne's racist tirade. She also finds strength in Man Cia's assertion that she should be "a real drum with two sides" (61), drawing attention to the restorative qualities of female community. Valérie Loichot argues that the individual voices that populate Edouard Glissant's books "are those of the community. They mix, dissolve, and clash in the person of a 'nous,' allowing the reconstruction of a clearly Caribbean voice."[12] In a similar way, the words of wisdom provided by Reine Sans Nom and Man Cia merge in Télumée and allow her to locate and assert her own voice. The story she gives the reader offers a powerful insight into black Caribbean female experience and is a spectacular example of postcolonial resistance. As Rosello affirms, "Télumée réussit à incarner une résistance originale, propre à la femme, adaptée à la forme d'oppression qu'elle subit" [Télumée manages to embody an original resistance, specific to women, adapted to the form of oppression to which she is subjected].[13] She thereby subverts the racist system that oppresses her without falling victim to the destructive techniques of her employers.

Schwarz-Bart offers countless examples of the profound influence female solidarity has on strengthening the lives of individual women. One of the most memorable scenes is when Télumée slips into depression following her first husband, Elie's, physical and emotional abuse toward her. In a reaction reminiscent of Reine Sans Nom's own withdrawal from life after the death of her daughter, Télumée neglects herself and her house until they both resemble an overgrown garden. However, in Reine Sans Nom, Télumée is fortunate to have a person who understands the process unfolding inside her. When Reine Sans Nom pricks Télumée with a needle to remind her she is a living, breathing creature, Télumée emerges from her sadness with a newfound clarity. She once again resorts to song and nature to affirm her resistance to adversity. In an action intimately associated with her mother and orchestrated by her grandmother, Télumée sings herself back into life. Her repeated immersion in the river highlights the cleansing properties of water and marks her readiness to assume both the joys and pains of Caribbean womanhood. Reine Sans Nom observes that her granddaughter has taken on "the walk of a woman who's suffered" (116) and in her eyes, this ability to accept suffering as a part of life is the distinguishing characteristic of Caribbean female strength:

> we Lougandors are not pedigree cocks, we're fighting cocks. We know the ring, the crowd, fighting, death. We know victory and eyes gouged out. And all that has never stopped us from living, relying neither on happiness nor on

sorrow for existence, like tamarind leaves that close at night and open in the day. (80)

While Reine Sans Nom is the most prominent example of the fortifying effect of female solidarity, Télumée is fortunate to receive support from other women in the midst of her depression. Schwarz-Bart reveals that these demonstrations of female solidarity often emerge in unexpected quarters and that the smallest token of kindness can have lasting positive consequences. The first of these instances arises when a female neighbor compares Télumée to a dragonfly who lights up her own soul and shines for everyone else. In a subsequent incident, two other villagers, Adriana and Ismene, show their belief in Télumée by reassuring her that she "will come to shore" (111). Drawing on the metaphorical values of the boat, these women underline Télumée's robust personality and their faith that she will eventually emerge triumphant from her pain.

Further on in the book, Schwarz-Bart depicts a more practical example of female solidarity in Télumée's friendship with Olympe [Olympia], whom she will follow into the gruelling work of the canefields. From the simple gesture of food left on a doorstep, Télumée and Olympe forge a friendship that binds them together despite their different personalities. Their bond further fortifies them in the face of horrific working conditions. The positive force offered by this female community becomes an essential element in maintaining and deepening Télumée's personal strength.

Schwarz-Bart also focuses attention on the strength that can stem from a spiritual female solidarity. One of Télumée's greatest reference points later in life is the wisdom and support she derives from Reine Sans Nom and Man Cia after their deaths. Indeed, as Reine Sans Nom remarks to Télumée: "Can you imagine our life, with me following you everywhere, invisible, and people never suspecting they have to deal with two women, not just one?" (119). Man Cia, the sorceress, exerts her supernatural powers in a more concrete way with the rejuvenating bath full of magical leaves that awaits Télumée each time she visits her cabin.

In her protagonist's attachment to the spiritual world, Schwarz-Bart highlights a further synthesis between Télumée and this classical feminine trait. In her respect for the afterlife, Télumée shows her openness to the combined powers of nature and spirituality. Man Cia's initiation of Télumée into the spiritual and natural worlds provides her with an unyielding source of strength as she faces the trials and tribulations of her existence. The gift of healing and humanity bequeathed by Reine Sans Nom and Man Cia becomes a central part of Télumée and allows her to reach out and touch others, transforming their lives as her own has been transformed. Schwarz-Bart shows this powerful spiritual and practical

support as being a direct result of female bonding, which remains as potent a force in death as it does in life.

In striking contrast to the sisterhood that bolsters Télumée through the
joys and sorrows of her existence, Schwarz-Bart depicts several female
characters who actively undermine the successes of their sisters. The
reader discovers that the "most savage of all were those living with a man
on a temporary basis" (7). Minerve observes that "these women had nothing in their lives but a few planks balanced on four stones and a procession of men over their bellies" (8). This situation recalls the common
Caribbean phenomenon of men fathering children and then leaving their
partners to raise them. When the loving and reliable Jérémie proposes
marriage to Reine Sans Nom, she invokes the rage and jealousy of the
women around her. While marriage does not always guarantee the permanent presence of the male partner, Reine Sans Nom's neighbors perceive nonetheless that the relationship between Reine Sans Nom and
Jérémie has a greater chance of survival than the momentary liaisons that
they experience.

Like her grandmother, Télumée also finds herself the victim of a jealous
female attack when her childhood friend, Laetitia, steals Télumée's husband from her. Laetitia is an orphan and suffers from a lack of family and
known origins. Laetitia's detached behavior could be explained as the result of an early break with the mother, which impedes the possibility of
forming successful relationships later in life. Having missed out on a loving mother herself, Laetitia does not know what it is like to feel closely
connected to someone.

On another level, however, Laetitia finds some stability in the community around her for "the whole village was her mother" (43). As a young
girl, she manages to beg small amounts of food from her neighbors and
successfully eke out an existence for herself. Yet the feeling of connection
does not flow into her adult life and she remains removed from meaningful interpersonal connection. Her familial status is also symbolic of the
orphaning of slaves from Mother Africa and she displays the same alienation suffered by her ancestors, a theme that can also be explored in relation to Germain and Elie.

Alongside the countless descriptions vaunting Caribbean female
strength in the novel, Schwarz-Bart portrays a number of scenarios that
attest to the superior value attached to men in Caribbean society. An early
example is when Victoire loses a fully-formed male child after giving birth
prematurely. Despite the tragedy of the event, the fact that she has produced a son gives Victoire a dignity and purpose she had never experienced before. "People see me in the street, but who can know this belly
has carried a man, a man to laugh and cry and become Pope if he felt like
it? Who can know that, eh?" (18). Victoire reinforces the notion of female

inferiority when she refrains from speaking her mind to her husband because she thinks he always knows best because of his biological sex.
"Regina, Mama, and I followed [Angebert] at a distance, so as not to undermine him with our women's fears" (22). Victoire's self-imposed voicelessness illustrates the deeply entrenched belief throughout Caribbean society that men are more valuable despite the irresponsible behavior they
are renowned for displaying.

Fanta Toureh suggests that voicelessness is not confined to women and
that the colonized black male subject can also suffer from disempower-
ment. According to Toureh, Angebert is so discreet in his role as a father
to Télumée and husband to Victoire that when Germain kills him his existence is quickly forgotten.[14] Télumée herself observes that "Angebert
had led a reserved and silent existence, effacing himself so completely
that no one ever knew who it was who had died that day. Sometimes I
wonder about him, ask myself what anyone so kind and gentle was doing in this world at all" (23–24). To some extent, Angebert's gentle character does not conform to accepted images of Caribbean masculinity,
which tend to present an exaggerated, sexually charged vision of what it
is to be a man. By not fitting the more exuberant mold of French
Caribbean masculinity, Angebert appears destined to remain in the margins of history, a space traditionally reserved for the black postcolonial
woman.

Throughout the novel Schwarz-Bart reveals that stereotypical gender
roles still persist in French Caribbean society. This situation is particularly
evident in a consideration of male and female attitudes to sex, men being
encouraged to form sexual relationships from a young age and women to
maintain their virginity. When Télumée passes through puberty, for example, Reine Sans Nom encourages her to avoid the company of young
men so she will "stay as white as a tuft of cotton" (42). A discussion between Télumée and Elie's father, Old Abel, effectively encapsulates the
expectations of gendered behavior in the Caribbean. After first question-
ing Télumée on her capacity for patience, Old Abel then advises her not
to "go aboard Elie's barge, or on any other for that matter, for above all a
woman should be patient" (46). For men, however, the standard is radically different and Old Abel states that above all a man should be "a bit of
a swaggerer" (46). As Barry Chevannes notes, a "man is not a real man un-
less he is sexually active"[15] while women who engage in multiple casual
relationships are stigmatized as prostitutes or loose women. This brief ex-
change between Télumée and Old Abel captures the contradictions of
gender roles in the French Caribbean, which require women to be the responsible head of the family whilst still being submissive to men. Men, by
contrast, are perceived as superior to women and yet their actions are
characterized by irresponsibility and unreliability.

Télumée recognizes the contradictory nature of gender roles in the French Caribbean, arguing that "it seemed . . . the balance was in favor of the men, and that even in their fall there was still something of victory" (44). Schwarz-Bart includes some description of the evolution of these gendered patterns in her portrayal of the relationship between Télumée and Elie. In her depiction of Elie's interaction with his male friends, for example, Schwarz-Bart stresses the importance of the peer group in fostering particular attitudes toward the opposite sex. His friends criticize his uxorious behavior: "The real trouble is that though you belong to the race of men, you're getting Télumée into one bad habit after another—anyone would think she holds the strings of your will . . . A man doesn't carry on like that, for heaven's sake—how do you expect to train her?" (86). Such male bravado becomes a major contributor in perpetuating standards of gendered behavior that pivot on female subjugation.

Schwarz-Bart also stresses the discrepancy between male perceptions of gender relationships and their actuality. In the relationship between Télumée and Elie, for example, Télumée is clearly the one in control: "I looked after Elie as a mother looks after her child" (91). This attitude of indulgence toward one's partner is widespread in French Caribbean society and it acts as a substantial factor in the continuation of male attitudes of irresponsibility. Because of their inability to separate from their mother, Caribbean men remain immature in their expectations of adult intimate relationships. By tolerating and even indulging their conduct, female partners appear partly complicit in their fate, helping to create the kind of man that in the end causes personal anguish for them.

In his inability to withstand life's adversities and his consequent resort to self-destructive behavior, Elie is the character who provides the most detailed study of the image of the Caribbean man as a breadfruit. Beginning his life full of optimism, he quickly declines when his fortune starts to change. Following a bad season of drought in the village of Fond-Zombi, "Elie seemed to find the sun tarnished, dulled, and you could see from his glance that here was a man who had stopped seeing wonders" (98). In contrast to Télumée who focuses on the positive in times of hardship, Elie turns to drink and silently accuses Télumée of indulging in something as trivial and inappropriate as singing. Wallowing in his suffering, he imagines he is "out at sea amid the currents" (98) and wonders whether he is going to drown outright. While Télumée and Reine Sans Nom are both likened to boats in order to emphasize their sturdiness and their capacity to weather the storm, Elie appears instead as a victim of the elements, resorting to violence and alcohol abuse.

Olive Senior suggests a possible reason for such degeneration, stating that "a man's self-image and consequent treatment of his woman might . . . be a direct result of economic powerlessness."[16] Elie is let down by the colonial education system which could never have offered a poor child the qualifications necessary to achieve his dream of becoming a customs officer. Moreover, his father could not have afforded to send him to a high school in town. With the increasing precariousness of his financial situation following the drought, Elie attempts to reassert his failing sense of masculinity by crushing Télumée both mentally and physically. Elie's violent conduct represents a desperate proclamation of his weakening grip on life, illustrated in his need to prove his self-worth through oppression of others.

Télumée's failure to challenge Elie's abusive treatment of her brings to light a common phenomenon found among Caribbean women of silently accepting violence by men. Gisèle Pineau asserts that such submissive female behavior can be understood as one of the continuing effects of the slave period on gender identity. In her view, men and women created a sort of emotional game after the demise of the plantation system in which women accepted being the target of abuse out of a feeling of guilt for the slight advantages they experienced under slavery. "J'ai vu tellement de femmes comme ça qui restent sous les coups, qui acceptent les tromperies, qui acceptent la violence parce que . . . les hommes et les femmes ont créé ça après l'esclavage" [I have seen so many women like that who stay with the beatings, who accept the deception, who accept the violence because . . . men and women created that after slavery].[17] Beverley Ormerod also attests to the importance of history in understanding Elie's actions, pointing out that his "fall into despair and violence is linked with the earlier motif of 'West Indian madness' which was introduced in the story of Germain, and which later recurs in the story of the literally brain-damaged Angel Medard."[18] As Ormerod makes apparent, this negative masculine behavior is not confined to Elie in the novel and Schwarz-Bart paints portraits of male weakness in several other characters.

Of unknown parentage and an irredeemable outcast from society, Germain is renowned for his villainous and destructive actions. His angry stance toward life culminates in the murder of the only man who befriends him. In his defense he can only plead the external factors at play: "I stabbed Angebert, and you can kill me. Go on—you've every right. But I swear it's not my fault. No, not my fault" (23). Germain's refusal to assume responsibility for the murder underlines a tendency in French Caribbean society to excuse all actions committed by men because of the persistent psychological consequences of slavery. The story of l'ange Médard [Angel Medard] who forces his way into Télumée's life despite his terrifying reputation further illustrates the way the scars of the past continue to condition gendered behavior patterns in the present.

Like Germain, Angel Medard has only one friend, Télumée, who treats him with respect and humanity. However, he too turns against this single compassionate person, kidnapping Télumée's adopted daughter Sonore and attacking Télumée with a knife. When the attack goes horribly wrong, Télumée has the opportunity to end his destructive life, but she chooses instead to comfort the dying man. This action provokes the villagers to christen her with the new name of Télumée Miracle. The incident between Télumée and Angel Medard exemplifies the disparity between male and female attitudes to the injustices of Caribbean history. While Angel Medard reacts to the past by adopting a self-pitying and negative approach to present-day life, Télumée rises above these circumstances to embrace the gifts of humanity. As she declares at the end of the novel: "I have moved my cabin to the east and to the west; east winds and north winds have buffeted and soaked me; but I am still a woman standing on my own two legs, and I know a Negro is not a statue of salt to be dissolved by the rain" (172). In this scenario, the image of woman as chestnut and man as breadfruit come to the fore.

Against this backdrop of complex male and female relationships it is women who emerge as the great carriers of strength even while men undermine their fortitude in certain situations. The great variety of Creole proverbs related specifically to women attest to this force, calling attention to their faith, vision and ability to withstand the trials of life. Their acceptance of life unadorned in its joys and pains coupled with a refusal to bow down to hardships are portrayed as the defining characteristics of Caribbean women. Schwarz-Bart's female characters are buoyed by a sense of community that reinforces their strength and reminds them of their capacity to survive and resist. By contrast, the male characters appear trapped by the legacies of the past, condemned to forever reproduce destructive patterns of behavior. As the prevailing voice of wisdom in the novel, Reine Sans Nom's approach encapsulates the resilient philosophy of her female ancestors and descendants:

> In her view a human back was the strongest, toughest, most flexible thing in the world, an unchanging reality stretching far beyond the eye's reach. On it descended all the ravages, all the furies, all the eddies of human misery . . . The main thing, after all the changes and chances, the traps and surprises— the main thing was just to get your breath back and go on; that was what God had put you in the world for. (41)

Along with *Pluie et vent sur Télumée Miracle*, Maryse Condé's *Moi, Tituba, sorcière . . . noire de Salem* offers memorable examples of the image of the French Caribbean woman as chestnut and French Caribbean man as breadfruit. This novel imagines the untold story of Tituba, a black female slave from Barbados caught up in the Salem witch trials. It also explores her relationship with her dead ancestors, a series of male partners and a radical feminist she meets in prison. The central characters of the novel, Tituba and her husband, John Indien, correspond closely to the idea of the strong woman and the weak man in their varied approaches to life under slavery yet they also constitute a variation on the Creole proverb described throughout this chapter.

Like Reine Sans Nom and Télumée, Tituba demonstrates an affinity with nature and the spirit world and she displays a similar courageous and humanistic attitude to life. John Indien, by contrast, adopts a manipulative and sometimes deceitful stance in his determined quest to survive the injustices of his slave status. While he could certainly be viewed as morally weak when compared to Tituba, his kowtowing approach to his superiors allows him a series of privileges and eventually secures him his freedom.

Complementing these portraits of gendered strength and weakness, Condé explores the fluid nature of gender identity in her inclusion of characters such as Yao and Benjamin Cohen d'Azevedo who could be described as "feminine" men and in aggressive women such as Susanna Endicott. Condé also examines the preoccupations of modern-day feminists in the character of Hester Prynne and masculine violence taken to the extreme in Tituba's Puritan master, Samuel Parris.

In an interview with Ann Armstrong Scarboro, Condé warns against taking the novel too seriously, emphasizing that it has a mocking tone as well as representing a pastiche of the feminine "heroic novel."[19] She makes much use of irony in this work, which she uses to challenge stereotypes, particularly those related to feminist issues and women's emotional vulnerability. By deliberately drawing on clichés related to the sacrosanct grandmother and the spiritual nature of women to explode long-standing myths, Condé rejects any alignment with political correctness or received ideas. Nonetheless, the novel employs many serious motifs associated with female oppression, illustrating Condé's indignation at the injustices meted out to a black female slave by white Puritanical society. The reader can thus interpret the book from a theoretical angle whilst still appreciating Condé's ironic point of view.

Condé draws attention to Tituba's strength with her choice of the evocative title: *Moi, Tituba, sorcière . . . noire de Salem*. Declaring herself as "I" in the very first word, Tituba assumes her identity as an independent woman who is not afraid of speaking her mind. Condé's illumination of a character traditionally excluded from mainstream history indicates a significant move toward reversing the triple oppression imposed by the racist, colonial and patriarchal society in which Tituba moves. Tituba demonstrates an awareness of her marginalized status, stating that:

> There would be mention here and there of "a slave originating from the West Indies and probably practicing 'hoodoo.'" There would be no mention of my

age or my personality. I would be ignored . . . I would never be included!
Tituba would be condemned forever! There would never, ever be a careful,
sensitive biography recreating my life and its suffering. (110)

As well as being one of Condé's metatextual tricks with its blatant
anachronism and allusion to the presence of the author, Tituba's apprehension nonetheless stresses the major feminist concern about the exclusion of women from history. While Condé denies being influenced by the
feminist revival of witches as examples of strong and independent
women,[20] Tituba's empowered position succeeds in providing a counter-
narrative to the official version of history.

Tituba represents an autonomous speaking subject who is not only the
director of her own life but, by her example, also inspires a more general
understanding of marginality in society. For many scholars in the fields of
francophone literature, feminism and multicultural studies, Tituba has
become something of an icon, providing the voice of "a strong Third
World woman"[21] which can be harnessed to aid in the empowerment of
other oppressed women. Tituba's expression of her own point of view as
a black, lower-class woman also encourages Western critics to examine
their bias and reflect on their privileged position compared to women in
other cultures. Through an exploration of the multiple strands of Tituba's
identity, Condé examines the manner in which seemingly disempowering
elements can be transformed into a powerful means of self-affirmation.

There are a number of qualities in Tituba's character which are linked
to the positive feminine qualities of resilience and courage. These traits include a respect and love for nature, a belief in the healing powers of female solidarity, a relaxed attitude to her sexuality and an overwhelming
sense of optimism. The wise and mystical Man Yaya sows the seeds of this
personal philosophy when she takes Tituba into her care after the tragic
death of her mother and her beloved stepfather, Yao. One of the most profound and lasting lessons Man Yaya teaches Tituba is "that everything
lives, has a soul, and breathes. That everything must be respected. That
man is not the master riding through his kingdom on horseback" (9). Man
Yaya's thoughtful words emphasize the necessity to locate the human in
every person and to treat people with a respectful openness.

This generous capacity for relationships reflects the observation of
object-relations theorists that women are more equipped for such an approach than men because of the different ways in which boys and girls react to being mothered. As a result of Tituba's successful, if unconven-
tional, experience of the mother figure—she is showered with love by Yao
during his life and by her mother, Abena, and Man Yaya after their
deaths—she is able to effortlessly re-create bonds of intimacy in her adult
life. By contrast, Man Yaya and Abena warn Tituba against forming rela-

tionships with men who do not share this capacity for loving openness. "Men don't love. They possess. They subjugate" (14). Condé emphasizes the limitations of this defensive male attitude toward relationships in characters such as John Indien who always seems to have another agenda alongside his professed love for his partner. To some extent, John Indien re-creates the lack of kinship systems of the slaves who were newly arrived in the Caribbean, developing a stance of him against the rest of the world. While John Indien clearly gains material advantages by resisting deep bonds with others, Condé depicts a superior form of strength in the character of Tituba who is sincere and forthright in her connections to people. Tituba is also able to derive a sense of purpose and belonging from the community around her, whether it be from her "invisibles" or from her relationships with Judah White or Hester Prynne.

A consideration of the presentation of maternity in the novel contributes to an understanding of the way in which gender identity is constructed in French Caribbean society. As in *Pluie et vent sur Télumée Miracle*, *Moi, Tituba, sorcière . . . noire de Salem* depicts a selection of biological and nonbiological mothers who display varying degrees of influence in raising children. These mother figures are predominantly women, reflecting the historical phenomenon of extensive female kinship networks, but Condé also includes two men, Yao and Benjamin Cohen d'Azevedo, whom she depicts as loving and nurturing carers. The diverse group of people who mother Tituba illustrates the way in which motherhood frequently extends beyond the bounds of the biological mother.

Abena finds herself unable to raise Tituba because her daughter is a constant reminder of the rape that caused her pregnancy. Tituba's stepfather, Yao, takes on the role of mother and father in her upbringing with such success that Tituba "did not suffer from this lack of affection, because Yao's love was worth the love of two" (6–7). In her positive portrayal of a nurturing man, Condé highlights the strength associated with the maternal role. Yao gains further significance in the novel for his selection of Tituba's name, which is symbolic of the rebuilding of the family structure after the scattering of family bonds caused by slavery. Condé's additional identification of Yao as African rather than Caribbean amplifies his role from the individual to the historical level in his tangible link with the African slaves' past. The certainty of Yao's origins helps to give Tituba a firm sense of her own identity, sparing her the traumatic quest for connection to an unknown ancestry that haunts many Caribbean people. Yao's influence is thus twofold in the constant source of affection which he provides for Tituba and in his positive alliance with history, both of which succeed in offering Tituba a firm concept of her own selfhood.

In addition to Yao, Man Yaya also acts as a significant mother figure to Tituba, offering her an infusion of love and the bountiful fruits of her wisdom. One of her primary gifts to Tituba is her initiation of the young woman into the healing properties of nature. Like Reine Sans Nom and Télumée, Tituba utilizes the curative potential of plants to help the people around her. These acts of selfless kindness are nowhere more evident than in the magical potions she prepares to help Samuel Parris' wife and daughter despite Parris' loathing of Tituba. Through her teachings to her adopted daughter, Man Yaya thus performs a similar role to Yao in her connection of Tituba to her African past, as magic is a cultural legacy from Africa. Simonne Henry Valmore draws attention to the distinctly feminine nature of this capacity for healing, asserting that the traditional rivalry between doctor and witch in the Caribbean replicates the old war between the masculine and the feminine.[22] Condé thus underlines the feminine quality of natural healing whilst also pointing to the empowering nature of nonbiological maternity for "mother" and child.

Condé problematizes the concept of motherhood in her illumination of the positive characteristics of nonbiological mothers and the frequent negative associations of biological maternity. The reader learns, for example, of the pain associated with Tituba's birth for Abena and Hester's punishment for adultery because of the physical evidence of her pregnancy. For Tituba too, motherhood is related to negativity and she chooses to abort her unborn child because she does not want to subject her/him to the deprivations of slave life. The decision by many female slaves to kill their unborn children is an established historical fact,[23] illustrating a certain (albeit painful) resistance to the colonial order. When Tituba becomes pregnant a second time she is determined to change the oppressive state of the world by militant action before giving birth to her daughter, but, tragically, she dies first. Despite her inability to bring any biological children into the world, Tituba spiritually adopts a girl called Samantha after her death in Barbados. As she describes it: "A child I didn't give birth to but whom I chose! What motherhood could be nobler!" (177). Acting as a sort of spiritual guide, Tituba fulfils a function similar to that of Man Yaya in the transmission of her wisdom and unyielding love to her young charge, affirming the value of motherhood by choice. These alternative visions of the mother figure allow women to become empowered through their rejection or acceptance of maternity. They also point to the rewards for mothers of passing their wisdom down through the female line. Condé expands the concept of motherhood to embrace the men in the novel who successfully take on the maternal role.

Despite her flexible approach to motherhood, Condé portrays a distinctly female community as a vital element in buoying Tituba in her times of trial. Emotionally sustained by Abena and Man Yaya, as well as by Yao, in the wisdom they communicate to her after their deaths, Tituba demonstrates the spirit and optimism that arises from a feeling of connection with others. This female kinship system also arises in the relationships between black and white women in the novel, both of whom are oppressed by patriarchal society although the racial aspect necessarily divides them. Abena and her mistress, Jennifer Davis, mutually comfort each other during the perils of night while Tituba and Elizabeth Parris form a firm friendship until the witch trials tear them apart. These cross-racial female relationships highlight the relative strength of the black female slaves who display a robustness and resilience that is in striking opposition to the ethereal nature of the white women. As well as being the recipient of female strength and guidance, Tituba also demonstrates her female solidarity in the attachment to nature she shares with Judas White and in the mutual understanding she and Hester offer each other in prison. Female community is instrumental in fostering Tituba's courageous attitude to life.

A further aspect of Tituba's strength is the stance she adopts in her sexual relationships. Condé transforms stereotypical understandings of female sexuality in which women represent the passive objects of male desire, pointing instead to the way sexuality can become an empowering element for women. Tituba derives great delight from her intimate relations with men and is easily accepting of her sexuality. While white men typically construct black women as exotic and promiscuous, Tituba reverses these expectations and makes sexuality a place of subjectivity. In her hands, sexuality becomes a tool of empowerment in a patriarchal society that has traditionally restricted women's autonomy in this field. Her attitude forms a contrast to the negative image of sexuality that arose as a result of the plantation system in which rape and sexual attacks against women were common. Sexuality for Tituba ultimately allows her to assume the fullness of her identity and leads to a deeper sense of self-expression. Her status as a fully autonomous individual allows her to better negotiate the hardships in life and to make choices from a position of strength.

However, Condé underlines the negative aspects of this enjoyment of sexuality in Tituba's sacrifice of her freedom. Despite Tituba's quiet independence in her rural lifestyle, she chooses to leave her life of isolation and communion with nature when she falls in love with a slave, John Indien. For the first time, she becomes aware of her sexuality and desire for male companionship. Although she has been depicted as a strong and independent female up to that point—maybe even the perfect radical feminist in her world without men—Condé draws her as a woman who still has a primal need for a man. So potent is this desire that she is willing to jeopardize her own freedom to pursue the relationship with John Indien.

> I wanted the man as I had never wanted anyone else. I desired his love as I had never desired any other. Not even my mother's. I wanted him to touch

me. I wanted him to caress me. I was merely waiting for the moment when
he would take me and the valves of my body would open wide, flooding me
with pleasure. (18)

Contrasting with previous descriptions of her character, Tituba appears
here as a stereotypical woman who cannot live without a man. Indeed,
she exemplifies Gisèle Pineau's statement that Caribbean women need a
man.[24] This overwhelming desire for John Indien comes as a striking contrast to Tituba's previous fiery independence. At the same time, however,
she demonstrates an awareness that she is voluntarily placing herself in a
position of powerlessness compared to her lover. Condé depicts Tituba's
departure from her rural idyll to join John Indien as a kind of self-
imposed expulsion from the Garden of Eden. When she becomes alienated from nature her life begins to change direction and she encounters
the negative elements associated with the fall from paradise. This highly
charged decision underlines the complexities of Tituba's character, highlighting her unequivocal ability to be the director of her life, but also detailing the consequences such choices may entail.

Tituba's relationship with John Indien brings into focus a number of
trends evident in Caribbean society in the relationships between men and
women. When John Indien is talking about his father, for example, he emphasizes the common phenomenon in the Caribbean of the "swaggering"
male who fathers many children and cannot provide for any of them. As
David Murray asserts, this exaggerated sexuality is considered one way
of asserting one's subjectivity over the emasculation of masculinity
caused by slavery and colonialism.[25] Tituba senses a force within John Indien that is beyond her control and therefore believes that she cannot rely
on him to remain permanently attached to her. "I had the intuition that
the main thing was not so much to attract a man as to keep him, and that
John Indien must belong to the species that is easily attracted but has no
intention of making any commitment" (17). Tituba's analysis of John Indien is confirmed in a night of musical hilarity when she learns that he has
led a life strikingly similar to that of his philandering father, producing
two children with a woman and then abandoning them.

While Condé describes the situation in a playful manner, it brings to
light a serious issue that carries important consequences for the women
left behind by such unreliable men. John Indien, for his part, takes the situation as a hilarious joke and his flippancy is a reflection of the cavalier
attitude many men are shown to adopt in their relationships with women.
It is significant also that women tolerate such male behavior and even, at
times, reinforce it. The mother of John Indien's children, for example, declares to Tituba: "Men, my dear, are made to be shared!" (33). In an echo
of Laetitia's proclamation to Télumée as she is about to steal her husband,

these words emphasize the presence of a jealous female "anti-community" that exacerbates the breaking of kinship patterns by denying any woman the chance at happiness with a man.

By allowing John Indien to get away with his actions, this woman is in effect perpetuating the child-like conduct of some adult Caribbean males who fail to form mature relationships with women. Through this character's failure to challenge her situation, Condé emphasizes the way in which Caribbean women repeat the patterns that victimize them. The scenario also constitutes a potent example of the way in which these male patterns of conduct provide the conditions from which strong women are born. Out of the pure necessity to survive and ensure their families' welfare, Caribbean women are forced to develop strength in order to withstand the adverse conditions presented to them by men.

In the characters of Tituba and John Indien, Condé demonstrates two ways in which black slaves reacted to their position at the bottom of the social ladder. While Tituba remains steadfastly true to herself and her principles throughout her life, her husband adopts a different stance by choosing to "play the game." For John Indien, this path involves kowtowing to his superiors and behaving in the obsequious manner expected of him in order to gain favors. While Tituba consistently remains committed to her passionate ideals, John Indien manipulates the system to his advantage by conforming to the racial stereotypes expected of him.

The concept of *marronnage*, explored by writers such as Edouard Glissant and Patrick Chamoiseau, sheds light on these radically opposed approaches adopted by Tituba and John Indien toward the experience of slavery. For Glissant, the *marron*, or runaway slave, who is always identified as male, is the supreme symbol of resistance in his steadfast refusal to participate in the colonial system. Patrick Chamoiseau refines the conception of this celebrated figure of opposition, describing instead the phenomenon of *la grande marronne* which rejects the colonial system outright and *la petite marronne* relating to the slave who only partially absents himself from the system.[26] The latter, inextricably linked to the ideology of *débrouillardise* or the ability to survive and exploit the system that oppresses, is the strategy John Indien assumes in his ability to exist and flourish within the gaps of slavery. For Tituba, collaborating with this hostile and unjust social system is unthinkable and she prefers to undertake acts associated with *la grande marronne*, even if ultimately it leads to her downfall.

John Indien's governing doctrine rests on the notion that "the duty of a slave is to survive" (22) and all his actions are chosen in accordance with this aim. He voluntarily places himself in a position of degradation, referring to himself as a nigger and wheedling favors out of his mistress, Susanna Endicott. He actively encourages conformity to the stereotypes set

out by white people as a way of further manipulating the system that oppresses: "Let's play at being perfect niggers" (32). This plan of action succeeds in producing the desired result and by the end of the book John Indien has secured himself a position as the live-in partner of a white
woman. Clearly there are advantages attached to adopting this philosophy, not only for the instant privileges it brings but also for more long-
term goals like John Indien's desire to be freed. As Tituba discovers, however, there is also a cost involved, particularly when the question of
relationships comes into play. In a consideration of strength and weakness, John Indian's behavior could be placed into either category depend-
ing on one's perspective. If strength is conceived in terms of personal survival and subversion of the system wherever possible, John Indien would
be a shining example of a resilient chestnut with his ability to manipulate
people to his advantage. However, if integrity of character is a defining
feature of strength he would be more comparable to the soft and rotten
texture of the fallen breadfruit.

In contrast to John Indien, Tituba refuses to submit passively to the injustices that she experiences as a result of her race although it ultimately
leads to her death back in Barbados. Participating in a maroon uprising
with her "son" and lover, Iphigene, Tituba is hanged with him after they
are the victims of betrayal. While premature death could be considered
the colonial order's ultimate triumph over Tituba's persistently defiant
spirit, Mireille Rosello highlights the revolutionary opportunities that
death and the after-life afford Tituba, declaring that "le roman fait de l'é-
tat de mort un moment privilégié d'opposition" [the novel makes of the
state of death a privileged moment of opposition].[27] Rosello also asserts
that Tituba continues her resistance in death by placing herself in the
hearts and minds of the living. "I am hardening men's heart to fight. I am
nourishing them with dreams of liberty. Of victory. I have been behind
every revolt. Every insurrection. Every act of disobedience." (175). The
most potent symbol of Tituba's continuing state of resistance is the song
she bequeaths to her beloved Barbados, a song that can be heard from one
end of the island to the other. Like *Pluie et vent sur Télumée Miracle*,
Condé's novel features song as a distinctly female rallying point in its
connections with nature and its link with female solidarity. Tituba's musical legacy to her island symbolizes her jubilation in life and the cement-
ing of her character as an admirable figure.

An additional character who exhibits opposition to the colonial system
is Hester Prynne, a twentieth-century feminist who is imaginatively transposed to the seventeenth century by way of Nathaniel Hawthorne's *The
Scarlet Letter*. While a comparison between Tituba and John Indien
demonstrates two reactions to racial oppression, the contrast between
Tituba and Hester highlights diverse approaches to gender exploitation.

Satirizing the position of modern-day radical feminists in the character of Hester, Condé humorously stages an encounter between "first and third world feminisms as the accused witch and the alleged adulterous wife meet in seventeenth-century Salem."[28] With Condé deliberately employing an anachronistic vocabulary, Hester gently chides Tituba for her love of men and old-fashioned ways: "'You're too fond of love, Tituba! I'll never make a feminist out of you!' 'A feminist? What's that?'" (101). Despite her parodying of radical feminism in this episode, Condé acknowledges the specific role gender plays in Tituba's oppression, arguing that she was not rehabilitated in history as the other white women were because she was a black female.[29] Condé presents Hester as a victim of male power in her suffering from hypocritical moral standards that tolerate male infidelity, but not acts of adultery committed by women. Thrown together in a jail cell, Tituba and Hester forge an alliance which bolsters their spirit and resolve.

Condé's dramatization of two approaches to female liberation highlights some of the debates between "first world" and "third world" feminists, although both paths described in the novel represent only one strand of each group. Condé's treatment of gender in this novel has a tendency to conflate "first world" feminism with radical feminism and rejects any theoretical conception of gender issues. Hester questions many of the received ideas in relation to gender, drawing attention to the notion of naming, for example, which has traditionally been carried out by men. When she discovers Yao chose Tituba's name, Hester is disappointed to learn that male domination in the area of naming prevails as much in African societies as it does in her own. For Tituba, however, Yao's selection of her name reminds her of her origins and she carries it with great pride.

This simple difference of opinion comes to symbolize Tituba's and Hester's contrasted perceptions of the female position in society. Although Tituba does not always agree with Hester's radical ideas, she nevertheless recognizes that women have a more difficult time in life than men. As Hester makes clear, female oppression continues to flourish in the world: "Life is too kind to men, whatever their color" (100). In recognition of the difficulties men create for women, she proposes a new society to Tituba that is characterized by the absence of men: "We would give our names to our children, we would raise them alone" (101). Hester's utopian blueprint provides a vision of female liberation consistent with the preoccupations of some radical feminists. In contrast to Hester's ideal, however, Tituba is concerned to integrate men into a society that is accepting of both sexes in a conviction more in line with the perspective of Alice Walker's "womanism." While Condé reveals the incompatibilities of Tituba's and Hester's methods, she nonetheless underlines the fact that both are effective mechanisms of resistance against an oppressive patriarchal system. Both Tituba and Hester can thus be considered to participate in the phenomenon of *la grande marronne*, displaying strength of character and determination of spirit.

Condé depicts white slave owners as the dominant power brokers in the novel, but she also aligns them with moral weakness. The most prominent example is Samuel Parris, Tituba's and John Indien's master in America. Parris is associated with violence and aggression and demonstrates the way in which the domination of others is used to mask personal inadequacy. A graphic example of his cold and uncaring attitude is his relationship with his wife. While sex is depicted as a beautiful act between Tituba and John Indien, Parris' wife Elizabeth points out that for Puritans it is a shameful and despised activity. "If only you knew! He takes me without removing either his clothes or mine, so hurried is he to finish with the hateful act" (42). When Elizabeth falls ill and Parris calls on Tituba to help, his first thought is for her to dress herself properly when she leaps naked out of bed to come to his aid. In one of the most disturbing episodes in the novel, Parris and two other hooded men gang-rape Tituba, plunging a stick up her body and beating her in order to gain a confession that she bewitched the children. Parris manifests his disgust at sexuality in a distorted way through aggression against women, underlining the old religious prejudice against nature based on the idea that nature reflected the state of fallen humanity—in contrast with lost Paradise. His actions demonstrate the contradictions of a man who is at once ruthlessly true to his beliefs, and is at the same time profoundly morally weak. Condé uses Parris' considerable social power as a powerful judgment on the patriarchal system of slavery and religious fanaticism.

A final male character for consideration is the maroon leader, Christopher, who betrays Tituba and provokes her untimely death. Despite the positive mythology that surrounds the legendary figure of the Caribbean maroon, Condé depicts Christopher in a negative light with his sexist attitude toward women and the selfishness with which he treats Tituba. As he constantly reminds her: "A woman's duty, Tituba, is not to fight or make war, but to make love!" (151). While the maroon traditionally represents a figure of intense virility and opposition to the colonial system, Condé unravels this stereotype in the character of Christopher and reveals him instead to be a man of moral weakness. Taking advantage of others in his driven quest for self-promotion, Christopher looks only for what he can gain and never for what he can give in his approach to his relationships. Condé portrays Tituba's spirit as strong and irrepressible in life as in death. Christopher, by contrast, appears emotionally crippled by his self-interested and destructive stance toward the trials of existence. In his determination to resist death, Christopher displays a commitment to

survival similar to John Indien's. However, he also resembles John Indien's breadfruit-like interior with the sacrifice of his moral strength.

Moi, Tituba, sorcière . . . noire de Salem and *Pluie et vent sur Télumée Miracle* represent two dynamic examples of the image of the French Caribbean
woman as a chestnut and the French Caribbean man as a breadfruit. In
Schwarz-Bart's novel, Télumée and Elie exemplify this picture of gendered strength and weakness and in Condé's work, Tituba and John Indien reveal the contradictions of the male and female stance on life. The
subsidiary characterization attests to this trend, ranging from the courageous attributes of Reine Sans Nom and Hester to the negative qualities
of Germain and Samuel Parris. Alongside these portraits of strong women
and weak men, however, the authors have acknowledged the fluidity of
gender in their portrayals of "feminine" men such as Xango and Yao and
more aggressive women in characters like Laetitia and Susanna Endicott.
As an essential backdrop to the unveiling of these character descriptions,
Schwarz-Bart and Condé include observations about French Caribbean
society. Both authors have drawn on the legacy of slavery to provide the
context for their novels, although Condé always approaches the subject
with an ironic tone. The female point of view expressed by Télumée and
Tituba provides a rare insight into Caribbean female experience and represents an important contribution to postcolonial literature.

NOTES

1. Doris Y. Kadish, "Guadeloupean Women Remember Slavery," *The French Review* 77, no. 6 (2004): 1186.

2. Patricia Mohammed, "Towards Indigenous Feminist Theorizing in the
Caribbean," *Feminist Review* 59 (1998): 28.

3. Héliane Toumson and Roger Toumson, "Simone et André Schwarz-Bart: Sur
les pas de Fanotte," *Textes, études et documents* 2 (1979): 20.

4. Gisèle Pineau, unpublished interview by Bonnie Thomas, Paris, 12 July 2001.

5. Wendy Goolcharan-Kumeta, *My Mother, My Country: Reconstructing the Female Self in Guadeloupean Women's Writing* (Bern: Peter Lang, 2003), 26.

6. Clarisse Zimra, "Righting the Calabash: Writing History in the Female Francophone Narrative," in Carole Boyce Davies and Elaine Savory Fido (eds.), *Out of
the Kumbla: Caribbean Women and Literature* (Trenton, N.J.: African World Press,
1990), 156.

7. Ronnie Scharfman, "Mirroring and Mothering in Simone Schwarz-Bart's
Pluie et vent sur Télumée Miracle and Jean Rhys' *Wide Sargasso Sea*," *Yale French
Studies* 62 (1981): 91.

8. Goolcharan-Kumeta, *My Mother, My Country*, 190.

9. Yolande Helm, "Prolégomènes," in Yolande Helm (ed.), *L'Eau: Source d'une
écriture dans les littératures féminines francophones* (New York: Peter Lang, 1995), 1.

10. Philippe Seringe, *Les Symboles: Dans l'art, dans les religions et dans la vie de tous les jours* (Genève: Helios, 1985), 297, 299 and 303.

11. Mireille Rosello, *Littérature et identité aux Antilles* (Paris: Karthala, 1992), 77.

12. Valérie Loichot, "Negations and Subversions of Paternal Authorities in Glissant's Fictional Works (*Le Quatrième Siècle, La Case du commandeur, Tout-monde*)," in Eva Paulino Bueno, Terry Caesar and William Hummel (eds.), *Naming the Father: Legacies, Genealogies and Explorations of Fatherhood in Modern and Contemporary Literature* (Lanham, Md.: Lexington Books, 2000), 113.

13. Rosello, *Littérature et identité aux Antilles*, 81.

14. Fanta Toureh, *L'Imaginaire dans l'oeuvre de Simone Schwarz-Bart: Approche d'une mythologie antillaise* (Paris: L'Harmattan, 1987), 84.

15. Barry Chevannes, *Learning to Be a Man: Culture, Socialization and Gender Identity in Five Caribbean Communities* (Kingston: University of the West Indies Press, 2001), 217.

16. Olive Senior, *Working Miracles: Women's Lives in the English-Speaking Caribbean* (Cave Hill, Barbados: Institute of Social and Economic Research, University of the West Indies; Bloomington: Indiana University Press; London: James Currey, 1991), 180.

17. Pineau, unpublished interview by Bonnie Thomas.

18. Beverley Ormerod, *An Introduction to the French Caribbean Novel* (London: Heinemann, 1985), 123.

19. Ann Armstrong Scarboro, "Afterword," in Maryse Condé, *I, Tituba, Black Witch of Salem*, trans. Richard Philcox (New York: Ballantine Books, 1994), 212.

20. Françoise Pfaff, *Conversations with Maryse Condé* (Lincoln: University of Nebraska Press, 1996), 59.

21. Jane Moss, "Postmodernizing the Salem Witchcraze: Maryse Condé's I, Tituba, Black Witch of Salem," *Colby Quarterly* 85, no. 1 (1999): 5.

22. Simonne Henry Valmore, *Dieux en exil* (Paris: Gallimard, 1988), 50.

23. Gabriel Debien, *Les Esclaves aux Antilles françaises (XVIIe–XVIIIe siècles)* (Basse-Terre: Société d'Histoire de la Guadeloupe; Fort-de-France: Société d'Histoire de la Martinique, 1974), 363–66.

24. Pineau, unpublished interview by Bonnie Thomas.

25. David A. B. Murray, "Homosexuality, Society, and the State: An Ethnography of Sublime Resistance in Martinique," *Identities* 2, no. 3 (1996): 249.

26. Richard D. E. Burton, "Debrouya pa peche, or il y a toujours moyen de moyenner: Patterns of Opposition in the Fiction of Patrick Chamoiseau," *Callaloo* 16, no. 2 (1993): 473.

27. Rosello, *Littérature et identité aux Antilles*, 66.

28. Caroline Duffey, "Tituba and Hester in the Intertextual Jail Cell: New World Feminisms in Maryse Condé's *Moi, Tituba, sorcière . . . noire de Salem*," *Women in French Studies* 4 (1996): 101.

29. Pfaff, *Conversations with Maryse Condé*, 60.

4

History, Lack and Gender

Edouard Glissant published two of his most significant studies on Martinican identity in 1981: the philosophical *Le Discours antillais* and his fourth novel, *La Case du commandeur*. Drawing on his research at the Institut Martiniquais d'Etudes, Glissant painted an exhaustive portrait of the island's "missed opportunities" regarding independence from France and the possibility of creating a uniquely Caribbean identity. Driven by his passionate desire to overcome Martinique's absence from a tangible historical continuum, Glissant's theoretical and creative works are linked to his conviction that understanding the past provides the key to the present and future. Glissant's work asserts that Martinicans need to carve a place for themselves within the specific geographical and historical context of the Caribbean.

In Glissant's hands, literature offers a constructive medium for subverting Martinique's cultural domination by France. Through his proposal for a writing of opacity, which he perceives as an important counterpart to the oppressive transparent models of Western thought, Glissant draws attention to the contrast between writing and orality. With the former linked to France and the latter to Martinique, this contrast carries important implications for the place of Creole, an oral language, in the Caribbean context. Reacting to the universal models and denial of difference that are embedded in a writing of clarity, Glissant grounds his own work in opacity. Glissant sees obscurity as a function of the absence of history and the linguistic conflicts between French and Creole in the Caribbean. Glissant's desire is to celebrate diversity and thus his novels frequently feature an explosion of narrative points of view that subverts the notion of a single Truth.

While Glissant's works do not focus specifically on gender identity, two of his novels, *Le Quatrième Siècle* and *La Case du commandeur*, provide a revealing picture of the gendered undercurrents that surface in his interrogations of the Caribbean past. In *Le Quatrième Siècle*, for example, Glissant portrays the way in which qualities associated with masculinity and femininity are available to both sexes, sometimes moving freely between the two. In his extensive narrative cast, Glissant paints portraits of people who are firmly allied with the attributes of either the masculine or the feminine and others who identify with both.

La Case du commandeur, by contrast, is the only novel in which Glissant privileges a female point of view. Although Marie Celat's perspective dominates for only half of the book, Glissant nonetheless gives some insight into the female condition in Martinique. He also explores the figure of the *femme matador*, or the woman who courageously resists life's trials, in the character of Cinna Chimène. Glissant's novel reveals the way in which the forces of history intrude on relationships, expressed in his descriptions of the generations of couples which prevail in the first part of the novel. While the focal point of the two books is on the role of the past in shaping identity, it is clear that the question of gender is an important element in both texts.

First published in Paris in 1964, *Le Quatrième Siècle* represents Glissant's second venture into fictional writing. An epic tale tracing the genesis of two families, the Longoués and the Béluses, from their arrival in Martinique in 1788 until 1946, *Le Quatrième Siècle* pivots on an examination of the country's troubled relationship with history. Glissant frames and interrupts the story with a conversation about the past between the *quimboiseur*, or sorcerer/healer, Papa Longoué, the last living descendant of the maroons, and Mathieu Béluse, a young intellectual keen to know more about his ancestry. With the arrival of the first Longoué and Béluse on Martinican shores, Glissant explores two possible responses to the experience of slavery: the former escapes into the hills within minutes of setting foot on the island; Béluse opts for tolerance and resignation by accepting his slave status. Richard Burton draws attention to the value judgment Glissant attributes to these varying approaches, noting that "la partie supérieure—moralement comme topographiquement—appartient aux Longoué et la partie inférieure aux Béluse" [the superior part—morally as topographically—belongs to the Longoués and the inferior part to the Béluses].[1] Following this initial contrast, Glissant delineates a series of binary oppositions that are presented through antagonistic couples in the novel. While Glissant clearly contrasts past and present, History and histories, magic and logic,[2] there is also a place for the distinction between

sex and gender, which is particularly appropriate in a novel that Burton
describes as "patrifocal, patrilinear, even patriarchal, in structure."[3] This
book, which has traditionally been viewed in terms of history and politics, is also important in the study of gender.

In the figure of Longoué, first evoked in *La Lézarde*, Glissant returns to
the mythology surrounding the maroon in Martinican culture. Symboliz-
ing "not only the spirit of revolt . . . but also the African element in the
composition of the Caribbean man,"[4] the maroon represents the ultimate
symbol of resistance to the plantation system. As well as epitomizing defiance of the colonial order and the capacity to adapt to a new environment, this figure has also come to be identified as an overarching emblem
of masculinity. Romuald-Blaise Fonkoua, for example, asserts that one of
Longoué's first tasks after his escape to the safety of the *mornes* is that he
"conquiert la femme, l'oblige à oublier son nom issu de l'habitation et
donc de l'esclavage" [conquers the woman, obliges her to forget the name
given to her by the plantation and therefore by slavery].[5] Jacques André is
even more emphatic in his association of *marronnage* and masculinity, stating that in the maroon world of the hills, "tout est *affaire d'homme*" [every-
thing is *men's business*].[6] This masculine dominance contrasts sharply with
the feminine law that prevails on the plantations.

A powerful testament to the virility of the maroon in *Le Quatrième Siècle* is the recognition Longoué finds in the eyes of the powerful estate
owner, La Roche, who is his official "owner." Described as "an absolute
and maniacal Patriarch" (128), La Roche embodies the force associated
with the domination of others. However, in a curious way, these two figures of dominant masculinity form a symbiotic relationship in which each
accepts and affirms the other's difference. This mutual recognition is
nowhere more evident than in the scene where they meet in the hills. Instead of killing each other, they begin speaking each in his own language,
unable to understand the other's words, but somehow able to communicate. The spirit of understanding that occurs between these two figures of
virile patriarchy attests to the exclusion of the maroon from the process of
emasculation that occurred under slavery. Glissant thus portrays in the
character of Longué a man recognized for his potent strength and ability
to exist outside the dominating system.

Despite the virile side to Longoué's character, he also displays an alliance with nature that is more typical of the feminine principle. When the
slave ship docks on the island of Martinique for the first time, it takes less
than an hour for him to flee to safety in the hills. While Glissant pays tribute to Longoué's masculinity with his insistence on the active role Longoué plays in his escape, describing him as "the pioneer, the vanguard,
the discoverer of the new land" (16), he also reveals that this action occurs
not through the domination of nature but by collaboration with it. It is the

natural environment that offers Longoué his first roots in the new country, permitting him "to assert around the forest, at this boundary to
known existence, his incomprehensible and ineradicable presence" (78).
To some extent, Longoué appears a conqueror of the natural world, but he
maintains a respectful understanding of the environment as he builds up
a maroon community. Longoué's relationship with nature thus exhibits a
merging of the masculine and the feminine.

Nature also provides Longoué with his vocation in the new country
when he begins imparting advice as a *quimboiseur*. Considered to be at the
heart of Caribbean identity, the spiritual healing of the *quimboiseur* was
born in resistance to the declaration in Article Three of *Le Code Noir* that
the only valid religion was Catholicism. The *quimboiseur* represents a figure outside the colonial system in a similar manner to the maroon, with
these two roles frequently coinciding in the same person.

According to Simonne Henry Valmore, a *quimboiseur* is always male
while women are confined to the roles of healer or mother.[7] Barry
Chevannes affirms this difference between male and female approaches
to healing, stating that the notion of women as healers "is directly linked
to a woman's nurturing role, which she begins training in from the childhood stage when she is assigned to model her mother's role in taking care
of her younger siblings."[8] In a similar manner to the maroon, then, the status of the *quimboiseur* is heavy with masculine connotations. Thus, while
Longoué operates in the medium of nature traditionally associated with
the feminine, his position as maroon and magician reinforces the masculine side of his character.

Although Longoué is firmly identified with virility, he experiences a
paradoxical relationship with his partner, Louise. Louise is described as a
"warrior woman" (47) who exercises a compelling power over Longoué
following her release of him. Sparking a yearning in him so overwhelming that he risks the threat of approaching the plantation to meet her, he
seeks to reestablish his authority by kidnapping Louise "so she could
know the taste of the earth and have her back marked by acacia branches,
because he would lay her down there on the ground and she wouldn't
even struggle" (68). According to Jacques André the act of making Louise
submit by laying her on the ground is also symbolic of taking possession
of the earth,[9] attesting to Longoué's need to feel he is the master of his domain. While Longoué forces Louise to accompany him into the hills, she
departs with a struggle and repeatedly along the journey Longoué realizes that she is gathering her resources in a display of resistance against
his control. Moreover, he soon realizes that "he had never conquered
Louise. He had been reduced to demonstrating affection, weakness, as he
would to a creature who was his equal. Even superior to him, perhaps. He
had not taken her; she had accepted him" (91).

The arrival of Louise in the *mornes*, despite the forced circumstances of her departure from the plantation, in effect signals a challenge to Longoué's masculine credibility. This imbalance of power is further evident in the fact that Louise is the one who initiates him into the new world, offering Longoué the power of communication by teaching him the language. While Louise gradually occupies a more stereotypical gender role, metamorphosing from a young and rebellious girl to a wife and mother who earns the nickname Man-Louise, Glissant shows that the energy and determination with which she approaches life keep a check on Longoué's domination of the maroon community.

Alongside this tale of predominantly masculine potency associated with the maroons, Glissant depicts an alternative existence in which the feminine principle reigns supreme. Representing a kind of female pyramid in its organization of power, the plantation leaves little place for men. Glissant describes this hierarchical arrangement of women in detail, ranging from the field slaves who are firmly at the bottom of the ladder, through to the house slaves and peaking with the plantation owner's wife, Marie-Nathalie Senglis. While the plantation slaves embody the qualities of passivity and weakness classically associated with femininity, Marie-Nathalie exercises a patriarchal rule over her subjects, thriving on her oppressive exploits. In the ultimate recognition of Marie-Nathalie's tyrannical reign, even her husband, the hunchback Senglis who is La Roche's binary opposite, knows he is "not exempt from the feminine law ruling the plantation" (64).

Reversing stereotypical gender expectations in which men have the upper hand over women, Glissant portrays the male slaves as the ones at the base of this social ladder, suffering from a figurative emasculation that strips them of mastery over their lives. "They had become accustomed to walking behind the domineering women . . . the all-powerful procreators" (64). This recognition of women's childbearing capacity is one of the few testaments Glissant makes to the significance of women in Caribbean society. Within the boundaries of the Senglis plantation, a constellation of gender roles thus emerges: the "masculine" woman in the character of Marie-Nathalie with her penchant for patriarchal domination, the resourceful and courageous slave women who claim a sense of sovereignty over their lives despite their exploitation and the drifting men who are valued only for the economic and reproductive functions they perform. In contrast to the virility of the maroon existence, the plantation emerges as a predominantly feminine affair, providing another example of a binary opposition in the novel.

It is within this female environment that Béluse ekes out his existence and founds the second family line in the story. In contrast to the freedom attached to *marronnage*, Béluse accepts enslavement on the Senglis plantation, losing all notion of personal liberty. Glissant renders this opposition between selfhood and otherness even more potent with the fact that Longoué's "owner," La Roche, is an overarching symbol of patriarchy while Senglis is a figure of weakness who suffers complete domination by his wife. The name Marie-Nathalie selects for Béluse is emblematic of his resigned attitude to his fate: "Béluse . . . Good-use. I named you Béluse for the good use I could make of you" (95). Béluse becomes part of an obsessive breeding program undertaken by Marie-Nathalie, eventually producing a son after six infertile years caused by a curse put on him by Longoué. Marie-Nathalie calls the child Anne, further feminizing the Béluse men.

As for the women, Glissant chooses to leave them anonymous in this family line because their only significance is in their reproductive capacity. Béluse thus emerges as Longoué's dichotomous opposite in his proximity to the feminine principle provoked by his failure to resist enslavement and female domination on the plantation. This contrast sparks a whole series of binary pairs, including maroon/slave, subject/object, masculine/feminine, virility/emasculation and resistance/resignation that highlight the gendered implications of these two responses to the experience of slavery.

Longoué's first son, Melchior, appears to have a more complex gender identity than his father, displaying masculine strength coupled with feminine tranquillity. While these traits are often pitted against each other, their coexistence in the character of Melchior points to a man who is at ease with himself. In contrast to his father who is permanently scarred by past hatred and injustice, Melchior evolves to a point where love reigns as the most important element in life. Reversing standard expectations of the role of the *quimboiseur*, a vocation practised by both father and son, Glissant depicts Louise as the one who initiates Melchior into the secrets of the forest. He thereby injects a feminine element into a realm traditionally grounded in masculinity. Moreover, Glissant describes a mutual understanding between mother and son in their desire to connect with the opaque forces of night, demonstrating the far-reaching influence of maternity in the development of children. "I spent too much time with my eyes open in the dark while I was expecting him, he is tranquil as night and like night he cannot be understood" (125). The quality of opacity attributed to Melchior aligns him with resistance to the colonial order, but, unlike his father, he achieves this oppositional stance in a peaceful spirit. His behavior emphasizes the potential compatibility of masculinity and femininity.

In contrast to the communion that exists between Melchior and Louise, the relationship between father and son underlines the discrepancy in their gender roles. While Longoué enjoys establishing his paternal authority through long, drawn-out monologues, Melchior is content to absorb quietly the fruits of his father's experience. Indeed, "Melchior's strength and courage lay entirely in his calm" (140). A perfect melding of masculine and feminine, then, Melchior breaks down the binary oppositions relating to gender, creating a harmonious dialogue between the two in his approach to life.

Longoué's second son, Liberté, emerges as the dichotomous opposite to his brother, representing sunshine and light-heartedness where Melchior embodies strength and sturdiness. Like a carefree butterfly plucked from nature, Liberté displays no aptitude for the serious pursuit of healing, contenting himself instead with supporting Melchior's career. Liberté appears as the perfect "wife," occupying a supportive role in the private realm while the "husband" busies himself with important affairs in the public arena. This image of femininity linked to Liberté takes on greater resonance in his affinity with nature and the satisfaction he finds in nurturing and caring for others. However, while Melchior represents a positive meeting of the masculine and the feminine, Glissant reveals contradictions in Liberté's character which result in a lack of synthesis between the competing gendered forces within him. Glissant further dramatizes this imbalance in the contrast between Liberté and Anne Béluse who display radically different gendered attributes. While Liberté is described as a man of "naturally gentle tendencies" (139), Anne emerges as a ruthless killer when a childhood game goes horribly wrong and he stabs Liberté to death. Glissant highlights the potential risk of masculine domination over the feminine and in this particular context, depicts masculinity as the unequivocal victor.

The character of Anne highlights the effect of the environment on one's identity and the way it enhances the personality traits developed from birth. The circumstances of Anne's conception condition his negative attitude to life and help to foster the violence that burns inside him. According to Richard Burton, the act of bearing a feminine name "incarne son tiraillement entre le monde à dominante féminine, voire matriarcale, d'en bas et celui, fortement masculin et patriarcal, d'en haut" [embodies his conflict between the dominantly feminine, indeed matriarchal, world of down below and the strongly masculine and patriarchal world of the hills].[10] From the outset, Anne experiences a crisis of gender identity in which he must constantly assert the masculine side of his character over his domestic surroundings brimming with powerful women. Jacques André asserts that Anne is the character who most "vit la blessure insupportable" [lives the unbearable wound][11] that results from the feminization of the plantation and the consequent emasculation of men. Indeed, this situation is emblematic of Chevannes' assertion that male identity suffers when women appropriate the same symbols men traditionally use as signifiers of their masculinity.[12] Like the male slaves subject to female authority in the house, Anne experiences a loss of autonomy to which he reacts with aggression and destruction. "He was high-strung and violent, fighting with everything, a river rock, a dog, a child his age" (137).

Growing up as a figure of defiance, Anne develops violent tendencies to affirm his identity against the predominantly feminine universe in which he lives. He exemplifies the scars of a lack of parental role models, displaying little respect for the enslaved life Béluse has chosen and banishing his mother, known only as "the old woman his mother" (139), to the sidelines. When Béluse dies and his undetected restraining effect on his son disappears, Anne wrenches free from life on the plantation and escapes into the hills with a girl he and Liberté had been courting. However, the masculine world of the maroons proves incompatible to his personality and Anne learns that he "did not have this strength, nor did he have patience" (141). He thus becomes an outcast, ill-at-ease with the masculine culture that dominates maroon existence, but unable to return to the feminine law of the plantation. In his final violent action, Anne dramatizes the tragedy of a person who is not able to balance the masculine and feminine qualities within.

In the next maroon generation, Melchior produces a daughter called Liberté whom he names in memory of his brother. Reflecting the invisibility of women in history, Liberté occupies little space in the story and particularly in her father's eyes. Her mother also gains no illumination in the book apart from reference to her name: Adélie. This anonymity of women emerges in Glissant's failure to name Béluse's wife and the young girl over whom Anne and Liberté the uncle fight to the death. While Liberté the daughter seems set to take her place in the margins of history, Glissant underlines the significance of this character through her influential role in the establishment of a new family line, the Celats. The lack of detail in Liberté's character, despite her place in perpetuating the maroon line, is a testament to the relative invisibility of women when compared to men. It is the male characters who emerge as the predominant actors of history in this novel.

While Glissant explores most of his male characters in the book in detail, drawing attention to their far-reaching influence on their surroundings, there is one man who stands out instead for his ineptitude. This character is Apostrophe, Melchior's son, who, in a reversal of patriarchal expectations, emerges more in relation to his wife, Stéfanise, than he does in his own capacity. Significantly, Apostrophe is born one year after Stéfanise and in this time she "accumulated the light dew of living that made her someone who was always *a little more* than Apostrophe" (160). While Stéfanise appears as the stronger of the two, Glissant is concerned to keep the standard gender arrangement largely intact, noting that Stéfanise would stay modestly behind Apostrophe and would never demonstrate any awareness of this *little more*. Stéfanise appears to adopt an attitude of indulgence toward Apostrophe in a manner similar to the Caribbean women who treat their partners like their children. While Apostrophe occupies the role of *quimboiseur* in the tradition of his male ancestors, he seems to have entered this vocation almost by chance. Despite the masculine connotations of the *quimboiseur*, Apostrophe appears more aligned to the feminine quality of tranquillity than he does to the masculine influence of the healer.

In contrast to Apostrophe, Stéfanise is a vibrant and active character in the novel. As Anne Béluse's daughter and Apostrophe Longoué's wife, Stéfanise forges the first enduring link between the two antagonistic families. Glissant's portrayal of Stéfanise underlines the diverse facets of her gender identity and his descriptions present her in an androgynous light. While Glissant depicts Stéfanise as a pivotal force in the synthesis of the two family lines, he consistently draws on images of nature in order to emphasize her feminine qualities. "The river current led to her! Stéfanise was almost a delta . . . this instinct that was entirely womanly, sometimes assaulted, sometimes urged on and sometimes rejected by the man, but always victorious" (158). Stéfanise's capacity to withstand life's adversities and emerge triumphant mirrors the courageous spirit embodied in the image of the *femme matador*. She also exemplifies the feminine attribute of mediation as she smooths over personal differences and creates peace between previously estranged family members such as Melchior and Apostrophe. While highlighting the strength with which Stéfanise approaches life, Glissant leaves traditional gender patterns largely unchallenged by insisting on the centrality of her feminine characteristics.

Given this backdrop, it is ironic that it takes Stéfanise fourteen years to conceive a child of her own. Alienating her from standard notions of femininity, Stéfanise's extended period of barrenness further complicates her gender identity. During this time when she longs to have children but is unable to, she devotes herself to her husband and gradually absorbs the secrets of his healing abilities. She thereby incurs Apostrophe's disapproval for her intrusion into the male-dominated arena of the *quimboiseur*. When she eventually produces a son, Papa Longoué, Stéfanise discovers a realm in which she can unequivocally assert her authority. She takes it upon herself to show her young charge "*who's the master*. She was crazy about the boy and took him in hand, even stepping ahead of his grandfather Melchior, and making all the decisions" (208). Stéfanise assumes the role of the dominant female figure responsible for all aspects of her child's upbringing, conditioning Papa Longoué's development and illustrating the effects of female parenting on children. Glissant amplifies this influential maternal position even further with Apostrophe's death when Papa

Longoué is five years old, thereby depriving the young boy of a paternal role model.

As Papa Longoué matures, Glissant highlights the impact of a dominant mother and an absent father on gender identity. Papa Longoué's name captures some of the complexities of this situation in his suspension between the feminine influence of his mother and the need to assert his masculinity: "Papa . . . means tenderness and kindness, and Longoué . . . is rage and violence" (10). In a further acknowledgment of the femininity linked to Stéfanise, Papa Longoué blames his mother for the "shortcoming of gentleness and weakness" (11) she passes on to him from the Béluse line rather than the masculine force of the maroon family. This feminine upbringing means that Papa Longoué only just manages to perform the functions of *quimboiseur* and he constantly searches for a means to assert his masculinity. Papa Longoué's birth invests Stéfanise with a masculine independence and influence and Papa Longoué with a persistent battle against the feminine elements of tenderness and kindness. Although Glissant depicts these qualities as an important contribution to the exercise of Papa Longoué's healing powers, he nonetheless underlines the dissonance in his character, which is at the mercy of the conflicting forces of masculinity and femininity.

Papa Longoué's wife, Edmée, is little developed in the novel, but she remains a powerful anchor in the confusion of his life. A thin and self-effacing woman who barely utters a word in her noisy family, Edmée eventually escapes to the *mornes* to take up residence with Papa Longoué. Her father is so outraged by this defiant action that he organizes a wake in which he mourns the "death" of his eldest daughter. Forcing her mother and siblings to participate, Edmée's father is an example of extreme authority gone wrong. He ruthlessly divides his family, which he sees as necessary to ensure his patriarchal rule over his wife and children. By adhering to his principles at all cost, this man represents the extremes of masculine violence, which establishes authority through the domination of others.

In contrast to Edmée's father, Papa Longoué is a soft and tender man. Edmée's weakness and fearfulness, however, awaken Papa Longoué's masculine tendencies as he responds to her calls for help. She thereby helps to balance the masculine and feminine elements competing within her husband. The extreme vulnerability of Edmée's character, appears ultimately doomed to self-destruction and Glissant takes her life prematurely in a horrific hurricane. It is as if he turns the feminine against Edmée as she is crushed beneath the forces of nature. The character of Edmée serves as an example of the extremes of femininity and is an important foil to the more complex gender identity of Papa Longoué.

René, the son of Papa Longoué and Edmée, further exemplifies the tragic male figure who falls victim to his own violent tendencies. Edmée's death in the hurricane when René is eight sparks a deep chasm between father and son that provides the breeding ground for hatred and wildness in the young René. Suffering from an absent mother, René confuses "Papa Longoué, the hurricane, and fear" (239), thereby establishing a state of total alienation from parental guidance and authority. In a similar manner to Anne Béluse, René attempts to assert the precarious boundaries of his identity through violence: "He liked to fight, not so much because he was a troublemaker as to convince himself that he was part of the community" (242). Papa Longoué is blind to his son's needs because he is so preoccupied with his own sadness. He thus provides a fertile ground for destruction and physical force to grow unfettered within René. The ultimate symbol of the domination of the masculine principle in René's character is his enlistment in the French army whose uniform he proudly wears on the way to war. The gap between the "feminine" father and the "masculine" son comes to the fore in their varied approaches to this event: René is a figure of pride where Papa Longoué perceives only a "savage." When René loses his life shortly after arriving in France, Glissant evokes again the dangers of extreme personalities. While Edmée identifies too closely with femininity and is conquered by nature, René clings too deeply to masculinity and is overcome by violence.

Glissant largely neglects the male figures in the Béluse family until he arrives at young Mathieu in his philosophical conversations with Papa Longoué. Until that point in the narrative, Glissant only underlines their unreliable and philandering conduct: "who could count the offspring they had outside, . . . all of [them] were apparently sterile in their own homes, but . . . [they] cast their seed everywhere outside with the greatest of freedom" (201). In this simple comparison between the Béluses and the Longoués, the maroon family emerges victorious with its production of talented healers and capable female figures. However, Glissant also makes the point that it is the former group that looks forward to a continuation of its descendants and the latter which is fated to die out. Although the feminine characteristic of plantation life appears to dominate over the masculine attributes of the maroon community in this scenario, Glissant depicts Mathieu as ill-at-ease with the fact that he springs from the slave line rather than the maroons, hinting at a crisis of identity which can only be resolved by projecting himself into the future.

Mathieu appears as largely dominated by women, his female upbringing caused by the absence of reliable support from his father. Mathieu is parented by a number of female caregivers who take on the role of providing for him while his father Mathieu Senior busies himself with multiple

adulterous relationships. Mathieu demonstrates the effects of being in-
dulged as a child by his female parents, maintaining a childlike attitude
in his adult relationships with women. His choice of the independent and
wilful Marie Celat, a descendant of the maroons, as his wife, attests to his
continuing desire for strong female leadership. From the firm and
grounded base that Marie Celat provides for Mathieu, he is able to indulge in intellectual flights of fancy which have little to do with daily reality. In a reversal of patriarchal gender expectations, Marie Celat embodies action where Mathieu incarnates static passivity when it comes to
practical matters. From a patriarchal perspective, Mathieu could be considered a "feminine" man and Marie Celat a "masculine" woman, underlining the fluidity of gender.

An examination of *Le Quatrième Siècle* reveals the gendered implications
of a work concerned primarily with history. While the narrative focuses
on the influence of the past on Caribbean identity, it is evident that gender identity is also a by-product of the historical process. Glissant's book
exemplifies a number of observations made by sociologists about the
Caribbean regarding the phenomena of strong women and weak men, the
female-dominated upbringing of children and the irresponsible attitudes
adopted by some men. However, he also highlights the fluid nature of
gender, detailing many characters who are a complex melding of masculine and feminine elements. Indeed, he draws on the gendered connotations of this binary opposition between masculinity and femininity to il-
luminate the basic contrast in the story between defiance and acceptance
of the colonial order.

Glissant's fourth novel, *La Case du commandeur*, also reveals the way in
which historical forces influence gender identity. Through his focus on
Marie Celat's viewpoint in the second half of the narrative, Glissant gives
a privileged insight into the female psyche, also describing several strong
female characters who correspond to the idea of the *femme matador*. By
contrast, the male characters in the book conform more to the notion of
the weak man through Glissant's portrayal of them as victims of the
Caribbean past. Glissant also depicts the influence of history on the life of
the couple, drawing attention to the external factors that condition relationships. Gender theory thus offers a valuable framework for analyzing
the impact of the past on the many facets of identity.

An essential backdrop to the presentation of gender identity in the
novel is the historical context in which it is set. Beverley Ormerod likens
the structure of *La Case du commandeur* to a pyramid in which Glissant's
unspecified narrative "nous" leads the reader backwards in time through
four generations, pausing at the apex in a section entitled "Mitan du
temps" [the Centre of Time] in which the narrative voice briefly changes
to an omniscient narrator, and continues down the other side to take up

the story of Marie Celat and her children.[13] The word "Odono" provides the driving interest of the story, simultaneously uniting the disparate generations in their search to unveil the meaning of this mysterious utterance. While its significance remains largely obscured from the characters in the novel, passed down the Celat family line in the form of incomplete and enigmatic tales, Glissant progressively reveals Odono to be the first ancestor to arrive from Africa via the Middle Passage. With Odono's story a legend on the slave ship, the reader uncovers a tale of treachery and betrayal in which two brothers, both with the name "Odono," become mercilessly divided over their love of one woman. In the end, both are transported on the ship to the Caribbean, escaping into the maroon forests where they continue to haunt their descendants' present-day lives, paralyzing them in a powerful reflection of the stagnation of contemporary Martinique. This troubled relationship with history also influences the portrayal of gender in the novel.

The character explored in the greatest detail in *La Case du commandeur* is Marie Celat, also known as Mycéa, whose life reflects the persistent psychological stresses of slavery. While Marie Celat takes her place in a tradition of *femmes marronnes* who embody the complexities, the anguish and the spiritual resistance necessary to combat the assimiliationist reality of the present, J. Michael Dash stresses that *La Case du commandeur* is not a feminist work nor a celebration of resistance despite its emphasis on female suffering and strength.[14] These women represent an alternative approach to history in their refusal to bow down to the scars of the past, yet Marie Celat and her female ancestors are equally poisoned by the lack of clarity in their collective and individual histories. Despite her strength and individualism, Marie Celat eventually descends into madness, and is forcibly institutionalized after the premature death of her two sons. Wendy Goolcharan-Kumeta explains Marie Celat's mental breakdown as a consequence of her lack of bonding with her mother who abandoned her at a young age, thereby exacerbating her state of alienation and exile.[15] In the character of Marie Celat, Glissant juxtaposes the psychological difficulties of living in a country under cultural domination with the complexities of being a Martinican woman.

Glissant highlights Martinique's gender values, in which men are considered more valuable than women, when Marie Celat's father, Pythagore, blows on a conch shell at the announcement of her birth. This gesture is usually associated with mourning and arises because she is not a son. Much to Pythagore's disappointment, Marie Celat proves not even to be a "vraie fille" [real daughter] (22) with the self-confidence, intelligence and independence she develops from an early age. She displays a sturdy determination when she refuses to follow her mother after she abandons the family home, preferring instead to stay with her father and apply herself to her studies where she achieves considerable success against all the odds. Glissant describes Marie Celat as "un figuier-maudit, avec des branches qui devenaient racines" [a cursed fig tree with branches that became roots] (24). This likening of Marie Celat to a sturdy tree sets her apart from other characters in the novel who remain deeply troubled by their lack of historical roots. In a continuing association of Marie Celat with nature, Glissant describes the resisting opacity of her personality in her fondness for "être perdue dans la nuit et à sentir le noir sur son dos comme une laine" [being lost in the night and feeling the black on her back like wool] (146). As a symbol of opposition to the colonial system, this opaque side to Marie Celat underlines her status as a *femme marronne*. She thus displays the attributes of courage, resistance and attachment to the earth, which characterize many Caribbean women.

Glissant draws a memorable distinction between feminine concreteness and masculine abstraction in the contrasting portraits of Marie Celat and Mathieu and in the gendered attitudes of their friends. Marie Celat reacts impatiently to the intellectual pontificating of men, becoming withdrawn, for example, when her school director begins to lecture her about universal man. In contrast to her female peers who reinforce classic gender roles by allowing men to take the lead in their relationships, Marie Celat refuses patriarchal domination. "Ses amies . . . avaient appris depuis longtemps, comme toutes les femmes dans le pays, à laisser dire les hommes. Marie Celat ne laissait pas dire" [Her friends . . . had learnt a long time ago, as did all the women in the country, to let the men speak. Marie Celat would not let them speak] (147). This attitude fostered by Marie Celat's friends highlights the role women play in reinforcing gendered stereotypes. By permitting their partners to take control and therefore indulging male conceptions of themselves as superior, these women are in part responsible for the perpetuation of negative male behavioral patterns. Marie Celat, by contrast, confines these men to the realm of voicelessness, inverting the patriarchal organization of gender relations that traditionally refuses women the self-assertive qualities attained through speech.

Mathieu is a particularly powerful example of male abstraction taken to the extreme. While Marie Celat demonstrates a steadfast dislike of theory, preferring instead to keep her eyes fixed firmly on present reality and action, Mathieu spends much of his time philosophizing as he imagines a glorious past for his island. For Marie Celat, by contrast, theories only obscure the harsh reality of Martinique's historical void and she chooses not to rule over things with words. This dichotomy established between action and theorizing, abstraction and concreteness illustrates the way in which gendered qualities are related to the historical process. History intrudes into the characters' private relationships and solidifies or challenges received ideas relating to gender. While Marie Celat's friends choose to reinforce stereotypical gender roles, she and Mathieu reverse these expectations in the former's emergence as a strong woman and the latter as a weak man.

Alongside her independence and fighting spirit, Marie Celat's approach to relationships underlines the continuing presence of the past in Martinique. She and other characters in the novel display a sexual alienation manifested in promiscuity or withdrawal into total indifference.[16] These destabilizing behaviors arise as a direct result of the shattering of family patterns under slavery and are further exacerbated by the lack of historical roots. A casual attitude toward intimacy defines many of the relationships portrayed in the novel and Marie Celat's own attitude to men exemplifies this inability to remain attached to others. When she ends her partnership with Mathieu with whom she has a daughter, Ida, she appears to feel no sense of loss, merely remarking: "[o]u bien je quitte mes hommes, ou bien ils me quittent" [either I leave my men or they leave me] (166). Following her termination of this relationship, Marie Celat engages in a series of meaningless sexual liaisons, until one day she meets a man by whom she has two more children, Patrice and Odono. After this relationship inevitably ends, Marie Celat remembers nothing about him. Marie Celat's inability to sustain intimate attachment points to a deep-seated psychological rupture that not only plagues her on a personal level but also torments Martinicans more generally. Her lack of connection with men leads her to deprive her children of a constant paternal presence, thereby maintaining a pattern of familial instability.

The question of maternity arises in the novel, shedding further light on the troubling consequences of unstable relationships that permeate family life in the Caribbean. J. Michael Dash emphasizes the constant intrusion of history into personal relationships by likening Martinique to "the kept woman of the French empire"[17] and drawing attention to a legend in which the Caribbean "is imagined in the figure of the woman . . . destined to suckle a snake all night long."[18] The dual images of a woman extravagantly accepting gifts through no effort of her own and being defiled by a snake reveal a state of "violated maternity"[19] which is graphically reflected in the novel. The maternal role that emerges is marked by irresponsibility and lack of attachment in contrast to the stereotypical conception of the Caribbean mother as the center of the family. As Richard Burton remarks, "*La Case du commandeur* is notable for the number of absent, unknown, or suspect parents and forebears that it contains."[20]

Glissant shows that an essential aspect of Marie Celat's questionable mothering skills is the lack of a parental role model provided by her own parents, Pythagore and Cinna Chimène. Adopting an attitude in which they treat her nicely and ask nothing of her, Marie Celat's parents suffer from a failure to grasp their place in history, which manifests itself in their withdrawal from intimate bonds. Eventually Cinna Chimène is so overcome by her unsatisfied search for meaning that she abandons the family and moves into town, embarking upon a series of meaningless sexual encounters. In his dramatization of the enduring consequences of history on personal relationships, Glissant emphasizes the way in which contemporary gender roles are continually influenced by the psychological scars of the past.

Glissant transforms the image of the unwavering Caribbean mother in this novel, depicting in Cinna Chimène a woman driven away from her family by her inner demons. Glissant also upturns the celebrated image of Caribbean women passing their gifts of wisdom down the female line, portraying instead the negative effects of generationally ineffective mothering. When Ida is born, the child's paternal grandmother quickly removes the child from her mother's influence to "assurer son éducation" [ensure her upbringing] (166), in a dramatic demonstration of mistrust in Marie Celat's mothering abilities. Moreover, with the birth of Patrice and Odono, Marie Celat begins to explore seriously her own feelings of maternal inadequacy: "est-il possible que je sois une mère dénaturée?" [is it possible that I'm an unnatural mother?] (172). In the character of Marie Celat, Glissant draws a direct link between childhood experiences and the patterns perpetuated in adulthood. Whilst attesting to the continuing dominance of the mother in Caribbean upbringing, this situation also represents the persistent scars inadequate mothering can cause in a child. Through Cinna Chimène's failure to connect with her daughter, she fosters a behavioral trend in which detachment is the dominant factor in relationships. Marie Celat's withdrawal from intimacy results in an unstable home environment for her children that in turn contributes to the creation of two unstable young men. The role of the mother, therefore, when coupled with the influential forces of history, has an instrumental part to play in gender identity.

Glissant nuances Marie Celat's initial appearance as a *femme marronne* in his portrayal of her descent into madness after the death of her sons, Patrice in a motorcycle accident and Odono in a diving accident, when both are aged nineteen. Affirming the role of history on the individual psyche, Marie Celat's personal loss turns into a profound crisis of origins when Odono fails to come up from the ocean and she frantically calls his name. Her grief over her son and her grief over her ancestors merges into the single word "Odono." While Marie Celat attempts to transcend the profound destabilization that occurs in her parents' lack of an ancestral past, she ultimately finds herself the victim of this same psychological curse. The various family responses to this tragedy offer another insight into gender relations, with traditional male and female roles emerging in greater clarity than in the banality of everyday living. These portraits are particularly apparent in Glissant's discussion of the aftermath of Patrice's death.

While Marie Celat's withdrawal into madness may appear as a sign of weakness and inability to cope, some critics have drawn attention to patriarchal society's perceptions of this mental condition. Certain feminist theorists equate madness with the feminine principle, declaring that this psychological state is yet another example of the patriarchal division of the world into binary pairs based on the fundamental opposition between man and woman.[21] Martine Delvaux suggests that the women society identifies as mad in fact act as scapegoats for social madness: the internment of these "mad women" serves to immunize society against such deviant behavior.[22] Glissant also represents an empowering facet to Marie Celat's madness, perceiving it as "positively deviant, . . . a kind of restorative counter-order."[23] Marie Celat's descent into madness therefore carries positive connotations as well as demonstrating her difficulty in assimilating painful events into her life. Whilst dramatizing the damaging effects of patriarchal colonialism, Marie Celat's experience also symbolizes a defiance of this social order by refusing to conform to traditional gender roles.

In contrast to Marie Celat's desperate struggle to make sense of Patrice's tragic death, Ida returns home to restore peace and order "au point qu'elle parut comme le chef de cette maison où elle ne vivait pas" [to the point where she seemed to be the head of this house where she didn't live] (186). Occupying the pivotal position in the family, Ida displays the strength and courage characteristic of the stoic Caribbean woman. In his physical and emotional absence from this Celat family crisis, Mathieu emerges as incapable of connecting with the painful realities of everyday life, employing the characteristic of *errance*, or wandering, as a means of avoidance. "Marie Celat décréta mornement que Mathieu n'était pas fait pour les malheurs, qu'il fallait le laisser tranquille. Ida Béluse protesta, demandant pour combien de temps encore les femmes devraient tout prendre sur elles" [Marie Celat declared mournfully that Mathieu was not made for unhappiness, that they had to leave him in peace. Ida Béluse protested, asking for how much longer women had to take everything upon themselves] (186). This brief vignette sheds light on the way the novel's protagonists react to the challenging circumstances that a tragic situation presents. Every person undoubtedly suffers from tragedy, yet women surface overall as the ones best equipped to resist such adversity. While Ida represents the supreme example of the strong and courageous Caribbean woman, Mathieu's strategy of *errance* attests to his fragile sense of identity. Marie Celat seems suspended between the two extremes: temporarily withdrawing from reality, but surfacing again in a testament to her tenacious character.

In addition to the peace she makes with history, portrayed in her trance-like discovery of her past in the abandoned *case du commandeur* of the book's title, a central component in Marie Celat's recovery process is her reattachment to her mother. This bond is indicated in the form of a unifying song sung by Cinna Chimène when she escapes into the forest as a little girl and is taken up by Marie Celat as she explores her ancestry in the overseer's cabin. Glissant then goes on to detail further parallels between mother and daughter.

Marie Celat finally realizes the significance of Papa Longoué's prediction a long time earlier that "la fille perdue allait se trouver dans la nuit, mais que ce ne serait pas sous un pied de quénettes" [the lost girl would find herself in the night, but that it wouldn't be under a guinep tree] (162). Referring to Cinna Chimène's discovery by Pythagore and Ozonzo under a guinep tree as a young child, Papa Longoué's prophecy acts as a binding element between Marie Celat and Cinna Chimène, providing the daughter with the strength necessary to reenter life. In this way, she is finally able to accept Cinna Chimène and to "'[find] herself' through a reconnection to her mother."[24] While Cinna Chimène is largely significant in the novel for her unstable mothering, her significance in her daughter's recovery is a powerful testament to the enduring influence of the mother in the psychic development of children.

Marie Celat's father, Pythagore, is a character profoundly affected by ignorance of his origins, which creates a rootless drifting that prevents him from forming meaningful relationships. In contrast to Marie Celat, Pythagore does not possess the intellectual resources or the cultural knowledge with which to transform his state of psychological paralysis. Glissant draws a distinction between Marie Celat and Pythagore in their different approaches to the gaping historical void that engulfs them, establishing an image of a strong woman and a weak man. Pythagore detects a pattern of distinctly female strength around him and with the birth of his daughter, he fears being confronted by another woman as powerful as Cinna Chimène. As he gradually realizes the poverty of his emotional resources when compared to his daughter, Pythagore withdraws into a fruitless quest for an imagined motherland he calls "la Guinée" or "le Congo" and an ancestor named Odono. Ridiculed by government officials when he attempts to conduct research into the African king Béhanzin, the last king of Dahomey whom the French exiled to Martinique at the end of the nineteenth century, Pythagore suffers the increasing emasculation of his identity. By the end of the novel he embodies the zombification of Martinican society in the mindless existence he leads in front of his daughter's television that he watches from four o'clock in the afternoon until the end of transmission at ten o'clock. With his inability to confront Martinican reality in the present, Pythagore exemplifies a man crushed by life's hardships. His uneasiness with his identity manifests itself in total withdrawal, depicting an alternative avoidance strategy to Mathieu's constant wandering.

Stumbled upon by Pythagore and his father Ozonzo one night, Cinna Chimène represents "the archetypal lost child, of unknown age and origin."[25] In the eruption of questions over her background following her discovery, and Cinna Chimène's refusal to elaborate on her past, this young girl comes to symbolize the forgotten history of her race. Described as "une Négresse matador" [a fighting Negress] (22), Cinna Chimène displays certain qualities linked to female strength. At the time of her first communion, Cinna Chimène escapes from her home and plunges herself into the "ventre inviolé de la forêt" [unviolated womb of the forest] (64) and undergoes a spiritual initiation directed by Papa Longoué. Associated with the visionary qualities of the *quimboiseur*, Cinna Chimène gains an inner strength that is characteristic of the *femme matador*. However, despite her capacity for vision and self-knowledge, Cinna Chimène becomes increasingly frustrated with the unanswered historical questions that she piles up in her mind in the form of a mausoleum. She eventually manifests this existential dissatisfaction by dressing in old rags and smoking a clay pipe. In an echo of Pythagore's defeated actions, Cinna Chimène also withdraws from life although she earlier achieves this separation in a far more dramatic manner by abandoning her family:

> Tout simplement prit ses hardes et son bagage, descendit le morne. S'installa sans drame chez une de ses tantes au bourg (c'est-à-dire, chez une femme qu'elle avait accoutumé d'appeler tante Ada), et n'entendit plus parler de Pythagore. Ce fut merveille qu'emmenant les six garçons (c'étaient les barreaux d'une échelle, de neuf à trois ans, qu'elle éparpilla bientôt chez autant de cousine, tante, voisine, grand-maman, da et marraine) elle pût si totalement oublier son existence de naguère, se mettre en ménage avec celui-ci ou celui-là au gré de la vie et garder une honnêteté de manière que nul ne songea un jour à lui dénier."

> [Quite simply took her old clothes and her bag, and went down the hill. Set herself up without drama at the place of one of her aunts in town (that is to say, at a woman's house whom she had become accustomed to calling aunt Ada) and no longer heard anything of Pythagore. It was a wonder that taking the six boys, (they were rungs of a ladder, from nine to three years old, that she soon scattered at a cousin's, an aunt's, a neighbour's, a grandmother's and a godmother's house) she could so totally forget her previous existence, setting up house with this man or that man drifting through life and keeping a decency that no one ever dreamed of denying her]. (40)

Cinna Chimène thus exhibits the overpowering indifference to relationships that is a direct consequence of slavery and a reflection of the continuing historical poverty of Martinican society as perceived by its citizens. Her apparently heartless desertion of her husband and children reveals a casual attitude to parenting in which children are simply objects without attachment, easily passed on to any number of alternative female carers. Cinna Chimène's scattering of her sons into a variety of homes attests to the continuing dominance of matrifocal households in the Caribbean, even if it is not always the biological mother who takes on this role. Moreover, Cinna Chimène's nonchalant drifting from man to man also indicates a detachment in intimate partnerships, which is a further consequence of the shattering of family bonds in the plantation period. However, like Marie Celat, Cinna Chimène ultimately emerges as victorious in her private battle with the legacies of history. Rejoining her family at the end of the novel, she appears full of enlightenment, seeing "avec netteté le contour des choses" [the shape of things clearly] (200). Cinna Chimène may not be an extreme example of a *femme matador*, but she appears to have attained a level of spiritual peace denied to the male characters in the novel.

The characters of Cinna Chimène's adopted parents, Ozonzo Celat and Ephraïse Anathème, are drawn as dichotomous opposites, revealing some of the challenges of the male-female relationship in Martinique. Described as a patched-up Negro, Ozonzo is a gentle man who is firmly under the authority of his outspoken wife. Alongside his passionate search for historical origins, Ozonzo is known for his ability to communicate with mules, culminating in his nickname of "papa-mulet" [father-mule] (48). While Ozonzo is a kind, but essentially ineffectual man, Ephraïse is depicted instead as a woman who has "trop de femmes dans [elle] déjà" [too many women inside [her] already] (71). This reference to the strength and resilience of Caribbean women takes on even greater resonance in the character of Ephraïse with the comment that she possesses the power of more than one woman. Glissant encapsulates their vast difference from each other in his image of Ephraïse's capacity to separate sixteen dollars in a handkerchief compared to every four of Ozonzo's. The wide-ranging influence she wields not only highlights the need for her to compensate for her husband's lack of fortitude, it also provides an example of the common trope of the Caribbean woman who battles for survival. In many ways, Ephraïse demonstrates the overarching hardships faced by Caribbean women when Glissant shows her exhausting all her resources in the simple quest to survive. Ozonzo and Ephraïse symbolize the image of the Caribbean woman as a chestnut and the Caribbean man as a breadfruit: while Ozonzo displays the nurturing feminine quality of love toward animals and children, Ephraïse emerges as fighting and triumphant against life's adversities.

After tracing the history of Ozonzo's parents, Augustus Celat and Adoline Alfonsine, Glissant turns his attention to Anatolie Celat, a philanderer who is the father of thirty-five children and the first one in the Celat line to gain a family name. Before his relationship with Papa Longoué's aunt, Liberté, Anatolie is celebrated for his multiple sexual conquests and a mysterious narrative that he relates in small, disconnected pieces to each of his mistresses. Yet another version of the ancestor tale that Anatolie remembers hearing from his grandmother Eudoxie, a direct descendant of Odono, this story fascinates his convoy of women to such an extent that they meet to piece together the disparate fragments in a startling display of female community. Actively seeking to exclude men from the puzzle, Anatolie's lovers search for the thread to weave together the patches of his story and therefore to gain some mastery over their past. Their communal effort represents an example of Valérie Loichot's assertion that the reconstruction of history can be "patched up with the thread of fragmented voices that compose the community."[26] Community once again emerges as a powerful antidote to the alienating legacies of slavery and colonialism. While this episode underlines an unlikely manifestation of female solidarity, it also serves to highlight Anatolie's moral instability in his multiple sexual relationships.

With his ignorance of the beginning and end of the narrative, Anatolie's story remains an absence and it is only on meeting Liberté Longoué that he is finally able to trace the missing link. With her visionary gifts linked to female selfhood, she is able to shed light on much of the story of Odono passed down through the generations. However, even she is not able to explain everything and she admits that the beginning of the story "tombait dans un trou sans fond, où plus personne n'était visible" [fell in a bottomless pit, where no one was visible any longer] (106). Leading Anatolie down to a former prison cell for recalcitrant slaves, Liberté relates as much of the story as she knows, finally offering to use this point where past and present merge as the place to conceive their descendants. When Anatolie murmurs in response that "tout le monde avait oublié" [everyone had forgotten] (108), Liberté reassures him that women do not forget. Glissant thus stresses the place that women occupy as the keepers of history, for they are the ones who retain attachment to the past and who offer the key to understanding the future in this novel. Liberté becomes the centerpiece to the Celat story with her ability to translate the far-flung fragments of Odono's legend, providing a sense of historical origins for the many characters who suffer from their rootless background. The female characters emerge as better equipped to cope with the unruly legacies of Caribbean history, demonstrating an ability to rise above the constraints of the past and look to the future as an opportunity for change.

The men, by contrast, appear propelled by the greater power of history, which compels them into patterns of irresponsible behavior no longer appropriate to the postcolonial context.

In the middle section of *La Case du commandeur*, "the Centre of time," Glissant paints several portraits that graphically dramatize the atrocities inflicted upon Caribbean women, exacerbating the trend of sexual and emotional alienation. In his description of the early life of Adoline Alfonsine's mother, known only as the woman without a name, Glissant reveals the rampant sexual abuse of black female slaves by their white masters. He mentions one colonizer in particular who fathers two mulatto daughters and eagerly awaits the first girl's thirteenth birthday so he can impregnate her. When he attempts to rape the second daughter, Adoline's mother, the reader witnesses the destruction of innocence in a young girl who suffers in silence. "La fille ne bouge pas, ne pleure pas, ne crie pas. Elle commence à parler sans pouvoir arrêter. Elle continue de vivre, de marcher, de travailler" [The girl doesn't move, doesn't cry, doesn't shout. She starts talking without being able to stop. She continues to live, walk, work] (123). The dual crushing of this young spirit and her tenacious will to survive helps to explain the evolution of the Caribbean psyche from the time of slavery to the present day. As a woman without a name, this young girl symbolizes the silent suffering of the many Caribbean women abused by their white superiors and yet, at the same time, she refuses to be destroyed by it, drawing on her strength to overcome these painful obstacles. In some ways, the qualities of courage and fortitude characteristic of Caribbean women arise as a result of the many hardships they faced from the time of the plantation system and beyond. Glissant stresses the resourceful nature of these women who have successfully transformed a situation of exploitation into a determined means of survival.

Glissant includes an even more disturbing story in his depiction of a female slave on the Middle Passage who, along with the other female slaves, is raped day and night by the white sailors. Once again the image of silent suffering comes to the fore when he writes that none of them cried out. When this woman, also nameless, conceives a child, she decides to keep it, in contrast to other female slaves who chose to abort their pregnancies. While this woman refuses to abuse herself with these potent herbal mixtures, she enacts her own expression of revulsion at her inability to control her body when she offers herself to all the slaves in the area. In a procession of twenty or fifty men per night, the woman exhausts her body to such a degree that there emerges in her "quelque chose d'inexpliqué, une magie" [something unexplainable, a magic] (132). Opening up her body to anyone who desires it, the woman holds onto her soul and she becomes a symbol of hope in an environment starved of positive elements. One of her most touching gestures is to place a flower on the forehead of those who are tortured or executed by the white masters. Just as those around her begin to find hope in the birth of her child, the female slave smothers her newborn baby and dies. In an abrupt and violent acknowledgment of the tragedy of conditions under slavery, Glissant highlights the ephemeral nature of peace in slave society. This shocking incident buried amidst other stories on the plateau of "the Centre of time" remains an enduring testimony to the patterns of cruelty, alienation and lack of attachment that are born of the harsh reality of life in the Caribbean. It also exemplifies the extremes of colonial violence in the exercise of control over others through ruthless domination.

Le Quatrième Siècle and *La Case du commandeur* provide rich material for an analysis of gender despite their predominantly historical focus. Against the backdrop of Martinique's failure to come to terms with the absences of its past, Glissant reveals an array of gender relations which attests to the intersection of gender and history. In *Le Quatrième Siècle* he highlights the fluidity of gender and the way in which feminine and masculine qualities can be displayed by both sexes. The contrast between masculine and feminine in this novel pivots on the fundamental distinction between maroon and slave. He also demonstrates the effect of a matrifocal upbringing on the development of gender identity, emphasizing the overarching influence of maternity on children.

La Case du commandeur offers a varied portrait of the social conditions springing from Martinique's historical experience and also depicts characters who correspond in varying degrees to the idea of the Caribbean woman as a resilient chestnut and the Caribbean man as a vulnerable breadfruit. This book also brings to light the importance of community, particularly female community, in combating historical lack. These two novels thus provide an important insight into the nature of gender identity in French Caribbean society.

NOTES

1. Richard D. E. Burton, *Le Roman marron: Études sur la littérature martiniquaise contemporaine* (Paris: L'Harmattan, 1997), 70.

2. Celia M. Britton, "Discours and histoire, Magical and Political Discourse in Edouard Glissant's *Le Quatrième Siècle*," *French Cultural Studies* 5, no. 2[14] (1994): 156.

3. Richard D. E. Burton, "Comment peut-on être martiniquais?: The Recent Work of Edouard Glissant," *Modern Language Review* 79, no. 2 (1984): 309.

4. Vere W. Knight, "Edouard Glissant: The Novel as History Rewritten," *Black Images* 3, no. 1 (1974): 70.

5. Romuald-Blaise Fonkoua, 'Edouard Glissant et le langage: Du langage du cri à la raison du langage," *Notre Librairie* 127 (1996): 40.

6. Jacques André, *Caraïbales: Études sur la littérature antillaise* (Paris: Editions Caribéennes, 1981), 130.

7. Simonne Henry Valmore, *Dieux en exil* (Paris: Gallimard, 1988), 216.

8. Barry Chevannes, *Learning to Be a Man: Socialization and Gender Identity in Five Caribbean Communities* (Kingston: University of the West Indies Press, 2001), 209.

9. André, *Caraïbales*, 140.

10. Burton, *Le Roman marron*, 72.

11. André, *Caraïbales*, 138.

12. Chevannes, *Learning to Be a Man*, 219.

13. Beverley Ormerod, "Discourse and Dispossession: Edouard Glissant's Image of Contemporary Martinique," *Caribbean Quarterly* 27, no. 4 (1981): 6.

14. J. Michael Dash, *Edouard Glissant* (Cambridge: Cambridge University Press, 1995), 132.

15. Wendy Goolcharan-Kumeta, *My Mother, My Country: Reconstructing the Female Self in Guadeloupean Women's Writing* (Oxford: Peter Lang, 2003), 26.

16. Ormerod, "Discourse and Dispossession," 10.

17. J. Michael Dash, "Writing the Body: Edouard Glissant's Poetics of Re-membering," *World Literature Today* 63, no. 4 (1989): 610.

18. Dash, "Writing the Body," 610. Glissant uses this legend in his book *Soleil de la conscience*, 23–24.

19. Dash, "Writing the Body," 610.

20. Burton, "Comment peut-on être martiniquais?" 309.

21. Martine Delvaux, *Femmes psychiatrisées, femmes rebelles* (Le Plessis-Robinson: Institut Synthélabo, 1998), 11. Delvaux draws on Catherine Clément and Hélène Cixous' research in *La Jeune Née* (Paris: Union Générale d'Editions, 1975).

22. Delvaux, *Femmes psychiatrisées, femmes rebelles*, 16.

23. Dash, *Edouard Glissant*, 127.

24. Celia Britton, *Edouard Glissant and Postcolonial Theory: Strategies of Language and Resistance* (Charlottesville: University Press of Virginia, 1999), 130.

25. Ormerod, "Discourse and Dispossession," 7.

26. Valérie Loichot, "Negations and Subversions of Paternal Authorities in Glissant's Fictional Works (*Le Quatrième Siècle, La Case du commandeur, Tout-monde*)," in Eva Paulino Bueno, Terry Caesar and William Hummel (eds.), *Naming the Father: Legacies, Genealogies and Explorations of Fatherhood in Modern and Contemporary Literature* (Lanham, Md.: Lexington Books, 2000), 97.

5

Two Faces of the
femme matador

Two novels published in 1992, Patrick Chamoiseau's *Texaco* and Maryse Condé's *Les Derniers Rois mages*, reflect on the theme of the *femme matador*, or the fighting woman who courageously resists life's trials. These books are centered on productive and community-minded women who forge a prominent place for themselves within their respective societies. However, Condé and Chamoiseau refuse an idealized picture of their female protagonists, revealing both positive and negative ways in which external circumstances shape their characters' approach to life. Chamoiseau, for example, highlights the manner in which personal and social hardships foster Marie-Sophie Laborieux's unwavering determination to conquer adversity. In *Les Derniers Rois mages*, by contrast, Condé depicts Debbie's triumph over her surroundings, evident in her successful career and esteemed public status. However, she underlines that this power arises at a cost to close relationships. Chamoiseau and Condé each draw on a variety of flawed male characters in their novels, offering a point of comparison with these figures of female strength. Forming two faces of the *femme matador*, Marie-Sophie and Debbie illustrate how the environment can generate an attitude of positive determination in one character and a desire to control in the other.

Patrick Chamoiseau's *Prix Goncourt* winning novel, *Texaco*, offers a complex study of a resilient Caribbean woman set against the evolution of Texaco, a shantytown-like suburb on the margins of the Martinican capital, Fort-de-France. Chamoiseau is one of the leading advocates of *Créolité* and his political philosophy informs the aesthetic structure of his novel. Chamoiseau's style is intensely poetic and every word and phrase is crafted with precision and insight: Pierre Pinalie, for example, describes him as an "orfèvre" [goldsmith] of language.[1] Chamoiseau succeeds in creating an original language where literary forms coexist with Caribbean turns of phrase in a unique "regional French." Reflecting his ambitious linguistic projects, the themes Chamoiseau treats in his novels are equally complex. In the context of gender identity, *Texaco* provides scope for a consideration of the *femme matador* in his heroine Marie-Sophie Laborieux. He demonstrates the way in which she harnesses her difficult external surroundings to strengthen her character and ensure her ultimate triumph over hardship.

In his book *Le Roman marron*, Richard Burton characterizes Texaco as feminine and L'En-Ville, or City as it is referred to in the English translation, as masculine.[2] By transposing the question of gender onto this symbolic plane, Burton highlights the opposition between Texaco, the peripheral suburb of Fort-de-France, and City, the bustling and powerful town center. Drawing on patriarchy's ordering of the world into binary oppositions, Burton compares the curved feminine nature of Texaco to the fixed masculine rigidity of City.[3] Chamoiseau affirms these connotations of masculine and feminine in his writing, depicting the positive value of femininity and the devaluation of masculinity in a reversal of patriarchal expectations. For example, in his portrayal of the linear nature of City, Chamoiseau emphasizes the lack of spirit and heart he perceives in this architectural arrangement. "All the streets were straight, square-cut. Nothing evoked a city. Everything had been built with no regard for memory" (167). The flowing lines of Texaco, by contrast, encompass strength and hope in their feminine embodiment. The "valleys that are open to the sun offer a maternal, fertile soil, lavish with calm river water . . . Like God's carafes" (129).

Burton adds a further contrast in the battle between Texaco and City that is encapsulated in the gendered qualities of their leaders. Marie-Sophie Laborieux whose name carries connotations of maternity, wisdom and untiring work leads the fight for Texaco while City has a man, Papa Césaire, who exemplifies paternalism. By associating Texaco with the feminine and City with the masculine, Burton exposes a variety of gendered traits. However, he refrains from commenting on the social implications of these gender-based divisions. Burton also foreshadows the positive valuation of the leading character, Marie-Sophie, who is linked to femininity in her unwavering fight for Texaco.

In an extension of the gender model presented by Burton, Chamoiseau highlights the association of City and sameness, which is embodied in *francité*, or Frenchness, and that of Texaco and difference, which is exemplified through *Créolité*. Within Burton's gender framework, *francité* is associated with the masculine and *Créolité* with the feminine, thereby positively weighting the latter over the former. Burton alerts the reader to Chamoiseau's positive evaluation of feminine values, a theme that emerges throughout the novel. Indeed, he advocates the acknowledgment and celebration of these feminine characteristics, calling for Texaco to be "different from—but equal to—the metropolitan Centre."[4]

Chamoiseau draws on the image of a mangrove swamp to illustrate the way in which diversity creates extraordinary richness even if at first sight it appears to favor conflict. He also demonstrates the way in which the apparently chaotic merging and separation of different roots in a mangrove actually constitute a vital counterpart to City. A note from the urban planner to the word scratcher asserts: "City draws strength from Texaco's urban mangroves . . . Texaco needs City to caress it, meaning: it needs consideration" (263). Through the contrasting images of Texaco and City, Chamoiseau employs a geographical metaphor that can be harnessed not only to promote his philosophy of *diversalité*[5] but also to propose a path out of rigidly defined gender stereotypes. By affirming both sides of the dichotomous gender pair, he emphasizes that the masculine and feminine can achieve a state of coexistence. In *Texaco*, Chamoiseau is particularly concerned to promote, through the character of Marie-Sophie, the feminine which patriarchal society has traditionally devalued.

Texaco's main protagonist, Marie-Sophie, is the woman who takes on the task of fighting for and recording the history of Texaco. In contrast to more mainstream histories that privilege men as the writers and actors of the past, *Texaco* is woman-centered. This role is particularly significant given the prestige that is associated with the storyteller in Caribbean society. Straying from more classical approaches to the past, Marie-Sophie offers a distinctly feminine point of view on the evolution of Texaco, interweaving the public and private, the subjective and objective. The public and private domains merge in a harmonious whole in Marie-Sophie's hands, suggesting the possibility of their coexistence. Marie-Sophie's confident voice also allows the possibility of the postcolonial experience to come to the fore, unmediated by white, colonial historians. The splintering of the narrative viewpoint into the voices of Marie-Sophie, the *marqueur de parole*, or word scratcher, and the *urbaniste*, along with Marie-Sophie's fictitious notebooks, adds a postmodern element to the book that destabilizes the notion of a coherent and linear historical narrative. The frequent authorial intrusions in the form of footnotes, glossaries and explanations further contribute to the promotion of a mosaic of histories in the story of Texaco, rather than an authoritarian History.

The choice of a woman as the storyteller of Texaco is not incidental given that it was founded in reality by a Madame Sico, but it also reflects the important position women occupy more generally in French Caribbean society. In an interview with Maeve McCusker, Chamoiseau explains that Marie-Sophie is a mixture of Madame Sico and his mother. When asked if his novel serves to some extent as a eulogy to the Martinican woman, Chamoiseau replies in the affirmative: "la réalité sociologique de la Martinique, c'est que les femmes sont très présentes, et ce sont de fortes femmes" [the sociological reality in Martinique is that women are very present and they are strong women].[6] Speaking more specifically about his mother as an example of a strong Caribbean woman, Chamoiseau states that she is "une femme-à-graines, une femme virile, et toutes les femmes antillaises sont comme ça" [a woman with balls, a virile woman, and all Caribbean women are like that].[7] While there is an element of romanticism to Chamoiseau's classification of *all* women as *femmes matador*, he nonetheless draws attention to women's attachment to the earth and their overwhelming responsibility for the home and children.[8] Against the sociological realities of the matrifocal society, Chamoiseau portrays Marie-Sophie taking her place in the tradition of strong Caribbean women.

Through the course of her existence, Marie-Sophie draws strength from adversity and develops the outstanding vigor that allows her to take on the fight for Texaco. "I had suddenly understood that it was I, around this table with this poor old rum, with my word for my only weapon, who had to wage—at my age—the decisive battle for Texaco's survival" (26–27). While those around her may bow before overwhelming pressures, she takes the experience as a challenge. When Texaco comes under threat, for example, Marie-Sophie adopts the warlike pose of her Creole sisters and prepares for battle. Part of her fortitude derives from the symbolic importance of place. On the advice of the healer, Papa Totone, she gives herself a secret name which she reveals at the end of the book to be none other than "Texaco." The potency of this name fills her with courage when she is ready to surrender to her suffering. Indeed, with its connotations of *Créolité* and feminine strength, Texaco replenishes Marie-Sophie's flagging energy and transforms her into "a fighting cock" in a memorable echo of Reine Sans Nom's words to Télumée. With her display of courageous optimism and a determined quest to survive, Marie-Sophie exemplifies the qualities of the *femme matador*.

Part of Marie-Sophie's success in withstanding the difficulties of the war she wages for Texaco is her capacity for *débrouillardise*, a postcolonial technique that allows Marie-Sophie to subvert the system that oppresses. It is Marie-Sophie's father, Esternome, with his links to the plantation system, who most clearly highlights the need for crafty techniques of self-preservation. Through the marriage of the public and private realms that she inhabits, Marie-Sophie develops a unique ability to endure the trials of life and emerge fighting. For example, she draws on her intense sadness at the departure of her lover as the definitive starting point of her fight for Texaco. Adopting "the defiance of a Creole woman" (275), Marie-Sophie gathers strength from the empowered images she perceives in the women around her. She also draws on the fortifying survival technique of singing discovered by Télumée and Tituba. Marie-Sophie employs a number of mechanisms for survival that are frequently identified with women and fuses them into the larger system of *débrouillardise*. Her determination to triumph over public and private distress underlines her resilient, chestnut-like toughness.

Despite her courage and spirit, Marie-Sophie suffers from her decisions to terminate a series of pregnancies when her children are conceived as a result of violence, hate or infidelity. When she discovers her first pregnancy to Basile, a man for whom she is but one of many lovers, Marie-Sophie decides to induce an abortion. Following the advice of her neighbor, she succeeds in aborting her child and becomes one of the many Caribbean women who have chosen to spare their children an unhappy existence. Marie-Sophie's situation highlights that she is not alone in this refusal of maternity, underlining the consequences of a society in which men seem to impregnate women casually and then abandon responsibility: "How much women suffer behind closed louvered shutters . . . oh women's sorrows" (240). Marie-Sophie repeats her potent abortion-inducing cocktails on several occasions to the extent that she ultimately loses the capacity for conception. She thus joins the growing list of wise and spirited women in French Caribbean literature, including Télumée and Tituba, who are not biological mothers.

This noteworthy phenomenon of key female literary characters rejecting biological maternity raises important questions about the role and expectations of French Caribbean mothers. As the protagonist Marie-Sophie shows, women may have more chance of survival without children and an increased capacity to give spiritually and practically to their community in the absence of binding family ties. It is clear in *Texaco* that she adopts a prominent role in the public arena typically occupied by men. It is possible that if Marie-Sophie had accepted motherhood, she would have been so bound up in the daily quest for survival that she might have had no energy left with which to defend Texaco. Significantly, many authors reveal that their nonmaternal characters are capable of producing children, thereby avoiding the social stigma of infertility and emphasizing the element of choice these women claim for themselves. The acceptance or rejection of maternity becomes one way in which women assert sovereignty over their lives. While maternal qualities are generally portrayed positively in French Caribbean literature, Chamoiseau suggests that traits such as assertiveness and force are still necessary to make an enduring mark in patriarchal society. Marie-Sophie therefore exhibits a certain association with the masculine principle in her successful mastery of the public domain, a characteristic that she harnesses in the battle for a more just society.

Marie-Sophie's mother, Idoménée, illustrates the importance of the maternal role in French Caribbean society and the way in which the mother's presence shapes gender identity. Despite her fleeting appearance in the book, Idoménée is a paradoxical character who embodies the fighting spirit of the Caribbean *femme matador* and the unconditionally loving mother-figure who ultimately abandons her family through her premature death. With her humble origins and lack of a stable family environment, Idoménée had to fight life early on, developing the quality of *débrouillardise* that is later displayed by her daughter. Given her adaptable and determined spirit, nothing proves too challenging for Idoménée, even the progressive loss of her eyesight, which eventually leaves her blind. Demonstrating the tenacious faith in life evident in other memorable Caribbean women such as Reine Sans Nom and Télumée, Idoménée hits rock bottom, but shows her resilience and rises to the surface again. As a result of her blindness, Idoménée develops a deeper connection to the nuances of relationships, a skill she harnesses to guide others. Representing a kind of Tiresias figure in the wisdom she achieves through blindness, Idoménée counsels Esternome as he drifts through life without understanding his path or its purpose. The phenomenon of the wife who "mothers" her husband recurs in the relationship between Idoménée and Esternome, encapsulated in the image of her cradling him like a child to protect him from his painful memories. Esternome's consistent inability to gain mastery over his life can partially be explained by the attitude of indulgence Idoménée displays toward him.

In her status as a mother to Marie-Sophie, Idoménée embodies maternal nurturing, but she also requires a certain level of mothering from her daughter. As a young girl, Marie-Sophie does not at first understand the consequences of this filial responsibility until her childish lack of attention causes Idoménée to slip and fall in some undetected mud. At this point, Marie-Sophie finally realizes that she is the "mother" in this parent-child relationship and that she must conduct herself conscientiously and with initiative. While Idoménée does her best to ensure she at least provides her daughter with adequate love, her untimely death leaves Marie-Sophie to cope with life independently from a young age. Despite her failure to fulfil her daughter's needs in life, however, Idoménée represents a powerful source of strength for Marie-Sophie in death:

> Idoménée Eugénie Lapidaille, I think of you every first day of the year, that white day, that day of hope, that day of renewal which you would clothe in white, white tablecloths, white linen. With rum, ash, and lemon you would rub everything. You would cram the house with hibiscus flowers as if you

wished to gather up the certain movement of their sap. You would unravel the money from an old praline bag. To our surprise you would unveil the whiteness of nougat. With a piece of nougat the world is wonder, life sings, happiness goes by. (195)

Idoménée's extraordinary influence from the grave illustrates the way in which absence may function as powerfully as presence. Despite her brief appearance in the book, the character of Idoménée focuses attention on the significance of maternity in the French Caribbean. Through her courageous and independent example, she provides a positive role model for Marie-Sophie who goes on to develop many of the spirited qualities linked to her mother. As a result of her early departure from her daughter's life, Idoménée underlines the paradoxically beneficial effect an unstable family environment can have on a child. In the face of Esternome's inability to adequately assume responsibility for Marie-Sophie's upbringing, the latter must develop self-sufficiency and resilience from a young age, characteristics which equip her well in the fight for Texaco later in life. Idoménée also reveals the common trend in Caribbean male-female relationships in which the wife is mother to her husband as well as to her children. Her character therefore highlights many important themes in relation to gender.

Esternome and several other male characters in the novel serve to focus attention on Marie-Sophie's image as a resilient chestnut through their contrasting moral weakness. Constituting a foil for Marie-Sophie's character, Esternome displays a strikingly different attitude to life. Where Marie-Sophie is strong and decisive, Esternome is slow and deliberating: "a true characteristic of my papa is this calculating, calculating, calculating before lifting a finger or moving a muscle" (50). Indeed, Esternome receives his official name of Laborieux because the secretary had found him laborious in thinking of a name. As a result of his dreamy and idealistic nature, Esternome often attaches himself to strong women whom he happily accepts as the director of his actions. These capable female partners appear once again to foster an attitude of irresponsibility in their relationships with men by treating them with a childlike indulgence. While these women display genuine feelings for Esternome they are marked by a much more pragmatic approach to relationships than he, who remains ruled by his heart.

When he suggests to his first love, Osélia, for example, that they embark upon life together, she answers: "If you wish, dear boy . . . but only until I meet my mulatto or my white man" (64). In this simple contrast of an intellectual and instinctual approach to love, Chamoiseau highlights Esternome's identification with feminine softness and Osélia's with masculine pragmatism. Their relationship represents a powerful illustration of a woman who is so preoccupied with the quest for survival that love for love's sake is not always enough. Esternome, by contrast, is so out of touch with reality that romance counts for everything.

Alongside this reversal of stereotypical gender images, however, Chamoiseau depicts another side to Esternome's character that is more in line with the Caribbean stereotype of the "swaggering" male. Unable to cope with Osélia's job as a nightclub dancer, Esternome finds refuge in drink, gambling and bawdy games. Esternome thus disguises his inability to face life's trials by resorting to the irresponsible behavior that Chamoiseau believes is characteristic of Caribbean men. The dichotomous opposite to Marie-Sophie who resolutely refuses to surrender to hardship, Esternome reinforces the portrait of his daughter's strength through such demonstrations of moral weakness.

Chamoiseau amplifies this image of Esternome's weakness through his reaction to the demise of his relationships to Osélia and Ninon. Unlike Marie-Sophie who uses her failed romance to draw strength for the future, Esternome drowns in his sorrows for years. In a section entitled "Barbecued Love," Chamoiseau describes a man who "lived for many years like flowers in a vase. His brain was clotted with sadness. His eyes became faucets and his heart was a hot iron brand lodged inside his chest" (146). As his life falls apart around him, Esternome manufactures fairytales for himself as to why his lover left him to avoid the painful impact of reality. Significantly, it is another woman, Idoménée, who saves Esternome from himself, allowing him to escape responsibility for his previous failed relationships. Exhibiting the feminine qualities of passion and emotion in a male body, Esternome proves unable to exploit the empowering nature of these traits in the way that characters such as Xango and Yao do in *Pluie et vent sur Télumée Miracle* and *Moi, Tituba, sorcière . . . noire de Salem*. Indeed, Esternome emerges not as a positive "feminine" man, but rather, as a man limited by a debilitating weakness. Chamoiseau brings this depiction of a breadfruit-like man into even sharper focus when he sets it against Marie-Sophie's success in combining masculine and feminine characteristics.

Chamoiseau includes several meditations on the status of men and women in the book which highlight the difficulty of being a woman in French Caribbean society: "To raise a hutch was, as in the hills, the duty of men alone. The women had to face the rest of life, including the duty of finding food for a swarm of little ones, and all without a garden" (173). While there is an obvious contradiction between Chamoiseau's statement here and his comment in a 2001 interview that "l'implantation des jardins, des cases, des enfants, tout ce qui est construction de vie, c'était les femmes" [the setting up of gardens, cabins, children, everything that is about the construction of life, was done by women],[9] he nonetheless highlights the notion that women are the sustainers and nurturers of Caribbean life. Françoise duRivage comments on the extension of the female role from the private to the public in *Texaco*, asserting that "it is women who have the responsibility to build the Creole society of tomorrow."[10] Marie-Sophie echoes this idea herself, writing that the women "had to wage the battle alone, because the men . . . would not organize anything, would not plant anything" (336). Women thus emerge as *femmes matador* as a direct response to the pressing need to survive and the inability of men to help them. Chamoiseau's reference to planting fortifies the alignment of a female power achieved through harmony with nature. In a specific example, Ninon is the one who instructs Esternome in the ability to coexist with the land by living according to the seasons. It becomes clear, then, that Chamoiseau conceives of women as the courageous maintainers of life through their respect for nature and their skill in survival under adverse conditions.

There are a number of female characters in the novel who dramatically illustrate another side to the hardships faced by Caribbean women. As a mosaic of inhabitants of Texaco gradually assemble around her, Marie-Sophie meets Adélise Canille, a mother of nine children and a woman evidently living the phenomenon of the unreliable Caribbean man who impregnates and then leaves. Péloponèse discovers her lover is about to marry a rich widow rather than stay with the woman who has provided him with everything, choosing material gain over loyalty in an echo of John Indien's approach to life. A further addition to Texaco is Eugénie Labourace, a *chabine*, or mixed-race woman with light-colored skin, from Macouba, escaping from a drunken and incestuous partner. The negative image of men is further compounded when Sérénus Léoza arrives with five children "and a half-useless piece of meat supposed to be a man" (301). Marie-Sophie effectively underlines the female opinion of Caribbean men and her principle for survival, with "men being worth nothing, the stick of courage was the only stick that helped women to stay on their feet in life." (284).

Against these suffering, strong women, the first man to join the community of Texaco is Milord Abdond who again reinforces the bad reputation of the Caribbean male. "He lived off fighting cocks raised in a hole in Pont-de-Chaînes. The rest of the time, he hung around pits and in the shade of fatherly mistresses to whom he unfailingly entrusted a package to keep for nine months" (302). These brief gender portraits as Texaco's inhabitants begin to congregate illustrate some of the more general patterns of male-female relationships in French Caribbean society. The incidence of unreliable men appears particularly high, with portrayals of their numerous mistresses, abandonment of their families and damaging treatment of their children. While these descriptions certainly underline women's ability to triumph over adversity, they also suggest female implication in these male behavioral patterns. By failing to challenge their partner's destructive habits, women in some part contribute to their own unhappiness. Marie-Sophie, however, refuses to subject herself to such self-destruction. Chamoiseau also depicts these abuses across a variety of ethnic groups, spanning black, mixed-blood and Indian people in an acknowledgment of the Creole nature of Martinican society.

Chamoiseau provides several detailed analyses of male characters in the novel that exemplify the idea of the weak man and emphasize Marie-Sophie's intolerance toward them. He includes a number of humorous depictions of men who are mocked for their weakness by the strong women around them. Speaking of her first lover, Basile, Marie-Sophie comments that his muscles "indicated nothing, they seemed of no use, and I even suspected them to be somewhat inflatable" (234). Her initial surprise at his misplaced vanity grows into an embittered lack of respect when she discovers he has a string of other mistresses. Disgusted at his deception, Marie-Sophie confronts these women and gathers her strength for revenge. When Basile learns of these encounters he is outraged and attempts to return Marie-Sophie to a place of subservient womanhood. For Marie-Sophie this action is the final straw and she teaches him a lesson he will never forget, throwing Basile and his possessions onto the street and screaming out her triumph for all to hear. Her reclaiming of her voice is a striking testament to her refusal to be dominated by a man.

Marie-Sophie's other significant relationship, with Félicité Nelta, offers an additional dimension to the image of male weakness. Unable to cope with the realities of Caribbean life, Félicité Nelta places all his faith in the French word *partir* [to leave], which he had looked up in the dictionary. Nelta's dream of *errance* prevents him from connecting to others in a meaningful way, representing a form of escapism from life's challenges. For Marie-Sophie the experience is intensely frustrating and she finds him as absent as someone who has physically deserted his family. In a similar manner to Glissant's Mathieu, Félicité Nelta's eternal quest for departure underlines the fragility of his identity. He reacts to his inner lack by isolating himself from relationships. Although he is not physically violent or unfaithful toward Marie-Sophie, Félicité Nelta's emotional instability remains a sign of his inherent moral weakness. It is from the demise of this relationship that Marie-Sophie determinedly gathers her inner resources in the fight for Texaco.

There are a number of instances of sexual violence toward women in the novel, reinforcing the idea of men asserting their power through domination of the physically weak and vulnerable. Marie-Sophie experiences sexual violence herself on a number of occasions, although for her, they become opportunities for personal growth. On the first occasion, her landlord, Lonyon, attempts to rape her soon after she reaches physical maturity. However, in her typical defiance, Marie-Sophie defends herself with an explosive power: "I never would have thought I could let forth so much strength" (208). Marie-Sophie's reaction to this intimate invasion sows the seeds of her determined character and her decision never to be oppressed by anyone. On the second occasion, her employer, Monsieur Alcibiade, succeeds in sexually violating her, but Marie-Sophie is quick to reestablish the balance of power. "Well, I can tell you that that poor dirty man paid dearly for what he did to me, in blows to the head, flying pots, bowls, jars" (255). While these instances of sexual assault could be conceived as the ultimate demonstration of male power, Chamoiseau shows, by contrast, that the men who commit these crimes have little autonomy. The clash of Marie-Sophie and her sexual predators becomes a powerful indication of the way in which some Caribbean men become crippled by weakness.

Marie-Sophie's courageous qualities exemplify the ability of Caribbean women to draw strength from their arduous external surroundings. Through her comparison with characters such as Esternome, Basile and Félicité Nelta, Chamoiseau underlines that the social environment is sufficiently potent to crush weaker personalities, in particular Caribbean men. Caribbean women, however, consciously or unconsciously learn from their mothers and the female figures around them that adversity is part of life and thus that the best must be made of it. Despite her brief time in her daughter's life, Idoménée offers Marie-Sophie an empowered female role model which helps her to develop her outstanding capacity for resistance. Alongside the sociological observations that buoy this image of female strength, Chamoiseau offers an additional vision of the symbolic value of gender. With his fundamental alliance of Texaco and the feminine and City and the masculine, Chamoiseau amplifies the power of his female protagonist through her positive identification with femininity. Marie-Sophie thus emerges as an impressive example of the *femme matador* in French Caribbean literature.

Maryse Condé provides an alternative image of the *femme matador* through the character of Debbie in *Les Derniers Rois mages*. While Marie-Sophie positively harnesses the challenges of her environment for society's good, Debbie seeks to master it in what is frequently an oppressive manner. Condé draws on irony in her approach to her subject matter in *Les Derniers Rois mages*—the incompatibility of the Caribbean and African-American cultures—and this postcolonial literary strategy runs like a thread throughout the novel. Satirizing the concept of feminism, for example, Condé exaggerates her portrayal of Debbie, depicting her as a feminist and social activist who takes political correctness to the extreme. However, as in *Moi, Tituba, sorcière . . . noire de Salem*, there are serious

undercurrents which highlight the problems caused by incompatible relationships and the continuing intrusion of the past into present-day life.
Condé states that *Les Derniers Rois mages* may be read as an invitation for
African-American women "to undergo a sort of self-criticism"[11] based on
her perception of them as too harsh toward their male partners. She also
hints at the role women play in producing the weak men that surround
them, declaring that Debbie's and their daughter Anita's desire for Spéro
to be a superman in fact exacerbates his feelings of inadequacy and failure. The impact of external factors on the development of gender identity
informs the themes of the novel, illuminating—despite Condé's frequent
exaggeration—this portrait of a disintegrating marriage.

On the surface, Debbie and Spéro conform perfectly to the image of a
resilient chestnut and a spongy breadfruit. Growing up in Charleston,
South Carolina, Debbie is a dynamic, focused woman who works as a college history professor. While on a cruise financed by her mother as a re-
ward for her brilliant academic success, she meets Spéro in Guadeloupe.
From the outset there is a clash of cultures as Debbie, the sophisticated
American, meets this struggling artist trying to sell his paintings to im-
pressionable American tourists. Despite his overall lack of ambition and
success, Spéro has one glittering asset—he is the descendant of an African
king. For Debbie, obsessed with the search for historical roots, this genealogy outweighs everything else. After their marriage in Guadeloupe and
return to the United States, Debbie and Spero embark on increasingly
alienated paths from each other: Debbie immerses herself in her work and
ceaseless social campaigns out of a growing frustration at her husband's
inadequacy; Spéro dabbles in different occupations, but never succeeds in
any of them, dealing with his sense of failure in work and love by indulging in a series of adulterous affairs. Condé offers numerous reflections on gender relations throughout the novel, encapsulated in Spéro's
declaration that the "Good Lord was a terrible director of humankind. On
the stage of life he had cast women with strength, courage, and ambition.
Men had to make do with the frantic need to be steeped in love like a fe-
tus bathing in its mother's womb" (207). In this evocative description,
Condé summarizes many of the book's main themes related to the question of gender: she highlights, for example, the qualities of strength found
in many Caribbean women, the way in which Caribbean men remain attached to and influenced by their mothers long into adulthood and the influence of the mother figure on gender identity.

Condé's depiction of Debbie aligns her with an impressive strength regarding the promotion of black culture and racial equality in her society.
Driven, intellectual and ambitious, Debbie has a rigorously organized
schedule that sees her taking on a significant social role at her local church
and college. While the author celebrates the important contribution Deb-

bie undoubtedly makes, it is evident that Condé's portrayal of her character is steeped in irony and exaggeration. Condé further parodies her female protagonist by employing Spéro's mocking point of view toward
Debbie's feminist activities, which are framed in the light of radical feminism. When she invites a feminist writer "who gave the impression she
wanted to banish men from the face of the earth" (95) to speak at a local
bookstore, Debbie is subject to Spéro's ridicule when he states that he
would prefer to get drunk rather than find out the details of that evening.
Despite Condé's conflation of feminism with radical feminism, a form of
activist thought that seems personally distasteful to her, the satirical elements of her portrayal underline the exaggerated personality of her protagonist. Nonetheless, Debbie emerges as a successful career woman with
an impressive list of socially minded activities to her credit, which forms
a striking contrast to her husband's lack of ambition and talent.

Condé alerts the reader to Spéro's vastly contrasted approach to life
through her description of him spending his days in an old tracksuit that
he puts on over his dirty pyjamas. Spéro's lack of attention to his appearance is symbolic of his failure to succeed professionally, displaying an attitude of aimless *errance* that sees him drifting from job to job. He emerges
as a seeker rather than a finder in his constant and unfulfilled quest for
understanding, displaying a rootlessness that permanently alienates him
from a meaningful existence. Condé includes a comic episode in the novel
in which she gently mocks Spéro's complete inability to survive in the
modern world, underlining also the more serious consequences of his defeated stance toward life. Alluding to Albert Camus' *L'Etranger*, Condé
writes that he refused a job in Le Moule because the sun was too strong
and hurt his eyes, which were weak like his ancestors'. As well as highlighting Spéro's inherent fragility, this extract also places weakness in a
specifically male genealogical progression. In contrast to the Lougandor
women in *Pluie et vent sur Télumée Miracle* who bequeath strength and
courage to their female descendants, Spéro and his male ancestors breed
moral weakness and inadequacy and all are professional failures. Condé
intensifies the deficiencies of Spéro's identity by portraying him at the
complete mercy of his dominant wife. Spéro's failure to identify with a
strong masculine role model leads to the exaggeration of this characteristic in Debbie, a woman who aggressively pursues her ambitions in the
public arena. Spéro, by contrast, is content to confine himself to the domestic realm and occupy himself with his ceaseless mental meanderings.

While Spéro, his father Justin and grandfather Djéré, the illegitimate descendants of the king of Dahomey, find a sense of self-worth in their royal
blood, Condé reveals that this glorious heritage is in fact the product of a
leopard's supposedly raping a young woman many years earlier. The creation of a royal family through the marriage of human and animal offers

an element of myth to the story as well as suggesting a satire on the search for origins. In the context of gender, the most important repercussion of this fated mingling of woman and leopard is the moral confusion that arises from the event and that persists down the male genealogical line. Sam Haigh focuses attention on the distinctly masculine nature of this dynasty that depends for its survival on the "erasure of the maternal-feminine as guarantee of Antillean legitimacy."[12] It is significant that this family produces a line of sons that fosters the continuation of their paternal genealogy. However, with Spéro's creation of a daughter, which brings this masculine dominance to a halt, Condé questions the legitimacy of the obsessive quest for paternity in a predominantly matrifocal society. Drawing on Fritz Gracchus' research into Caribbean fatherhood, Haigh asserts that "the idea that 'legitimacy' is conferred solely by the paternal side is perhaps inappropriate, and its pursuit thus doomed to failure."[13] Ironically, it is Spéro himself who first suggests that the maternal heritage is as important as the masculine one. By depicting Spéro in a morally ambiguous male royal line, Condé underlines one response to the Caribbean obsession with origins. In their compulsive battle to fit themselves into legitimate African royalty, Spéro and his male ancestors prove unable to live in the present, allowing the scars of the past to become a convenient excuse for avoiding responsibility.

Against the backdrop of this male dynasty, Condé depicts another response to the past in the character of Debbie. Religiously ensuring the commemoration of the royal ancestor's death on the tenth of December every year, she becomes increasingly resentful at what she feels is her short-changing in relation to Spéro's African ancestry. It seems that Spéro's failure to provide her with a glorious royal heritage provokes further obsessive campaigning in Debbie as if she is trying to compensate for some genealogical lack of her own. While Debbie worships her prominent black bourgeois family, she discovers that the Middletons conceal some dark secrets when she begins writing her adored father's biography. Despite his illustrious reputation, Debbie learns that George Middleton's passionate fight for the black cause stems from rather questionable and racist origins. Given that reverence is her religion, Debbie quickly abandons her literary project and throws herself into her quest for racial equality. Condé thus uncovers a certain hypocrisy in Debbie's character which she plays out in relation to Spéro through her humiliating and distant treatment of him. As Mildred Mortimer maintains, "[i]n effect, she parodies the racist tactics she abhors; Debbie becomes responsible for 'putting a Nigger in his place.'"[14] Debbie's obsession with the past emerges in contrast to Spéro's and yet it is equally as potent in its force. Not only does it condition her extremely socially aware attitude to life, but it also influences her relationship with her husband through her overwhelming demands on him.

A behavior Spéro develops in partial response to the magnification of Debbie's character is his frequent recourse to extramarital liaisons. The perception of this moral conduct varies widely according to which society provides the interpretative framework. From an American point of view, Spéro's infidelity is morally reprehensible, representing a cowardly escape from dealing with his feelings of inadequacy and failure. For the Caribbean man, however, an abundant collection of lovers attests to successful sexual prowess, a quality revered by men in Caribbean society. In this scenario, Condé depicts Debbie as the betrayed but accommodating wife who looks past her husband's behavior despite her feminist principles.

> Thanks to women, Spero had made his discovery of America. The good souls of Charleston—and there was a good many of them—informed Debbie of each of his infidelities, and she treated them with the utmost contempt. It's a common fact—isn't it?—that African, American, or Caribbean, the black man is not hewn from the wood of monogamy. In private she likened herself to a bara muso, a first wife sharing her husband with co-wives yet managing the household finances. She was caught off her guard only once. And that was because of Tamara. (24)

This passage brings into focus a number of important issues relating to gender, including Debbie's acceptance of her husband's infidelity. A curious aspect to the situation is that the religious old women of the town inform Debbie of her husband's liaisons, leading to the question of why she tolerates Spéro's adulterous affairs. Condé suggests that Debbie is also profiting from the situation, whether achieving a certain power over her husband in his mistreatment of her and thus a powerful means of justifying her neglect of him or perhaps linking herself more intimately to the African past she craves by identifying herself as the head wife of a polygamous husband.

The issue of female solidarity is also raised in this context, as Spéro's lovers are on several occasions close friends or relatives of Debbie. In contrast to the positive female communities that support characters such as Télumée and Tituba, Condé depicts Debbie as steadfastly solitary in the battles she wages at home and work. In a merging of the public and private domains, it is significant that Debbie constructs a boundary to her accommodation of Spéro's behavior, refusing to tolerate his racial betrayal of her by his sleeping with Tamara Barnes, a white woman. As Lydie Moudileno asserts, in Debbie's eyes making love with a white woman is equivalent to sleeping with the enemy.[15] This act of treason committed by Spéro results in his permanent banishment from Debbie's bed, triggering the inner reflections that drive the novel's narrative. While bearing witness to his own moral imperfections, Spéro's unfaithful behavior also deepens Condé's portrait of Debbie, highlighting the contradictions of a character who places herself in a submissive position despite her fervent independence.

There are a number of instances in the novel in which double standards between men and women emerge with clarity. These hypocritical moral values contribute to a deeper understanding of Debbie's character by pointing to the limitations of patriarchal society for women. A prime example of these restrictions is the contrasted approaches men and women adopt toward the question of fidelity. When Spéro suspects Debbie of having an affair with a young historian while in her forties, he is aghast at his wife's despicable actions. Requiring only his heart and instinct as evidence, Spéro goes on to state that the coupling of an older woman and a younger man "has been the abomination of abominations ever since the sun has lit up the earth" (193). Several comments could be made here including the obvious hypocrisy of the fact that Spéro himself has pursued many extramarital relationships throughout their marriage. To begin with, Spéro is referring to a time more than a decade earlier, although his own latest sexual conquest is still fresh in his mind. Second, he bases his accusation on a feeling rather than concrete evidence. If Debbie had accused him of infidelity based on her heart, it is certain that Spéro would discard the argument as ridiculous. Third, Spéro paints himself as a victim, an abandoned and betrayed husband, despite the irony that he has spent many years deceiving his wife in exactly the same manner. Spéro takes this isolated incident to condemn women globally for their destructive conduct toward men. It is extremely revealing of the inequalities that continue to exist between men and women.

In the wake of his own adultery, Spéro continues to portray himself as the victim in a powerful testament to his crippling inadequacies. "Forsaken, he spent most of his time at the Montego Bay, wondering what use he was on this earth". (187). Through his self-victimization Spéro avoids taking responsibility for his actions and therefore forges a reliable alibi for his lack of achievement in life. Debbie's reaction to her husband's latest affair exemplifies a collective female disappointment at the unreliable conduct of their partners, encapsulated in the continuities between Debbie and her mother-in-law. "Debbie was sitting slumped at the table, motionless, her head clutched between her hands, immediately bringing to mind the picture he had of Marisia, his maman, crying because of Justin" (187–88). Despite the fact that he is the betrayer and therefore the powerholder in this situation, Spéro is the one who embodies fragility. The scene is reminiscent of a naughty child who wants his mother to pardon him so he can crawl into the safety of her arms again. However, in an illustration of his personal deficiencies, Spéro pursues the path of adultery for the temporary sense of self-esteem it offers him. Spéro's questionable moral conduct has dual importance for the context of gender in the novel—on the one hand it constitutes powerful evidence for Spéro's poor sense of identity and the consequent weakness he displays; on the other, it underlines a painful reality that forms part of the existence of many women.

Condé emphasizes that a substantial part of the problem of such irresponsible male conduct stems from the way boys are mothered in Caribbean society. As Spéro's mother, Marisia, indicates, women have long had to compensate for the unreliable men in their lives. "African king or not, Djéré's papa had behaved like all the other black papas on this earth. He neglected his child. He left him behind in the care of his poor single mother" (8). However, Condé is concerned to demonstrate the active role women play in the creation of weak men by treating their sons like little gods long into adulthood. The perpetuation of this negative trend is particularly apparent in the way Spéro's grandmother brings up her son and grandson, spoiling them to such an extent that there is no need for them to make their own way in the world. Marisia further fosters Spéro's development into an immature man by mollycoddling her husband so much that he does not even know how to boil a pot of water. She thereby establishes a gendered norm that Spéro carries into his own adult relationships. Spéro's enduring image of his father is being bathed by his wife in a tub of hot water, underlining Justin's infantile nature and hinting at the male desire to return to the safety of the womb. Condé herself declares that "all men are children"[16] and that because of the way mothers bring up their sons, they remain dependent on women for the most basic life skills. Thus, while it is patently obvious that it is the women who are the strength of the family, they are partly responsible for the suffering that is inflicted upon them through their acceptance of entrenched gender roles.

Object-relations theory shows that the overwhelming presence of the mother in the upbringing of children has far-reaching consequences on gender identity. Spéro's relationship with Marisia dramatically illustrates this momentous maternal power and the way it shapes boys' and girls' assumption of their gender roles. Playing out the established trend of the Caribbean man's prolonged dependence on his mother, Spéro appears paralyzed in his adult life by his unfulfilled Oedipal love for Marisia. As psychoanalysts from Freud onwards have pointed out, the resolution of the Oedipus complex marks the entry of children into adulthood and consequently their readiness to assume an independent identity. For Spéro, however, this process never completes itself and he remains trapped in an unhealthy obsession with his mother: "No woman ever had the same effect on him" (39). This inability to evolve beyond the psychological bounds of childhood also features in his quest for the reassuring security of a mother figure in his marriage, illustrated by his frequent appearance as a little boy in need of love. At one of the lowest points in his life, alone at the jetty waiting for Debbie, Spéro contemplates drowning in a futile attempt at a return to the watery security of the womb. The role of the mother in the evolution of Caribbean male identity emerges as paramount. By neglecting to provide their sons with clear boundaries for their behavior and by indulging them to the point where they grow up dependent on women for everything, mothers thus appear complicit in the fostering of weak Caribbean men.

Condé underlines men's contribution to the continuation of these gender patterns by focusing on the role models fathers provide for their sons through their absence rather than through their presence. While it has been documented that Caribbean girls grow up with clearly defined examples of female behavior due to the predominance of women in the family, it is evident in the upbringing of Spéro and his ancestors that boys absorb images of masculinity as a result of their fathers' failure to assume their parental responsibilities. As they perceive the lack of male participation in the family, it seems quite natural for boys to grow up and display these same gendered attitudes toward their domestic obligations. Justin, Spéro's father, for example, is an unsuccessful musician who chases after women and dulls his mind with rum, a pattern that Spéro unquestioningly repeats in his own adult life. Condé thus highlights the important effect men have on gender relations in the Caribbean by drawing attention to the potency of negative role models as well as positive ones.

Condé includes a disturbing episode of incest in the novel that illustrates the dangerous potential for these negative male role models to go to extremes. Indeed, such sexual abuse toward children represents "a manifestation of men's power over the powerless."[17]

> On the Morne Verdol lived Amédée, a papa who raped his daughters. He had given a belly to his eldest daughter, Emma, then another to his second, Emmeline. The neighbors gossiped about it all day long; the men were quite prepared to find excuses for him. After all, he was the one who made them! He could use them any way he wanted! The women were more recalcitrant and offended. Méralda, his companion and mother of his children, went about her business as if she were oblivious to what was going on in her house. But when Amédée approached the youngest daughter with the same intentions Méralda stuck a knife used for scraping hogs in his stomach. Public opinion and the magistrates from France acquitted her unanimously. A woman can do anything to protect her child. (127–28)

With incest a theme that is frequently dealt with by French Caribbean writers, this passage links incestuous men to the masculine qualities of violence and aggression. At first glance it appears that women are equally responsible for this unforgivable act of abuse, until the balance is restored when the mother reasserts her maternal power and kills her husband.

This scene highlights the unstable and brutally irresponsible nature of many men who have such a poor sense of identity that the only way they can assert themselves is by oppressing the physically weak and vulnerable. Women, by contrast, are depicted as the stable providers of the family and the ones who are permitted to go to any lengths to protect the honor of their loved ones. The implication of this incident for Spéro is that it leads to a further instalment of self-questioning where he admonishes himself for his failed attempt at parenting. While Condé depicts Spéro as hopelessly inadequate in his daughter Anita's upbringing, his repeated critical reflections further disempower him. This self-destructive behavior results in his abdication of parental duties and Debbie's eager adoption of the roles of both mother and father. Spéro's failure to take responsibility for his actions prevents him from participating actively in his destiny, exacerbating his already fragile self-concept and increasing Debbie's "woman's burden."

Debbie and Spéro express their marital dissonance and character incompatibilities to a large degree in their treatment of Anita. In typical fashion, Debbie seizes the opportunity of a child's presence to isolate herself from Spéro and to fill her daughter's head with stories of her ancestor and the passionate cause of the race. Debbie is highly ambitious for Anita and wishes to instil in her all the "right" values. Spéro's ambitions, however, are far more humble and he wonders why "Anita had never asked [him] if the full moon gives birth to rabbits or if a rainbow in the morning brings sorrow and one in the afternoon brings hope" (69–70). Experiencing the state of parental exile imposed on him by Debbie's "kidnapping" of their child, Spéro relinquishes all authority over the situation and withdraws instead into self-pity. "He had given [Anita] nothing. He had guided her nowhere . . . He had been a bad father! A very bad father!" (184). While Anita's distance from her father aggravates his sense of worthlessness, Debbie's attempts to control her daughter emphasize the extensive influence she exerts in the maternal role. Reversing the stereotypical image of the selfless and self-sacrificing mother, Debbie's approach to motherhood appear as yet another mode of manipulation in which she attempts to impose her views on others. To a certain extent, then, Debbie represents a negative mother-figure who uses her maternal influence as a means for self-advancement.

Les Derniers Rois mages provides considerable material for reflection on the question of the *femme matador*. While Condé consistently refuses to typecast her characters, Debbie both conforms to and challenges the stereotypical nature of this gender category. At first glance Debbie is a confident social activist and feminist who dominates her husband and strives to make a difference in the world. She has carved a successful career for herself and she manages to juggle her public and private roles with apparent ease. However, Condé undermines Debbie's achievements by drawing attention to the flaws in her character caused by excessive political correctness. It is through Spéro and his wayward reflections that Condé challenges Debbie's status as a strong woman, offering an alternative vision of coping with the scars of the past. History is a constant backdrop to the novel and both Debbie and Spéro remain influenced by the past. In the characters of Debbie and Spéro, Condé stresses that "the historical ties between Africa and the New World are neither simply the key to the present nor a cultural burden to deny."[18]

Debbie and Spéro's varied reactions to history dramatically influence the construction of their gender identity. Spéro adopts a defeated stance to the injustices of the past, falling into a family tradition of morally weak men. Debbie is rigidly defiant and determinedly fights for racial equality. However, the achievement of her social goals often arises by stifling others' difference. Through Debbie's contrast with Spéro, Condé nuances her portrait of Debbie as a *femme matador* and highlights the contradictions of gender in Caribbean and African-American societies.

Texaco and *Les Derniers Rois mages* provide two versions of the *femme matador* in French Caribbean literature. In the first, Chamoiseau depicts a generally positive image of the strong Caribbean woman in Marie-Sophie's ability to find strength in adversity. The author does not focus attention on any major flaws in her character apart from her human failing of falling in love with a string of unsuitable men. Furthermore, Marie-Sophie demonstrates the possibility of coexistence between the masculine and feminine principles. Chamoiseau's focus on a woman in *Texaco* contrasts with his other novels in which he does not privilege a female perspective. It also represents a challenge to the predominantly masculinist nature of *Créolité*. In *Les Derniers Rois mages*, Debbie emerges as a more complex example of a strong woman, displaying both positive and negative qualities. Both novels place their figures of female strength in a specific social context that underlines the importance of the environment in shaping gender identity. Their response to their circumstances introduces two alternatives to the experience of historical exploitation. Together these books nuance and question the celebrated figure of the *femme matador* in French Caribbean society.

NOTES

1. Pierre Pinalie, unpublished interview by Bonnie Thomas, Martinique, 28 June 2001.

2. Richard D. E. Burton, *Le Roman marron: Études sur la littérature martiniquaise contemporaine* (Paris: L'Harmattan, 1997), 192.

3. Burton, *Le Roman marron*, 189.

4. Lorna Milne, "From *Créolité* to *Diversalité*: The Postcolonial Subject in Patrick Chamoiseau's *Texaco*," in Paul Gifford and Johnnie Gratton (eds.), *Subject Matters: Subject and Self in French Literature from Descartes to the Present* (Amsterdam: Rodopi, 2000), 167–68.

5. Chamoiseau states that unity can be achieved only through the recognition of human diversity. Refusing the monolithic tendencies associated with universality, he coined the phrase "diversalité." See Jean Bernabé, Patrick Chamoiseau and Raphaël Confiant, *Eloge de la Créolité* (Paris: Gallimard, 1993), 114.

6. Maeve McCusker, "De la problématique du territoire à la problématique du lien: Un entretien avec Patrick Chamoiseau," *The French Review* 73, no. 4 (2000): 730.

7. McCusker, "De la problématique du territoire à la problématique du lien," 730–31.

8. Chamoiseau, interview by Bonnie Thomas, Martinique, 26 June 2001.

9. Chamoiseau, interview by Bonnie Thomas.

10. Françoise duRivage, "Texaco: From the Hills to the Mangrove Swamps," *Thamyris* 6, no. 1 (1999): 40.

11. Françoise Pfaff, *Conversations with Maryse Condé* (Lincoln: University of Nebraska Press, 1996), 93.

12. Sam Haigh, *Mapping a Tradition: Francophone Women's Writing from Guadeloupe* (London: Maney Publishing, 2000), 115.

13. Haigh, *Mapping a Tradition*, 121. See also Fritz Gracchus, "L'Antillais et la question du père," *CARÉ* 4 (1979): 95–115.

14. Mildred Mortimer, "A Sense of Place and Space in Maryse Condé's *Les Derniers Rois mages*," *World Literature Today* 67, no. 4 (1993): 760.

15. Lydie Moudileno, "La Qualité de l'amour chez Maryse Condé," in Nara Araujo (ed.), *L'Oeuvre de Maryse Condé: À propos d'une écrivaine politiquement incorrecte* (Paris: L'Harmattan, 1996), 178.

16. Pfaff, *Conversations with Maryse Condé*, 19.

17. Jane Ussher, *Women's Madness: Misogyny or Mental Illness?* (Amherst: University of Massachusetts Press, 1991), 33.

18. Leah D. Hewitt, "Condé's Critical Seesaw," *Callaloo* 18, no. 3 (1995): 642.

6

~~

Gender in the
créoliste Satirical Novel

Patrick Chamoiseau and Raphaël Confiant paint humorous yet revealing portraits of French Caribbean gender identity in two of their novels: *Solibo Magnifique* and *Eau de café*. Both books are characterized by the
authors' use of magic and both employ satirical exaggeration as a technique for underlining more serious preoccupations in French Caribbean
society. However, their character portrayals also highlight the *créolistes'*
sexist approach to gender issues. Ethnographers Richard Price and Sally
Price, who have been Martinican residents for the past decade, argue that
"the *créolistes'* masculinist position emerges directly—and uncritically—
from the routine sexism of Martiniquan daily life."[1] According to the
Prices, writers such as Chamoiseau and Confiant reproduce familiar
Caribbean gender roles in their books "in which women serve primarily
as mothers and lovers, in which homosexuality is highly stigmatized or
denied, and in which authorial authority is the exclusive prerogative of
men."[2] *Solibo Magnifique* and *Eau de café* emphasize the ways in which the
créoliste writers' sociological background influences their presentation of
contemporary gender issues.

In an analysis of *Solibo Magnifique* and *Eau de café* it is important first to
consider the operation of magical realism in the novels. This literary technique is commonly attributed to Latin American writers such as Gabriel
García Márquez and is a frequent feature of postcolonial works. Magical
realism introduces unrealistic elements into a narrative and relies on the
reader's suspension of belief. Beverley Ormerod asserts that this stylistic
approach is a recurrent feature in the writings of many French Caribbean

novelists, employed both as a literary game and a testament to the continuing presence of magic in Caribbean folk culture.[3] By offering center stage to supernatural or magical occurrences such writers forge a tangible link with the Caribbean's African heritage, celebrating the persistence of these folk traditions in the face of French cultural imperialism. Magical realism can thus be considered part of *Créolité*'s promotion of the enduring and oppositional nature of Creole culture.

Solibo Magnifique centers on a police investigation into the mysterious circumstances surrounding the protagonist's death, while *Eau de café* focuses on mystical occurrences in the small Martinican village of Grand-Anse. Chamoiseau and Confiant present their vision of gender identity as a series of stereotypes, including the *femme matador*, the philandering Caribbean man and the Creole *conteur*. They set their characters against Martinique's evolution from a plantation society to a country dominated culturally and economically by France. The philosophy of *Créolité* runs like a thread through their work, contributing to the panorama of colorful characters spanning all manner of racial and ethnic groups and every stratum of the social scale, but which, notably, excludes the complexities of gender identity.

Créolité's positive valuation of the Caribbean storyteller also features in these novels, a figure they identify as unequivocally male. Chamoiseau and Confiant effectively establish a dialectic between male and female storytellers in their novels by depicting a situation in which the female voice is silenced by the male *conteur*. This privileging of the male perspective over the female in *Solibo Magnifique* and *Eau de café* emerges in dramatic contrast to the vision presented by women writers such as Simone Schwarz-Bart and Maryse Condé. These *créoliste* works represent contemporary examples of female voicelessness and absence in the master discourses.

Richard Burton asserts that the *conteur* acts as a present-day example of Chamoiseau's conception of *la petite marronne*, relating to the slave who only partially absents himself from the colonial system.[4] It is therefore not surprising that the *créoliste* writers tend to identify themselves as storytellers or *marqueurs de paroles*. According to Burton, Chamoiseau's writing shows that it is almost impossible to adopt the absolute oppositional stance of *la grande marronne* in contemporary Martinique where France's cultural and economic dominance is unrivalled. By contrast, the phenomenon of *la petite marronne*, inextricably linked to the ideology of *débrouillardise* or the ability to survive and exploit the system that oppresses, becomes the supreme image of contemporary resistance.

Edouard Glissant, however, warns against adopting a "folklorized" image of Creole culture in which French Caribbean people think they are representing themselves, but in reality are collaborating with France's policy of assimilation. As he writes in *Le Discours antillais*, "le 'folklore,' soigneusement évidé de signification, présente un double avantage . . . pour le système: il entretient l'individu dans l'illusion qu'il se représente, et le distrait de toute autre tentation d'existence collective" ['folklore,' carefully emptied of meaning, presents a double advantage . . . for the system: it maintains the individual's illusion that they are representing themselves, and distracts them from any other temptation of a collective existence].[5] For Richard and Sally Price, *créoliste* literature manifests a certain complicity with this "folklorization," evident in "the celebration of a museumified Martinique, a diorama'c Martinique, a picturesque ad 'pastified' Martinique."[6] The folkloric aspect of *Créolité* plays an influential role in Chamoiseau's and Confiant's approach to their subject matter and informs the way they portray their characters' gender identity. These writers frequently resort to cultural shortcuts in the form of exoticized gendered stereotypes that have little to do with a postcolonial reality.

While Patrick Chamoiseau affirms his allegiance to *créoliste* literature and his intellectual debt to Glissant,[7] he expresses more sympathy toward women and portrays a greater spectrum of female experience in his books than Raphaël Confiant. The focus of *Solibo Magnifique* undoubtedly rests on the figure of the male *conteur* under increasing cultural threat from France. However, Chamoiseau introduces brief vignettes into the novel that attest to the vital role women play in preserving Creole cultural traditions. When the *créoliste* hero Solibo suffers from depression, for example, it is the female market vendors who rally around him with their stories of hope and courage. Affirming women's place as communicators of oral culture, Chamoiseau offers one of the few male insights into the importance of women in the cultivation of *Créolité*.

Richard Burton underlines the significance of Chamoiseau's choice of market women as symbols of *Créolité*, stating that "from the slave period onward, [they] have sustained the whole alternative Creole economy that functions in the interstices of the plantation complex."[8] Within this framework, women achieve a status comparable to that of the storyteller in their link to the phenomenon of *la petite marronne* and *débrouillardise*. Despite this acknowledgment of female culture-building, however, the intrusion of these resourceful women into the narrative remains ephemeral. *Solibo Magnifique* appears mid-way between the overwhelmingly masculinist works produced by certain male *créolistes* and the many texts by female writers who celebrate women's role in oral culture.

Solibo Magnifique engages with the question of gender by illuminating a series of stereotypes in a humorous fashion. Declaring this book to be his most Creole with its structure based on the Caribbean wake and magical realism, Chamoiseau draws on a unique Creolized French to convey his perception of Martinican reality. His work cleverly captures the two modes of expression that exist in the French Caribbean as a result of the dual presence of French and Creole. Chamoiseau's subtle linguistic techniques contribute to the images of gender identity presented in the novel, emphasizing the way in which gender intersects with race and class. The characters in *Solibo Magnifique* also illustrate the fluidity of gender. While the principal action of the novel revolves around the investigation into Solibo's death, and, symbolically, the death of Creole culture, Chamoiseau nonetheless provides a varied portrait of French Caribbean gender identity.

In his capacity as a "Master of the Word," Solibo appears in the novel as the ultimate *créoliste* hero, a living embodiment of the persistence of Creole cultural practices. Drawing on language to communicate Martinique's cultural traditions, Solibo exemplifies the masculinist tradition of the *conteur*. Moreover, he displays many of the characteristics associated with the irresponsible and philandering Caribbean man. Chamoiseau illustrates Solibo's penchant for rum, for example, in his "tafia expert's red-yellow eyes" (13) and his regular pauses at Chez Chinotte for a drink. Solibo is also depicted as a man who cannot resist the pleasures of the flesh. However, Chamoiseau softens his depiction of Solibo as a womanizer by mischievously highlighting Solibo's seizure of his multiple sexual experiences as an opportunity for learning:

> Ah, here comes Margaret from St. Lucia, and here's Haiti, tell us about Haiti, Roselita, Mama! This is Clara from Dominica and here's Puerto Rico *como esta uste*? Well I'll be damned! Who's this, is it Sacha from Barbados . . . the whole Caribbean's here! the Caribbean is here! (120)

As an ever-observant *conteur*, Solibo quickly transforms his interaction with this vast spectrum of Caribbean women into a source of material for his stories and an occasion for nonstop talking. Chamoiseau gently mocks this Caribbean male tendency to exercise the tongue with his description of Solibo talking "at every step, he talked to everyone, to a woman tattling tongue-crazy, available and useless, oh mama! what a gust of blah-blah" (9). While Chamoiseau's portrait of Solibo emphasizes his role as the custodian of cultural tradition, his light-hearted approach to Solibo's vices demystifies the exemplary figure of the storyteller. Chamoiseau's use of humor both underlines and challenges the stereotypical masculine image of the Creole *conteur*.

Chamoiseau also reveals a feminine side to Solibo with his qualities of nurturing, attachment to his family and affinity with nature. After his death, Solibo's one-time lover, Antoinette Maria-Jésus Sidonise, offers a moving tribute to these feminine traits in his character, detailing his enduring if not permanent presence in her family: "If times were bad and he didn't have a good sou left, he made sure we had the sea-given fish, the freshly picked vegetable" (42). While Sidonise acknowledges that she is not the only woman in Solibo's life, she continues to welcome him into her home. To some extent she exemplifies the Caribbean woman who values her love for a man over his capacity for constancy.[9]

Sidonise momentarily abandons her relationship with Solibo for the security offered by marriage and a regular income from her husband Dalta's job as a customs officer, yet this bond soon disintegrates out of her love for Solibo. Sidonise thus replicates the Caribbean female phenomenon of contributing to her own unhappiness with her voluntary separation from Dalta, "a good man [who] was always good with the children" (42). This portrait also attests to Sidonise's fidelity and discretion in her relationship with Solibo, highlighting the strength of her character and her ability to endure the hardships life offers her: "I am like that, my braids aren't braids, but vines of pride and when my heart chokes, when I feel like I'm drowning, it's pride that I live, that I eat, that I breathe" (79).

Solibo's nurturing capabilities come into sharp focus as Sidonise recalls the time when he prepares a shark stew at her home. This sensitive description of Solibo revelling in culinary sensuousness underlines the atmosphere of warmth that arises in his company. In his link to the enticing smells of the kitchen, one imagines being in the presence of a nurturing mother who fills her children with nourishing food and kind words. Solibo successfully re-creates this peaceful sanctuary in his slow preparation of the shark stew that he shares with Sidonise, her children and her neighbors. The scene culminates in Solibo's declaration of his eternal affection for Sidonise. The gentleness of this situation emphasizes Solibo's ability to connect to others, marking him as a feminine man in certain aspects of his character.

Solibo's human qualities come into play when one of the old village women, Man Gnam, dies and is destined to disappear from the earth without the slightest acknowledgment. Solibo takes it upon himself to give her a dignified burial followed by a wake dedicated to her life, paying for all the expenses and leading the reminiscences about Man Gnam. As one of the witnesses recalls, "[w]ithout the Magnificent, she would have left like a dog" (108). This declaration echoes the villagers' declaration to Télumée that if it had not been for her l'ange Médard [Angel Medard] would have died without dignity. By transforming the sorry event of Man Gnam's death into an event that values her contribution to the community, Solibo demonstrates a remarkable capacity to open himself to others. By transposing this predominantly female characteristic onto the male plane, Solibo exposes once again his feminine side. These qualities set him apart from the rigidly defined masculinist vision of the *conteur*.

Solibo's appreciation of nature is a further example of his proximity to certain traits classically associated with femininity. There are two particularly vivid scenes in the novel in which Solibo displays his connection with the natural world; the first, an encounter with a yellow snake and the second, his meeting with a pig that refuses to die. After heroically saving Man Goul from her terrifying encounter with a venomous snake in the market place, Solibo reflects on his position in nature: "I will never drown. In water, I become water, before the wave, I am wave. I will never burn myself either, because fire does not burn fire . . . Each creature is but a chord which you just have to tune in to" (44). This statement of deep understanding underlines Solibo's harmony with the elements and indicates a view of nature rarely found in male characters in French Caribbean literature. While connection to the environment is often considered a typically feminine quality, this bond between man and earth becomes a source of power in *Solibo Magnifique*.

When Man Gnam is unable to kill an uncontrollable pig fattened especially for Christmas Day, Solibo is the one she calls upon to save the day: "Strength. He hadn't even peeked into the yard when that Master Pig stopped squealing" (48). Solibo demonstrates a keen awareness of this capacity to communicate with the physical world around him, a gift that is also appreciated by other characters in the novel. Describing the exceptional quality of the charcoal Solibo sells at the market, Solibo's peers note that it "was no accident that he sold charcoal, since that's what he was in our lives: the charcoal is the wood, it's the trunk, the branches and leaves, and also the root" (124). Solibo's communion with the earth not only sheds light on his tie to the feminine, it also highlights the way in which strength is found in the melding of masculine and feminine. The character of Solibo thus provides a complex view of the traditionally virile figure of the Caribbean storyteller, drawing attention to both his conformity and nonconformity with this role.

The female character most developed in *Solibo Magnifique* is Doudou-Ménar, a fat woman who sells candied fruits in the market. Described in a series of satirical labels including "the Tigress," "the Enormous One," "the formidable street vendor," "the stuffed tomato," "the maniac," "the Big Bag," "the Terrible One" and "the Fat One," Doudou-Ménar is a larger-than-life character who offers a vision of the *femme matador* at its most extreme, tempered by Chamoiseau's depiction of her initially as a simple and innocent country girl.

When Solibo's listeners finally realize that he is dead, Doudou-Ménar is the first to rush off to the police to get help. Chamoiseau contextualizes his character's energetic reaction to this event by reflecting on the inherent strength in her character. In an allusion to the burden many Caribbean women must carry in life, Chamoiseau, tongue-in-cheek, recasts the Creole proverb first made famous in Simone Schwarz-Bart's *Pluie et vent sur Télumée Miracle* that a woman's breasts are never too heavy for her chest, applying it instead to Doudou-Ménar: "Her big breasts jumped up and down, but the fat woman ignored them (never burdensome for a chest, these things cannot fall, no)" (24). According to H. Adlai Murdoch, this intertextual reference "tacitly [inscribes] Doudou-Ménar as an icon of female cultural resistance,"[13] an identification amplified in Chamoiseau's description of her everyday life:

> [S]he drew upon the strength her long day had not been able to exhaust: getting up at sunrise to scald the grapefruit, sweep the house before waking up her son Gustave (a ne'er-do-well, my dear, who wears Pierre Cardin clothes and sings in Spanish in a band where other ne'er-do-wells pretend to be Latins), and sells candied fruit through the favor of the festivities, a way of dealing blows to her debts with the hard swing of a full purse. Her man, Gustave's father, had vanished from the midst of life's traffic, slumped in a festive stupor from which he emerged only after the Carnival, but with empty balls and the muscle all mushy. (24)

Doudou-Ménar's struggle to survive in the absence of reliable men highlights some of the hardships common to Caribbean women. Her partner's lack of responsibility is evident in his drunken collapse after the Carnival, a behavior that overflows into other aspects of their shared life. His failure to provide an adequate role model for his son partially explains the perpetuation of male patterns of unreliability in French Caribbean society. In the absence of a strong father figure, Doudou-Ménar's son shows little promise of breaking with this destructive trend. The passage also hints at Doudou-Ménar's own contribution to the problem by allowing the immaturity of father and son to continue. The immediate consequences for Doudou-Ménar, however, are that she must assume almost complete responsibility for the running of the home. She therefore develops the qualities of resilience and tenacity needed to survive. In this light, she appears as a *femme matador* who must shoulder the consequences of male irresponsibility.

Whilst the portraits of these fighting women generally attract admiration from the writers who describe them, Chamoiseau reveals a more serious consequence of this female struggle to survive. It is evident that material and emotional necessity succeed in producing a warrior spirit in Doudou-Ménar, which she draws on in her quest for survival in a hostile environment. However, the determination with which she clings to life grows to such an extent that she becomes prone to acts of violence that are more reminiscent of masculine aggression than they are of feminine resistance: "In this woman, street champion, any threat, any gurgle in the stomach, launched a desire to massacre" (26). Doudou-Ménar's considerable physical strength and bold spirit, presented with comic exaggeration, make her a potential danger to anyone who crosses her path. Within this framework Doudou-Ménar appears as a particularly aggressive woman, although Chamoiseau emphasizes that this excessive warrior spirit arises as a specific result of the hardships dealt to her by men. Nuancing the alliance of Doudou-Ménar and certain masculine qualities, Chamoiseau shows that she employs a distinctly female strength in order to control some of the threatening external circumstances that unfold around her: "Her breasts came down more destructive than sacks of gravel" (27). Colette Maximin asserts that the humorous side of this scenario—particularly when she attacks the policemen—also needs to be acknowledged in the series of unlikely pairings brought about by this explosion of violence: "[f]éminin contre masculin, un contre plusieurs, grosse contre maigres" [feminine against masculine, one against several, fat against skinny].[11] Against this backdrop, Doudou-Ménar emerges as a complex character who embodies both masculine and feminine qualities developed as a result of her socioeconomic circumstances, focusing attention on the oppositional rather than the harmonious nature of these gendered traits.

Chamoiseau parallels the harshness of Doudou-Ménar's adult fighting spirit with his depiction of her as a naïve girl from the country. With his inclusion of a memorable love scene shared many years earlier with Bouaffesse, the chief sergeant in the investigation into Solibo's death, Chamoiseau stresses the innocence of a young female who has not yet encountered the realities of Caribbean womanhood. Although he satirizes Doudou-Ménar's naivety, he also shows how she is exploited. In his poignant description of her disappointed expectation that Bouaffesse would remember her as he had promised all those years ago, Chamoiseau underlines her transition from the freshness of youth to the jaded and hardened woman who seeks help aggressively for Solibo. He draws further attention to Doudou-Ménar's simplicity and fundamental goodness in a humorous but poignant way with his description of her puffed up with pride when she travels to the crime scene in a police van. Brief vignettes such as these constitute a moving and subtle tribute to the women who suffer in their daily bid for survival. Doudou-Ménar becomes, therefore, a model of the contradictions of the female experience in French Caribbean society.

Chief Sergeant Bouaffesse illustrates a particular kind of Caribbean man in his location midway between the Creole witnesses to Solibo's death and the Frenchified policeman who leads the investigation. Embodying strength and self-confidence, Bouaffesse displays no vulnerabilities and is ruthless in his quest for answers to the mystery of Solibo's death. Indeed, two witnesses are killed in the process of his investigation. Throughout the book Bouaffesse demonstrates an obsession with proving his superiority over his subjects, drawing on violence and trickery in order to maintain his advantage. When interrogating Congo, for example, he deliberately suggests conducting the session in French which he knows this witness can barely speak: "The French language makes their heads swim, grips their guts, and then they skid like drunks down the pavement" (66). This same pleasure in domination is evident in Bouaffesse's confident exit from his office "with the light footstep of a boss who wants to catch an employee screwing up" (28). Situated in a higher social position than the Creole characters he interrogates, Bouaffesse nonetheless retains the ability to communicate with them, in contrast to his superior, Chief Inspector Evariste Pilon, who is unable to bridge the chasm between the witnesses at the bottom of the social ladder and his own elevated status. Bouaffesse continually reveals himself to be unafraid of getting his hands dirty in the investigation, appearing as a particularly strong male figure from a Caribbean point of view with his imposing physical presence and his easy recourse to violence.

Chamoiseau intensifies the virility of this male character with his detailed description of Bouaffesse's philandering activities that advance his social status among Caribbean men. Right back to the time of his first meeting with the young Doudou-Ménar, Bouaffesse was already a seasoned skirt-chaser who "justified (to his coolie concubine) his nocturnal absences with stories about Disaster Protocol Drills, [while he] haunted the feminine fishponds of small parties, balls, and other events where the juices flowed" (33). Chamoiseau's exaggerated portrayal of Bouaffesse's techniques of seduction focuses attention on the admiration this attitude toward women attracts from other Caribbean men. One of his young employees, for example, becomes consumed by jealousy when he observes Bouaffesse about to rekindle his sexual relationship with Doudou-Ménar in his office. As the object of male esteem and admiration for his physical strength and prowess with women, Bouaffesse displaces even Chief Inspector Pilon in his status as a strong Caribbean man.

From the point of view of object-relations theory, however, the character of Bouaffesse presents a different image of Caribbean manhood. In the background material he provides on Bouaffesse, Chamoiseau reveals him to be the victim of an unstable family environment caused by an absent father. "For Gros-Désors, the sire, the future Chief Sergeant became only the sixteenth of the unrecognized children he fathered every nine months, competing with his friends" (29). Despite his ironic tone, Chamoiseau's inclusion of an episode between Bouaffesse and a French psychologist, in which the former "would invariably reply to the questions *Mother?* and then *Father?*: Stéphanise Laguinée! . . ." (29), indicates another side to Bouaffesse's conception of his identity. With the lack of a consistent male role model against which he can develop his sense of masculinity and separate from his mother, Bouaffesse learns to assert himself instead through violence and aggression. Chamoiseau reveals that the massacre of

women, children and the elderly was a particular specialty of his regi-
ment in the Algerian War. Bouaffesse's over-identification with the masculine principle, evident in his continual affirmation of brutality, reinforces the perception that he is uncertain in his status as a man. In striking
contrast to Solibo, Bouaffesse displays no feminine side to his character
and his treatment of his wife is noteworthy for its absence of affection or
respect: "he made sure she could give birth ten times before marrying her
without even the simplest dinner or party" (29). Through the character
of Bouaffesse, Chamoiseau unveils some of the effects of a mother-
dominated upbringing on male identity. The diametrically opposed perspectives adopted by Caribbean society and object-relations theorists toward this stereotype of male strength highlight the complex nature of
Caribbean gender roles.

Chief Inspector Pilon presents another, more overtly satirical, view of
Caribbean male identity, encapsulating the contradictions of a man who
occupies a more secure social position than Bouaffesse with his elevated
role in the police force, but who displays greater uncertainty of character.
While Pilon has spent a long period of his life in metropolitan France and
exudes authority through his proximity to the power structures of
Caribbean society, Chamoiseau underlines his ongoing concern with
maintaining his social status. Pilon's wife is a *chabine*, a woman with light-
colored skin, illustrating his preoccupation with rising up the social scale.
With the social valuation of color one of the poisonous legacies of the
plantation system, it is significant that Pilon has chosen a partner with the
highly prized light skin that is linked to a higher social status in the
French Caribbean. Moreover, as a testament to his insecure sense of identity, Pilon demonstrates a distinct uneasiness in his position in the Martinican middle class. For example, while he "petitions for Creole in the
schools [he] jumps when his children use it to speak to him" (76) and
Chamoiseau comments that in the end "he lives like all of us, at two
speeds, not knowing whether he should put on the brakes when going
uphill or accelerate going down" (76). Chamoiseau highlights the fragility
of Pilon's self-concept by showing that any encounter with someone from
a lower social class threatens his character's perception of his own status.

Pilon's wavering sense of self comes into sharp focus when he and
Bouaffesse become embroiled in a specifically Creole manner of approaching Solibo's case, concentrating not on locating Solibo's killer but
on understanding the question: "Who is Solibo?" (127). Thereby forced to
abandon his logical and organized investigation and revert instead to the
insights of a *quimboiseur*, Pilon ends up "soaked in an unhealthy sweat,
[looking] like one of those poor old blackmen that you come upon at the
police station every day making impossible statements about running
into devils and zombies" (104). Pilon's instability when plunged into a

world that he has forsaken to strengthen his ties with the French high-lights the way in which conflicts of identity permeate all levels of the social scale. Pilon may appear to Bouaffesse and the witnesses as confident and influential in his position of power, but he emerges as less self-assured than they are because of his constant need to prove he belongs to this superior social environment. The character of Pilon thus underlines the difficulties of being a black man operating in a French power structure, a status that offers him an elevated social influence but which simultaneously erodes his sense of self-worth.

A further significant male character in the story is the witness Congo, a man associated with Africa and marginalized in the investigation because he is unable to speak French. Congo presents a complex view of male gender identity in his dual display of gentleness and compassion toward Solibo and his quiet assertion of his strength. When the police want to cover Solibo's dead body with a few pieces of dirty cardboard, for example, it is Congo who "took off his shirt, his trousers, his undershirt, un-folded his handkerchief, . . . demanding in a broken voice that they be used to cover the body" (64). Congo's simple nurturing gesture highlights the feminine side of a man otherwise known for his masculine presence. Chamoiseau underlines the undisputed nature of Congo's masculine authority in a conflict with Bouaffesse who is anxious to display his authority over the old man: "just as he was about to strike, his eyes met those of the Relic: the graveyard hand remained stuck in the air, trembling with powerlessness" (68–69). Congo reveals the extent of his strength in his lack of a need to express himself through violence and aggression. De-spite Bouaffesse's ruthless interrogation of him culminating in Congo's death, Congo remains true to his principles and refuses to admit to Bouaffesse's false accusations. Bouaffesse's cross-examination of Congo is marked by unrelenting violence and humiliation of his subject, a potent reminder of the former's need to assert himself through oppression of others. It is noteworthy also that Pilon deliberately stays out of this session, preferring not to know of Bouaffesse's unprofessional practices. Congo's ultimate leap to his death represents a final act of defiance to-ward a man characterized by violence. In stark contrast to Bouaffesse, Congo's simple presence and palpable link to the past embody all the force that is necessary to affirm his existence. He thus emerges as a potent figure of male strength in the novel, satirically opposed to the policeman's dependence on brute force.

Solibo Magnifique explores a number of facets of Caribbean gender iden-tity, focusing particularly on the complexities of masculine gender iden-tity and on the figure of the *femme matador*. Through his light-hearted em-ployment of humor, magic and stereotypes, Chamoiseau draws attention to the more serious issues of male-female relationships and the influence of the past on contemporary conceptions of gender. He underlines the manner in which gendered characteristics may flow between men and women, highlighted in the coexistence of masculine and feminine in characters such as Solibo and Doudou-Ménar. He also reveals the discrepancies that may exist between characters' perceptions of themselves and alternative theoretical interpretations of them, evident in Bouaffesse's dual emergence as a strong and weak Caribbean man. *Solibo Magnifique* thus provides an insightful portrait of gender issues in the French Caribbean, exposing some of the factors which condition male and female identities.

While sharing Chamoiseau's commitment to *Créolité* and employment of magical realist techniques, Raphaël Confiant's *Eau de café* offers a very different image of gender identity. An adjective that frequently recurs in discussions of Confiant's work is "carnavalesque"[12] and in his attempt to encompass the mosaic nature of Martinican society, Confiant, like Chamoiseau, has created a hybrid language of French and Creole. While writing and publishing in "pure" Creole proved to be a largely unsuccessful venture for him, Confiant has mastered a voice midway between the two languages that draws on the positive aspects of both. Confiant's utilization of a creolized French and his magical realist approach to his subject matter highlight his allegiance to the ideals of *Créolité*. This philosophy not only conditions his stance on the cultural melting pot that forms the background to his narrative, it also influences his portrayal of gender identity in his novels. A consequence of this narrow view of gender is that Confiant pigeonholes his characters according to their sex to such an extent that Daniel-Henry Pageaux has described his characters as "une suite de stéréotypes" [a series of stereotypes].[13] In *Eau de café* Confiant's female characters remain closely allied to their functions as sexual objects, *femmes matador* or mystical beings while many of the male characters embody the image of the "swaggering" and unreliable Caribbean man.

Confiant employs a graphic sexual vocabulary that reinforces his stereotyped approach to male and female relationships. Beverely Ormerod, for example, points out that in *créoliste* writers such as Confiant "magical realism is often associated with the marvellous exaggeration of sexual phenomena."[14] Thomas Spear offers another perspective on this attitude to sex, declaring that Confiant reproduces the unbridled sexuality classically attributed to the exotic Caribbean islands and in one sense, therefore, resurrects traditional stereotypes.[15] Spear also asserts that the male obsession with possessing "deux graines" [two balls] that is evident in Confiant's work underlines the association of aggressive sexuality and power over women.[16] The potential fear of women that surfaces from this male need to constantly prove his superiority emerges in Confiant's limited descriptions of men. Confiant's depiction of lovemaking as a gen-

dered battleground highlights his male characters' difficulty in conducting relationships with women. Confiant amplifies this lack of male-female
reciprocity with his exaggerated objectification of his female characters.
With their promiscuous stance toward the opposite sex, his male characters consistently attempt to assert their authority over women. The female
characters, by contrast, exist primarily for male pleasure and most are little developed outside their sexual role, a status consistent with Richard
and Sally Price's observations about *créoliste* writers.

Confiant satirically, yet with apparent approval, depicts the philandering Caribbean man in the character of the half-Syrian, Ali Tanin. Lauded
as "a master-cock" (13), Ali Tanin commands great respect from his fellow
men who envy his outstanding successes with women. Dachine, the mu-
nicipal dustman with "miruscule intimate dimensions [which] ruled out
any chance of amorous success" (13), remarks, for example: "'Hey! My
friend! When you next get hold of those girls, give them one or two good
thrusts from me!'" (13). The choice of the name "Dachine" identifies the
character's Chinese ancestry and serves to signal the use of the stereotype
of the underendowed Oriental. With his exaggerated descriptions of Ali
Tanin's techniques of seduction, Confiant breathes life into the character
of the woman-chaser who is boastful about his virility. This male figure
recurs in works of French Caribbean literature by both men and women.
Ali Tanin eventually undergoes a startling conversion to become a pious
Christian following a meeting with the Madonna in Fort-de-France: "instead of broadcasting the tittle-tattle of his urban adventures, [he] began
prophesying, bible in hand, at the entrance to his shop" (118). This as-
tounding metamorphosis reminiscent of Gisèle Pineau's Sosthène in *La
Grande Drive des esprits* illustrates Richard Burton's assertion that the male
characters in the novel tend to congregate at one extreme or another.[17]
With his characters' failure to challenge Ali Tanin's exploits when he is at
his sexual peak, Confiant reveals an approving fondness for this virile picture of Caribbean male sexuality.

Confiant draws on heavily stereotyped language that emphasizes
women as sexual objects yet paradoxically, he idealizes female sexuality.
According to Daniel-Henry Pageaux, Confiant's female characters can be
roughly divided into two basic categories: the prostitute and the exotic
beauty.[18] The figure of the prostitute features prominently in *Eau de café*
and Confiant lyrically praises Grand-Anse's sex workers, Myrtha and
Passionise. He describes, for example, the way in which Myrtha's and
Passionise's clients "would emerge from the experience transformed,
with the sense of having tasted a fruit which conjugal love could never offer" (33). The prostitute in Confiant's hands exemplifies a particularly no-
ble kind of woman who appreciates men in a nonjudgmental and tangible way. The exotic beauty, by contrast, retains an air of mystery about her

and frequently remains elusive for men. Confiant depicts the mystical Antilia, for example, as a "woman with full breasts," "vanilla-colored skin" and "provocative motions" (8). Beverley Ormerod wonders whether the portrait of this mysterious and sexy character is meant to convince the reader of her magical connections, or whether it is simply Confiant's indulgence in a male fantasy.[19] Even the village priest, Father Le Gloarnec, a man supposedly immune to the pleasures of the flesh, is won over by the exquisite grace of a black woman's body.

Confiant's consistent stress on the capacity of women to satisfy a man sexually affirms the vision outlined in the character of Ali Tanin that they exist primarily as sexual playthings for men. As soon as women stray from this function, they are cast in an unfavorable light. Doris, for example, the woman who raises Eau de Café and is the source of evil spells, is described as devilish, thereby resurrecting the age-old dichotomy of "damned whores and god's police."[20] Even the narrator comments on the "exclusively female evil" (4) that surrounds the circumstances of Antilia's death, highlighting the negative association of female spirituality in *Eau de café*. Confiant's portrayal of women and the extent to which they conform to stereotypical gender roles highlights the patriarchal phenomenon of dividing women into the figure of the angel or the whore. In a unique reversal of this categorization, Confiant positively values the prostitute while rejecting the qualities of female spirituality that are embodied in the angel. Confiant thus displays a strikingly different vision of women and magic to that presented in novels such as *Pluie et vent sur Télumée Miracle and Moi, Tituba, sorcière . . . noire de Salem.*

One of the few complex female characters in *Eau de café* is the narrator's godmother, Eau de Café, a self-reliant and powerful woman who runs a shop in Grand-Anse. Depicted for the most part as steadfastly independent, Eau de Café embodies many of the characteristics of the *femme matador*. Confiant attributes this title to her at several points in the novel, referring to her as "a fighting cock" and "a fighting woman" although Eau de Café herself rejects this label. While Simone Schwarz-Bart and Maryse Condé describe the radiant qualities of the *femme matador* in characters such as Reine Sans Nom, Télumée and Tituba, Confiant paints a different picture by exaggerating the fighting side of his protagonist. In contrast to Schwarz-Bart's and Condé's perception of the strong Caribbean woman as allied with nature, nurturing and healing, Confiant's portrait of Eau de Café reveals her as a "heartless-hysterical-uncouth-rum-drinking-slut" (79). This derogatory representation of the *femme matador* draws attention to the difficulties of the female quest for survival in the Caribbean and the effect this constant drain of energy has on one's outlook. In order to endure these conditions Eau de Café must combine in herself "les cultures féminine et masculine à la fois" [both the feminine and masculine cultures].[21] Confiant's portrayal of Eau de Café thus offers an alternative vision of the *femme matador* in French Caribbean literature by focusing on the extremes of her character and the competing forces of masculinity and femininity within her.

A central characteristic of this exceptional female character is Eau de Café's determination to speak her mind on behalf of all the women who have suffered under patriarchal colonialism. Firmly locating the source of female misery with men, she makes the decision to refuse the constraints of cohabitation with a male partner:

> you mix me up with those little perfumed nymphets who've been trying to get a man from the day that blood began to trickle down their thighs and who waste their lives waiting at their windows as the days go by and no shadow ever appears at the path leading to their huts. As for me, pah! I don't need to be weighed down by all those stupid dreams that clutter up your life just to become moodier than a cat who's had her litter drowned when it's all over. (77)

Eau de Café's isolation from intimate relationships with men fosters her confident assumption of her own subjectivity, displaying an attitude reminiscent of radical feminism. Her steely belief in her self-worth allows Eau de Café to be the director of her own life and to avoid the objectification by men from which many of the female characters in the book suffer. Her hard-won independence forms a contrast with the women who choose to gain advantages by playing games with men. For Eau de Café, submitting to the male gaze as some women do arises at the cost of self-worth. While Eau de Café suffers at times for her life choices she nonetheless appears as a woman who has continually engaged in the brave battle for survival. On this level, she embodies the exemplary strength and courage of the *femme matador*.

Confiant provides a contrasting image of the Caribbean woman as healer in his characterization of Eau de Café as a "white folk's psychic" (18). While Tituba employs her healing powers for the good of her loved ones, Eau de Café is both feared and revered for her ability to communicate with the spirits. Moreover, in contrast to the white apprehension demonstrated toward Tituba's affinity with magic, Eau de Café's skills are highly sought after by the village whites. Despite her black skin, Confiant is concerned to distinguish Eau de Café's magical capabilities from those of the respected figure of the *quimboiseur* through his satirical portrayal of her rejection of dealing with blacks who "can always go and consult magicians or other dealers in evil potions" (24). Confiant also likens her primary task of conducting séances as a loosely veiled excuse for incessant talking, thereby undermining the potency of her spiritual gifts. In his devaluation of Eau de Café's spiritual occupations, Confiant presents a neg-

ative view of female healing powers compared to Schwarz-Bart or
Condé's positive depictions of the woman healer. Furthermore, he also
aligns this capacity for magic with female evil, embodied in the villagers'
suspicion of the mysterious occurrences in Grand-Anse. Confiant thus effects a certain demonization of the feminine in his distancing of Eau de
Café from the positive attributes of the *quimboiseur*, and the general mistrust that surrounds her actions.

In contrast to the independent stance she adopts toward life, Eau de
Café unveils another side to her character that confuses the reader's conception of her as a *femme matador*. Despite her declaration that men "are
nothing but a bad breed" (202), Eau de Café reveals at the end of the book
that she has formed relationships with a number of different men including Julien Thémistocle who raped her mother, Franciane, when pregnant
with Eau de Café. This vicious sexual attack following the breakdown of
Julien Thémistocle's marriage provokes Eau de Café's premature birth
and Franciane's death the very next day. The adult sexual relationship
that arises between Julien Thémistocle and Eau de Café is further compli-
cated by the fact that he is initially charged with bringing up the young
girl as a punishment for his crime. The situation thus appears as a kind of
reverse Oedipal complex in which the mother is killed and Eau de Café
sleeps with the "father." There is also an overturning of the image of the
Caribbean matrifocal family in which the mother is absent through her
death and the "father" present, although in an irregular and distorted
fashion. Julien Thémistocle remains a recurrent if unreliable feature in
Eau de Café's life and when the sexual side of their relationship eventually fades she feels there is nothing left to live for. Eau de Café's involvement with this morally reprehensible man forces the reader to question
her role as a *femme matador*. In some ways she appears no different to the
nymphets she condemns for their dependence on men as it is the loss of
Julien Thémistocle that finally causes her determined quest for survival to
falter. Her own reliance on a man proves even more troubling given his
fatal mistreatment of her mother. Through this facet of Eau de Café's character Confiant criticizes her overall appearance as a strong and independent Caribbean woman.

As the most prominent example of the irresponsible man in the novel,
Julien Thémistocle reveals some of the complexities of male gender identity in the Caribbean. Confiant identifies his character as "a maroon" (18),
which immediately associates him with a tradition of male virility and opposition to the colonial system. For his acts of destruction, such as setting
fire to the canefields the day before milling, Julien Thémistocle attracts
widespread admiration from his male counterparts. Richard Burton
maintains that he becomes a kind of hero as a "tafiateur, coqueur de
femmes, manieur de jambette effilée et de maître-parole que personne

n'ose prononcer son nom ou le regarder en face" [rum drinker, woman chaser, manipulator of knives and master storyteller such that no one dares to say his name or to look him straight in the eye].[22] Combining all the elements that attest to virile masculinity in the Caribbean, Julien Thémistocle represents Confiant's glorification of the "swaggering" Caribbean man.

At the same time, however, the terror his character provokes through his sexual abuse of women emphasizes a more sinister product of the Caribbean past. Constituting part of the fabric of French Caribbean experience, sexual violence dates back to the time of the slave ships where black women were routinely raped by white sailors and the plantation system where white masters forced sexual favors from female slaves. In a firm affirmation of the legacy of history, Edouard Glissant emphasizes that "n'y a-t-il pas de Martiniquais qui ne compte au moins une femme violée parmi ses ancêtres" [there are ro Martinicans who do not count at least one woman who has been raped amongst their ancestors].[23] Julien Thémistocle displays the enduring effects of Caribbean history on male identity and he conducts himself with a disturbing violence. One of *Eau de café*'s *béké* characters, Honoré de Cassagnac, further underlines the persistence of scars left by the denial of black identity under slavery, declaring that Julien Thémistocle "wandered because wandering was his only way of existing. His only way of shouting to the world that he existed" (170). Maryse Condé states in *La Parole des femmes* that in some ways Caribbean men appear as victims for whom fate decides the direction of their lives.[24]

For the brief period when Julien Thémistocle takes responsibility for himself and returns from the French Army decorated and proud, he finally appears the director of his life. However, as a testament to his fragile sense of identity, he soon returns to "being an incubus, an outlaw, a hard man, a follower of the gods of Guinea" (234). Other examples of this negative male behavior include Chief Thimoléon who "wasted all his money drinking rum and gambling rather than raising a family like a true Christian" (42) and who "was screwing several women at the same time" (102) and a school headmaster "who specialized in making his pupils pregnant" (50). With their overwhelming reliance on alcohol, the sexual domination of women and physical destruction, Julien Thémistocle and his male counterparts highlight the way in which qualities revered as strong by many Caribbean men may appear instead as signs of moral weakness.

Eau de Café's relationship with Julien Thémistocle invites reflection on women's role in the perpetuation of their own unhappiness. Despite Julien Thémistocle's repeatedly violent conduct toward women, Eau de Café's continual openness toward him indicates her complicity in the situation. Indeed, Eau de Café takes her place among the many women from Grand-Anse who "mother" Julien Thémistocle into an attitude of irresponsibility by refusing to challenge his behavior. This male retreat into self-destruction and aggression is an example of Condé's claim that the frustrated and dispossessed Caribbean man finds refuge in unreliability.[25]

Using folk belief as a source of humor, Confiant creates Julien Thémistocle's most memorable role in the novel through his transformation into an incubus who preys on young virgins between two and four o'clock each morning. When his reign of terror is ultimately foiled by the supply of protective black underwear to all the women in the village except for one, Julien Thémistocle proceeds to violently rape this sole defenseless woman. Confiant's portrayal of Rose-Aimée Tanin's greeting of this attack as a regenerative experience offers a powerful illustration of female complicity in male behavior: "I'm even having pleasant dreams now. Ah, thank you, God! Thank you!" (70). While this incident must be placed in the context of Confiant's flippant humor and irreverent desire to shock, it may be read as an example of the part Caribbean women play in the continuation of destructive male patterns of behavior. In the case of Rose-Aimée Tanin, she not only fails to condemn her attacker, but she also positively affirms him as if his approach toward women is exemplary. Whatever the author's original intention, *Eau de café* focuses attention on women's acceptance of their sexual oppression as well as providing the textual possibility of a powerful indictment of the negative Caribbean man.

The character of Rose-Aimée Tanin also offers insight into the hypocrisy that exists within some male-female relationships in the Caribbean. While there are elements of the *femme matador* in this woman who takes in Syrian, her future husband and Ali Tanin's father, when he is destitute and homeless, Rose-Aimée nonetheless experiences many of the inequalities common to Caribbean women. As the last victim of the incubus, Rose-Aimée may expect compassion and understanding from her husband. However, Syrian accuses her of infidelity and permanently banishes her from their home. His extreme reaction to what is effectively a situation of rape demonstrates the general intolerance of Caribbean men toward their wives' relations with other men. Although they are perfectly happy to indulge in extramarital liaisons themselves and indeed, consider such behavior natural and normal for a Caribbean man, this privilege is not extended to their female partners. Despite the fact that it is Rose-Aimée who provides Syrian with the solid domestic foundation from which he develops into a highly successful merchant, it is she who is turned out of her own home without so much as an attempt at understanding by her husband.

Richard Burton asserts that there is a fundamental tension that exists between Creole masculine culture founded upon the four elements of rum, games, words and conflict and Creole feminine culture that is built on providing for the family.[26] In his view, this masculine oppositional culture can only threaten the survival of the matrifocal family, evident in Syrian's shattering of family bonds through his rejection of his wife. Condemned to wander the streets in desperate poverty until she mysteriously disappears, Rose-Aimée is a haunting reminder of the extent of male insensitivity toward women, also indicating that Confiant has, after all, some awareness of the damage men do to women.

A consideration of maternity gives a further illustration of the complex nature of Eau de Café's character as well as to the more general question of French Caribban gender identity. While Eau de Café is reputed to be barren for most of the book, replicating the phenomenon of childlessness found in many strong Caribbean women in the literature of the region, progressive revelations to her godson culminate in her confession that she is the mother of the elusive and mystical Antilia. The victim of a curse passed on to her by her mother, Eau de Café is swiftly separated from her child at birth by her female carer, Doris. Eau de Café's experience of motherhood renders her acutely aware of the obstacles facing the Caribbean mother: "since the days of slavery, our women have killed their babies in their wombs so as not to provide workers for the masters" (251). Transposed to the modern day, Eau de Café demonstrates that little has changed for the Caribbean woman when she too attempts to end her child's life while still in the womb.

The lack of mothering Eau de Café receives as a child and her inability to mother Antilia underline a more widespread phenomenon in the novel of the absence of the maternal, encapsulated in the experience of Martinicans wrenched from their homeland due to the slave trade. With her lack of insight into her origins—"I have come from nowhere, . . . or, if you prefer, from this very place, from here itself . . . " (9)—the character of Antilia incarnates the notion of the Caribbean as an orphan of Mother Africa. Confiant shows that this physical and psychological displacement carries dramatic consequences for the individual. Many of the villagers in *Eau de café* demonstrate an obsession with genealogy that attests to a fragile sense of personal identity. Julien Thémistocle, for example, finds himself the victim of Honoré de Cassagnac's tirade about his ancestors while other inhabitants of Grand-Anse feel intensely threatened when the motherless Eau de Café first strides into the village, bombarding her with questions about her ancestry. The slaves' uprooting from their country of origin coupled with the breaking of the African family upon their arrival in the Caribbean establish a situation in which the psychological scars of the past continue to condition personal identity. The symbolic failure of Africa to mother her children bequeathed a sexual status quo characterized by personal alienation.

The overwhelming maternal image in the novel arises in the figure of "that mad mother, the sea" (16), despised and feared by the villagers of Grand-Anse. Reflecting the barrenness of the relationships that occur between men and women in *Eau de café*, the sea is in fact the victim of a curse that causes all life within it to dry up and die. The characters seem to suffer from this lack of maternal nurturance and it is not until the end of the novel that the narrator is finally able to declare that "every night the sea made me a gift of its loving warmth" (280). The chaos that reigns until this point in the narrative appears as a powerful indictment of the consequences of maternal absence. While the lack of involvement of the Caribbean father is well-documented and can be measured in the pattern of strong women and weak men that has evolved in French Caribbean society, Confiant demonstrates that the absent Caribbean mother creates a chasm that is too wide for the characters to bridge. The process of rebirth encapsulated in the image of the newly nurturing sea finds resonance in the relationship between Eau de Café and Julien Thémistocle who make their own new beginning in the way they relate to each other.

Reverting to the body and mind of a young child, Julien expresses his fundamental need for a mother, a role Eau de Café adopts by offering him her flat and withered breast: "The little boy sucked greedily at the milk and began to grow-grow-grow, thus regaining his original strength of a man taller than the Mississippi" (270). For a character who is known throughout most of the book for his violence and aggression, Julien Thémistocle illustrates that "*aucun* personnage masculin chez Confiant n'arrive à se libérer de l'image de sa mère ou de celle qui occupe sa place" [*no* male character in Confiant's work manages to liberate himself from the image of the mother or the woman who occupies her place].[27] This male character thus attests to the omnipresence of the mother and her enduring effects on the psychic lives of her children.

Eau de café is a richly imaginative book that embodies the mosaic nature of Creole identity. While Confiant acknowledges the criticism levelled at his excessively sexual and violent writing style,[28] he also provides important insight into contemporary French Caribbean gender identity. His heavily stereotyped approach to male and female relationships underlines a persistent fascination with the philandering man and the exotic Caribbean woman. Confiant's depictions of his female characters focus predominantly on their physical attributes and capacity for sexual activity yet he also uncovers the image of the *femme matador* and the obstacles that many Caribbean women face in their daily lives. Satirized male figures such as Ali Tanin step aside to reveal a more serious undercurrent of the continuing intrusion of history into contemporary gender roles. Confiant thereby offers an innovative perspective on male-female relationships in a Caribbean context through the upholding and overturning of gender stereotypes. At the same time, however, these solemn "lessons" are frequently undermined by his constant refusal to take things seriously.

Solibo Magnifique and *Eau de café* together represent two satirical perspectives of *Créolité* toward the question of gender identity. While each of these novels is primarily concerned with the place of Creole culture in French Caribbean society, the vision of male and female relationships that emerges offers a powerful testament to the influence of gender in everyday life. The various satirized and exaggerated gender roles presented by Chamoiseau and Confiant highlight the legacies of history on present-day conceptions of male and female as well as the authors' textualization of this history. These two authors draw heavily on satire to consider past and present images of gender. This literary techique thus provides a highly entertaining vision of gender identity whilst underlining some of the more serious consequences of this arrangement of male and female gender roles in French Caribbean society.

NOTES

1. Richard Price and Sally Price, "Shadowboxing in the Mangrove: The Politics of Identity in Postcolonial Martinique," in Belinda J. Edmondson (ed.), *Caribbean Romances: The Politics of Regional Representation* (Charlottesville: University Press of Virginia, 1999), 140.

2. Price and Price, "Shadowboxing," 141.

3. Beverley Ormerod, "Magical Realism in Contemporary French Caribbean Literature: Ideology or Literary Diversion?" *Australian Journal of French Studies* 34, no. 2 (1997): 216.

4. Richard D. E. Burton, "Debrouya pa peche, or il y a toujours moyen de moyenner: Patterns of Opposition in the Fiction of Patrick Chamoiseau," *Callaloo* 16, no. 2 (1993): 473.

5. Edouard Glissant, *Le Discours antillais* (Paris: Seuil, 1981), 213.

6. Price and Price, "Shadowboxing," 138.

7. J. Michael Dash, *Edouard Glissant* (Cambridge: Cambridge University Press, 1995), 24.

8. Burton, "Debrouya," 476.

9. See Olive Senior, *Working Miracles: Women's Lives in the English-Speaking Caribbean* (Cave Hill, Barbados: Institute of Social and Economic Research, University of the West Indies; 1991), 179.

10. H. Adlai Murdoch, *Creole Identity in the French Caribbean Novel* (Gainesville: University Press of Florida, 2001), 234.

11. Colette Maximin, *Littératures caribéennes comparées* (Pointe-à-Pitre: Jasor; Paris: Karthala, 1996), 183.

12. See, for example, Roy Chandler Caldwell Jr., "*Créolité* and Postcoloniality in Raphaël Confiant's *L'Allée des soupirs*," *The French Review* 73, no. 2 (1999): 301–11; Thomas C. Spear, "Jouissances carnavalesques: Représentations de la sexualité,"

in Maryse Condé and Madeleine Cottenet-Hage (eds.), *Penser la créolité* (Paris: Karthala, 1995), 135–51; Richard D. E. Burton, *Le Roman marron: Études sur la littérature martiniquaise contemporaine* (Paris: L'Harmattan, 1997), 202–57.

13. Daniel-Henry Pageaux, "Raphaël Confiant ou la traversée paradoxale d'une décennie," *Portulan* (1996): 52.

14. Ormerod, "Magical Realism," 223.

15. Spear, "Jouissances carnavalesques," 137.

16. Spear, "Jouissances carnavalesques," 139.

17. Burton, *Le Roman marron*, 215.

18. Pageaux, "Raphaël Confiant," 53.

19. Ormerod, "Magical Realism," 223.

20. Anne Summers coined this term in her study of women in Australian society, *Damned Whores and God's Police* (Ringwood: Penguin, 1994).

21. Burton, *Le Roman marron*, 248.

22. Burton, *Le Roman marron*, 220.

23. Glissant, *Le Discours antillais*, 297.

24. Maryse Condé, *La Parole des femmes: Essai sur des romancières des Antilles de langue française* (Paris: L'Harmattan, 1993), 39.

25. Condé, *La Parole des femmes*, 36.

26. Burton, *Le Roman marron*, 229 and 247.

27. Burton, *Le Roman marron*, 251. Burton's italics.

28. Alain Bullo, "Entretien avec Raphaël Confiant," *Caribana* 5 (1996): 42.

7

⌁

Moving Away
from Stereotypes

In contrast to *créoliste* writers such as Patrick Chamoiseau and Raphaël
Confiant who grew up in the Caribbean, Gisèle Pineau experienced the
influence of Caribbean culture in a far less immediate way. Born in a
Parisian *cité*,[1] Pineau watered her Caribbean roots with the vivid stories of
her live-in Guadeloupean grandmother, Man Ya. Despite her childhood
and adolescence in France, Pineau always harbored an attachment for her
parents' island and eventually moved to Capesterre, Guadeloupe, as a
young adult. After practising as a psychiatric nurse for many years in the
Caribbean, Pineau returned to Paris where she now devotes herself to her
flourishing writing career. Lucía Suárez asserts that Pineau's formative attachment to two cultures is reflected in a style of writing that "advocates
an individuality enriched by two communities, structured by multiple
cultural inheritances where the beauty and the challenge lie in mixing languages, styles, rhythms, colors and beliefs."[2] Two of her novels, *La Grande
Drive des esprits* and *L'Espérance-macadam*, provide a contrasting view of
gender identity, demonstrating a move away from the simple categorization of characters into stereotypes. In spite of their vastly different plots,
the first focusing on the spiritual occurrences in a twentieth-century rural
community and the second on the emotional, physical and sexual violence that breeds unrelentingly in an urban ghetto, these books each illustrate a different angle of French Caribbean gender identity. While
Pineau depicts a number of gendered types common to other French
Caribbean writers, including the *femme matador*, the philandering
Caribbean man and the female spiritual healer, she also portrays the fluidity of gender. This gendered progression is evident in a comparison of

the two books themselves, with the later *L'Espérance-macadam* offering a less stereotypical vision of gender than *La Grande Drive des esprits*.

While some critics have characterized Pineau's early works such as *La Grande Drive des esprits* as consistent with the ideals of *Créolité*,[3] others have noted her refusal to confine herself to one particular literary movement. Kathleen Gyssels, for example, maintains that in spite of Pineau's Creole identity, she approaches her work in a unique manner that could be defined as a "négritude féminine" [feminine *négritude*].[4] Pineau's works attest to the continuing presence of the past in male-female relationships and she likens the French colonization of the Caribbean to an assault on a woman's body.[5] While Pineau denies being a feminist, arguing that she is simply against all oppression, she is nonetheless concerned to portray the rawness of female experience in the Caribbean: "Dire, fouiller, raconter encore et encore l'existence de ces femmes noires déchirées par les hommes, trompées, violées, debout malgré tout" [to tell, to delve into, to recount again and again the existence of these black women torn apart by men, cheated on, violated, standing upright in spite of everything].[6] In her 1995 essay "Ecrire en tant que Noire," Pineau writes of her own connection with female suffering, encapsulated in the image of her grandmother craving a return to her miserable Guadeloupean existence with her "bourreau d'époux" [torturer of a husband].[7] The legacy of the Caribbean past—both on a political and a personal level—thus emerges as a fundamental element in the portrayal of gender identity in Pineau's novels.

Published in Paris in 1993, Pineau's first novel, *La Grande Drive des esprits*, highlights the author's move away from gendered stereotypes and her interrogation of French Caribbean gender roles. Pineau's satirical approach to the philandering Caribbean man, for example, undermines this well-known male figure whilst amplifying her more nuanced portrayal of other characters. Emphasizing the fact that men and women can no longer be placed into stereotypical categories based on biological sex, Pineau displays the complexity of contemporary gender identity in her characters' shifting status as strong and weak, feminine and masculine. Such fluidity of gender is particularly evident in the novel's protagonist, Léonce, who displays a vast spectrum of gendered characteristics. The drifting spirits of the book's title announces the presence of magic in the narrative and the spiritual occurrences of Haute-Terre serve to further interrogate classic notions of gender. *La Grande Drive des esprits* exhibits some similarities with novels such as *Solibo Magnifique* and *Eau de café* in its portrayal of Creole folk traditions and employment of magical realism, but it also foreshadows Pineau's gradual shift away from the ideals of *Créolité* to a more individual approach to French Caribbean gender identity.

The most stereotyped character in the novel is Sosthène, a "swaggering" Caribbean man who is unable to control his sexuality and who constantly betrays his long-suffering wife, Ninette. Described in a satirical fashion, Sosthène typifies the Caribbean philanderer who continually indulges in sex with no thought for the consequence of his actions: "his head would turn so quickly each time the scent of woman reached his nostrils or a skirt wiggled before his eyes. His entire body would grow stiff. All thoughts of Ninette, his lawful wife, would fly zing! right out of his brain" (6). While Pineau satirically portrays Sosthène within the framework of this well-known Caribbean stereotype, she also reveals more serious issues surrounding his marital infidelities. Time and time again Sosthène is brought back to the reality of his fleeting female conquests when the women he has impregnated demand support. Pineau acknowledges the appealing nature of her pleasure-loving character with a description of his blissful innocence and ignorance—"Should [he] have to pay so dearly for one tiny moment of pleasure? Was he to blame because his seed would always fall on distressingly fertile fields?" (7)—yet she also underlines the very real suffering these women undergo as a result of his reckless attitude.

The character of Sosthène appears consistent with Maryse Condé's declaration that Caribbean men find refuge from the scars of history in ongoing patterns of irresponsibility.[8] Ninette's tolerance of his conduct, "because she had said yes to the shackles of marriage" (65), exemplifies women's contribution to their own unhappiness. Never once challenging Sosthène's unacceptable behavior, Ninette becomes an active collaborator in the perpetuation of her husband's irresponsibility. She is thus a further example of a woman who "mothers" her adult partner through her indulgence of his immature ways.

Pineau reveals a more solemn repercussion of Sosthène's insatiable sexuality when his and Ninette's son, Léonce, is about to marry the voluptuous Myrtha. When Myrtha moves in with them for six months before their wedding following the death of her mother and her abandonment by her stepfather, Ninette immediately takes measures to ensure that she is not the illegitimate daughter of one of Sosthène's many brief liaisons. Moreover, she is acutely aware of the potential danger of this domestic arrangement, charging herself with the task of watching over her husband day and night in order to keep Myrtha safe from his lecherous gaze. Pineau thus hints at the occurrence of incest in French Caribbean society, a theme she explores in detail in *L'Espérance-macadam*. She also portrays a somewhat pathetic side to Sosthène's character in his complete lack of control over his sexual urges: "He prayed to resist the temptation which governed his feelings, but could not suppress the surges of his pointed blade, always ready to strike, that was clenched between his legs" (58–59).

To some extent Sosthène's inability to exercise mind over matter offers a convenient excuse for his continual indulgence in his romantic fantasies. This affirmation of irresponsibility is reinforced by other characters in the novel who tolerate Sosthène's adolescent approach to relationships. He can thereby happily continue dropping in and out of his young lovers' lives with no fear of reprimand, perpetuating the tradition of the unreliable Caribbean man.

Pineau adds an ironic twist to Sosthène's character by revealing that his unquenchable thirst for pleasure is the result of a spell put on him by the mother of one of his sexual conquests. After successfully seducing Five-finger-Nono's desirable young daughter, whose virginity her mother had desperately tried to maintain, Sosthène finds himself the victim of a life-long curse: "You will have all the women you desire but none will love you. You will be the slave of your long, fat prick" (175). Pineau draws attention to the power of the mother in this episode with Nono's successful revenge on the man who deflowered her daughter. By placing a woman and, moreover, a mother at the source of Sosthène's unbridled sexual passion with Nono's spell, Pineau cleverly undermines Sosthène's appearance as a macho Caribbean male. It is a rare example of a woman who articulates her opposition to male promiscuity. At the same time, however, this curse becomes Sosthène's alibi for indulging in a multitude of affairs, thereby perpetuating a negative sexual pattern and contributing to other women's grief.

Sosthène finds himself the object of yet another female curse when he impregnates a fifteen-year-old girl, Mona, and promptly forgets about her. In a twist of fate, the baptism of her child takes place at the same time as Sosthène's marriage to Ninette and it is on this occasion that Mona realizes the full extent of her insignificance to Sosthène. When Ninette becomes pregnant with Léonce, Mona places a curse on her so that the young boy is born handicapped. This vengeful action played out on the body of another woman is an example of Pineau's assertion that "il est parfois doux de voir souffrir autrui aussi" [it is sometimes sweet to see others suffer too].[9] Mona's collaboration with sorcery in order to damage Ninette's life and those of her descendants is reminiscent of Laetitia's stealing of Télumée's husband in *Pluie et vent sur Télumée Miracle*. In contrast to women such as Tituba and Hester in *Moi, Tituba, sorcière . . . noire de Salem* who form strong bonds of solidarity, Mona's actions toward Ninette form part of a tradition among some Caribbean women of undermining the potential for an empowering sisterhood. Furthermore, by directly punishing Ninette rather than Sosthène, Mona allows her lover to avoid culpability for his philandering.

Pineau draws attention to one of the results of this casual attitude to relationships with her depiction of Mona's son growing up without a stable male role model. By the time he reaches adulthood, Emmanuel displays many of the behaviors associated with the weak Caribbean man. In a powerful affirmation of the effect of an absent father on male gender identity, Mona wonders whether he "would not have sought out the company of shiftless and lawless rascals" (203) if his father had been more present in his upbringing. By providing a model of male conduct through his absence, Sosthène in effect teaches Emmanuel that unreliability is an acceptable behavior. This young man never achieves a state of self-direction and he dies tragically in setting fire to a cabin.

Emmanuel's fragile sense of identity, evident in his inability to commit to anything more than rum-drinking and games, is an example of the assertion that "the more father-absence (or absence of adult men) in the family, the more severe are conflicts about masculinity."[10] Emmanuel remains trapped in an adolescent approach to life in which he never has to take responsibility for himself, confident in the knowledge that his mother will provide for the family. Sosthène's lack of involvement in the lives of the many children he has fathered, coupled with the mothers' dominance in their upbringing, illustrates the way in which negative male patterns of conduct are fostered by both men and women in Caribbean society.

Pineau employs spirituality as a method to subvert gender stereotypes, refusing the more traditional links of women with spiritual healing and men with the powers of the *quimboiseur*.[11] Through the characters of Nono and Mona, both aligned with evil spells and witchcraft, Pineau overturns the positive images of female healing presented in novels such as *Pluie et vent sur Télumée Miracle* and *Moi, Tituba, sorcière . . . noire de Salem*. However, she does not associate such female sorcery with the distinctly feminine evil that Confiant explores in *Eau de café*. Pineau neatly sidesteps the issue of positive or negative female spirituality by emphasizing that these women draw on evil spells to combat male irresponsibility, avoiding their simple categorization into angel or devil.

In relation to Sosthène, one of the primary sources of female suffering in the novel, Pineau repeatedly portrays him "as well behaved as one of the wise men, sitting legs together, reading his Bible like a good boy" (59). While it would be easy to condemn him for his selfish attitude toward women, her continual insistence on his basic good nature and fervent desire for forgiveness undercuts his appearance as an entirely negative man. When he finally loses his sex drive Sosthène devotes himself to the work of the church, presenting himself in pristine white clothes for the Sunday services. Through her rejection of binary opposites and gendered stereotypes, Pineau thus highlights the fluid and continually evolving nature of gender.

Pineau's characterization of Ninette offers another perspective on the link between women and spirituality, emphasizing her rejection of stereotypical depictions of gender. At the beginning of the novel Ninette appears to be the perfect embodiment of the submissive wife. Despite her full knowledge of Sosthène's extramarital liaisons, Ninette docilely opens herself to his nightly sexual advances because she believes that is her marital role. This picture sets out a traditional pattern of gender relations in which the man occupies the role of the active sexual aggressor and the woman the passive participant. However, Pineau also portrays Ninette's considerable strength with her ability to hold together her family in the face of Sosthène's unreliable conduct and her unending tolerance toward "her husband's betrayals [that] came screaming and cursing before her doorstep" (7). Ninette's success in maintaining the family unit in spite of her wandering husband demonstrates a fortitude that is characteristic of many Caribbean women. Her strength gains further force when Sosthène finally loses his sex drive and for the first time in twenty-five years Ninette does not have to perform her conjugal duty. The release of this sexual burden completely rejuvenates Ninette and she soon earns a reputation for spiritual healing:

> when she hugged to her bosom her first miracle, Ninette was completely transformed. Her eyes sparkled, sometimes glittering with flashes of goodness. And her face shone with a pure selflessness that had been copied from the Blessed Virgin. When she went back down the hill that morning, wings in the air, her feet no longer touched the ground, so much had her new body, as patron saint of the sick with no hope of tomorrow, given a lightness to her mortal flesh. (111)

Pineau's satirical portrayal of Ninette's transformation into the figure of the healer—reflected in Ninette's decision to wear only white clothes as a sign of her virgin purity—draws attention to the difficulty of placing her characters into simple gender categories. In contrast to Simone Schwarz-Bart's and Maryse Condé's positive depictions of the female healer, Pineau undermines her image of Ninette's miraculous qualities by casting her in a humorously exaggerated light. Ninette becomes so carried away with her spiritual connections that it is difficult to perceive her as an example of divine and selfless good. At the same time, however, this personal metamorphosis allows her finally to erect firm barriers in her relationship with Sosthène. As Ninette gains in strength with her new calling, Sosthène reverts to an almost childlike status, passively accepting his wife's lead. Ninette's ascent to spiritual heights radically reverses the gender roles in their relationship, placing Ninette in the position of conjugal superior. Ninette's progression from a weak and compliant wife to a strong and self-assured miracle worker underlines the complexity of contemporary gender identity. Moreover, Pineau's insistence on the satirical nature of this transformation reinforces her individual approach to gender roles.

Ninette's maternal power is evident in her relationship with her eldest child, Léonce, who is born with a clubfoot. As a result of the emotional scars caused by this physical disability, Léonce develops a particularly close bond with his mother that he carries long into adulthood. Ninette's overarching influence in her son's life, together with his feelings of deficiency due to his disability, contribute to the creation of a character marked by an eroded sense of his masculinity. When Léonce falls deeply in love with Myrtha, for example, Pineau highlights the way in which virility is frequently perceived in terms of the possession of a woman. As Léonce lies in a ditch debating whether to approach the object of his passion or not, his interior monologue reveals his conviction of the link between masculinity and female conquest: "'Good God! I'm a man after all!' he said to himself. 'KOCHI! That's your name! Look at your foot, you upstart!' replied a voice from deep within him" (4). When Myrtha finally arrives at the cabin Léonce has lovingly built for her, he is so overcome he collapses into the dust, where he is severely admonished by a nearby ox for his pathetic attempt at being a man.

Pineau emphasizes that Léonce's wavering sense of masculinity can be traced directly back to his enduring attachment to his mother. It is Ninette who carves out a path of hope for him while he is wallowing in depression, convinced that he will never attain the woman of his dreams. Moreover, it is she who engineers the relationship between Léonce and Myrtha, visiting the latter's parents and singing the praises of her son. The result of this intense state of co-dependence is that Léonce grows up "[approving] of everything, [saying] amen to every word that issued from Ninette's mouth" (103). Léonce thereby appears as a "mummy's boy," evolving into a man who displays the qualities that would be heartily endorsed by a mother: "a hard worker who is not in the habit of chasing skirts, gambling, drinking rum with friends" (16). Joëlle Vitiello asserts that this untypical vision of a Caribbean male constitutes "une image masculine exceptionnelle chez Gisèle Pineau: il est presque le seul homme monogame de ses écrits" [an exceptional masculine image in the works of Gisèle Pineau: he is almost the only monogamous man in her writings].[12] In some ways, Léonce's inability to separate from his mother in order to assume his independent adult status, leads to his emergence as a "feminine" man rather than a "masculine" one. Ninette's overwhelming maternal influence results in a son who identifies more strongly with the feminine, a situation that is exacerbated by Sosthène's lack of active participation in his paternal role.

Léonce demonstrates a remarkable affinity with the natural world, intensifying his connection with the feminine principle. One of the first ways in which Léonce combats his failing sense of masculinity is by devoting himself to the cultivation of his garden, a task achieved so successfully that those around him liken it to the "garden of Eden" (26). While Léonce's tending of his fields is directed toward winning Myrtha's heart, he creates a luxuriant riot of color and flourishing crops. However, this same garden becomes a symbol of his downfall when he finds himself increasingly unable to deal with his lack of impact in the masculine realm. Indeed, the state of Léonce's garden becomes a powerful indicator of the deep psychological processes that plague him throughout his life, underlining his inability to settle into one definitive gender category.

Pineau depicts a decisive midway point in Léonce's metamorphosis from a positive "feminine" man to the more familiar image of the weak Caribbean male. His opportunity for salvation from his rapidly disappearing sense of masculinity arises in the form of his grandmother's, Man Octavie's, offer of the gift of spiritual powers. The potent synthesis of femininity and spirituality encapsulated in the ability to communicate with the nonphysical world gives Léonce the chance to become more closely connected with others. When Myrtha finally becomes pregnant for the first time and Léonce is spiritually reunited with his dead grandmother, the feminine element of nature reflects his contentment: "Around him the garden that he had left without a trace of fruit was bursting with fruitfulness" (80). Man Octavie's gift promises Léonce an eternal link to the empowering qualities of the feminine principle, permanently allying him to the natural, spiritual and healing worlds. However, his grandmother places one limit on this gift, forbidding him to indulge in drinking. As Léonce increasingly loses his grip on life, he falls victim to the bottle and becomes drunk to "the point of forgetting his name" (136), thereby dissipating his spiritual powers. This costly indulgence is a dramatic indication of Léonce's lack of strength when dealing with the realities of his existence.

Léonce's ultimate defeat arrives with the declaration of the Second World War when he wants to join the Free French to prove once and for all his masculinity. As a result of his clubfoot, he is rejected and this event profoundly affects him for the rest of his life. Reflecting his alienation from the positive feminine qualities associated with nature and spirituality, Léonce's "marvellous Garden of Eden produced nothing but sickly fruit" (139). His decision to find refuge in patterns of irresponsibility marks his transition from a man linked closely to positive feminine qualities to one characterized by negative masculinity. He thus represents an uneasy example of male gender identity.

Through the character of Léonce's daughter, Célestina, Pineau records the devastating effects of his decline on the family. Following his abdication of his parental responsibilities, Léonce leaves Myrtha to raise their children alone, banishing them from his mind: "Since that tragic night spent in the pursuit of glory, he had not looked at them. He had not spoken to them. He had not listened to them" (141). In this poignant description, Pineau underlines the way in which the masculine principle, whose ultimate signifier is war, destroys the feminine in Léonce, leaving him a broken man. Despite the fact that he began as a loving and proud father, he ultimately abandons his family and allows the common Caribbean phenomenon of the matrifocal family to occur. The ironic contrast is that Léonce first appears as the very opposite of this stereotype—"one of that breed of black men which you no longer find anywhere" (16)—and the situation is all the more heart-rending because he remains physically present. The devastating result for Célestina is that she starts stuttering, a trait which alienates her from almost everyone around her. In spite of her radiant beauty, Célestina repels future suitors as soon as she opens her mouth.

Through Léonce's treatment of his daughter "as if she had become completely transparent" (144), he effectively re-creates the patriarchal scenario of female voicelessness. Without the ability to affirm her subjectivity, Célestina is left drifting on the margins of society, condemned to degrading jobs which do not require her to speak. She remains completely alone apart from her friendship with the novel's narrator. Like Léonce, she forms bonds with the spiritual world, but her convictions rest on the belief of human evil rather than good. Pineau thus deprives her of the empowering qualities that characters like Tituba and Télumée find in their spiritual connections. An overwhelmingly tragic character, Célestina brings into sharp focus the consequence of an absent father on a daughter's psychological and physical development, a theme largely unexplored in French Caribbean literature.

Léonce's wife, Myrtha, also undergoes a transition of character, moving from a place of suffering in her upbringing as a child to joy at life with her devoted husband, and finally emptiness at Léonce's withdrawal from life. Initially portrayed as a kind of Cinderella figure, Myrtha is kidnapped as a baby by her aunt Boniface and is subjected to deprivation and cruelty. Her unstable upbringing represents a continuation of the distorted kinship bonds produced by slavery with Boniface and Barnabé, Boniface's twin sister and Myrtha's mother, growing up in a large family marked by the "bitter fruit from [their] Papa's wanderings" (38). In a revealing testament to the double standards of Caribbean gender roles, their father ruthlessly watches over his daughters and refuses them all access to men in a vain bid to preserve their virginity. His obsessive concern with Boniface and Barnabé's purity results in their indulgence in an orgy of sexual activity that ultimately leads to their isolation from the family. Myrtha's precarious background, marked by the absence of her biological parents and the unkind treatment of her aunt and stepfather, bequeaths to her a desire to create stability in her own family life and she declares that she will marry the first man who provides her with a home.

In line with Pineau's move away from stereotypes, Myrtha displays a contradictory gender identity. At the outset of the novel Pineau describes her principally in terms of her physical attributes, evocatively recorded in natural vocabulary: "Her eyes flashed with the fire of suns. A slender body which displayed for all to see its hills and valleys, contours in a landscape never before seen under heaven" (4). This view of Myrtha as an elusive source of desire serves to objectify her. Myrtha is little explored outside her capacity to satisfy Léonce and to compensate for his inner lack. When the two finally marry, Pineau continues her association of Myrtha with the feminine element of nature, highlighting her conformity to the role of virginal bride and adoring new wife:

> Myrtha's flower, the bud of a poppy clenched tight like a fist, bloomed pain-lessly during their wedding night. When they awoke next morning, a purple orchid nestled in the soft bed. Myrtha's deflowering brought her no grief. On the contrary, she kept on laughing while scrubbing vigorously this dried flower which sealed, better than ink on the marriage certificate, her union with Léonce. (51)

As Léonce becomes increasingly unable to cope with his problems, however, Myrtha metamorphoses from a decorative and loving wife into a resilient Caribbean mother who determinedly holds her family together in the absence of conjugal support. With her husband's failure to enter the army and his subsequent crippling depression, Myrtha adopts the role of both mother and father in bringing up her children. Moreover, in a scene reminiscent of Aimé Césaire's mother working tirelessly at her Singer sewing machine,[13] Myrtha's "sewing [becomes] the family's only source of income . . . " (141), placing the entire realm of familial responsibility in her hands. In this view, Myrtha appears as a kind of *femme matador* who is able to resist life's trials through her unfailing courage and spirit. The character of Myrtha thus presents an evolution of gender identity that is dictated by the need to support her family.

Myrtha's and Léonce's youngest daughter, Gerty, offers a contrasting vision of female identity. Expanding on her brief portrayal of Léonce's sister, Lucina, as "a fighting female" (145), Pineau paints a somewhat stereotypical portrait of Gerty as a radical feminist. In a passage reminiscent of Virginia Woolf's *A Room of One's Own*, she describes Gerty as living "alone in a big concrete house built on land bought with her savings" (209). On the question of marriage, Gerty reveals certain fixed ideas that closely mirror the vision fostered by some radical feminists:

> "Get married!" she laughed. "You mean submit to some man's control!" Use her breasts to feed a bunch of noisy children. Peel vegetables. Wash under-

wear. Scour out pots and pans. And wait for him to return from his adventures. Pray that some rival was not already pregnant. (209)

Far from being interested in marriage and motherhood, Gerty strives toward an independent existence marked by education and professional satisfaction. Inspired by first wave feminists Simone de Beauvoir and Betty Friedan, she models herself on the image of the strong woman presented in their works such as *The Second Sex* and *The Feminine Mystique*. However, in a consideration of the empowering qualities associated with masculinity or femininity, Gerty appears to have located strength with the masculine. By choosing to emulate de Beauvoir's ideal of womanhood, linking female independence to a rejection of the biological constraints of motherhood and success in the public arena, Gerty is in fact valuing the masculine over the feminine. Contrary to feminist thinkers such as Luce Irigaray and Hélène Cixous who emphasize women's strength in their difference from men, de Beauvoir's vision of womanhood aims to enhance women's similarities to men. From this point of view, then, Gerty's adoption of this feminist blueprint could appear as a sign of weakness with its disinclination to value female specificity. The fortitude of Caribbean woman presented in the works of Simone Schwarz-Bart and Maryse Condé, by contrast, lies primarily in feminine qualities such as nurturing, affinity with nature and capacity for healing. Pineau's view of radical feminism embodied in the character of Gerty thus introduces a challenging new image of the strong Caribbean woman.

Pineau problematizes this depiction of Caribbean female strength, however, by portraying Gerty's ultimate descent into madness as a result of her imaginary love affair with Victor Hugo. Representing a step outside traditional conceptions of gender, Gerty appears unable to maintain her difference in an environment surrounded by contrasting images of Caribbean womanhood. Despite Pineau's descriptions of Ninette and Myrtha as courageous figures, she seems to be highlighting the difficulty of adhering to the ideals of radical feminism in a Caribbean environment. Through her rejection of feminine qualities such as nurturing and spirituality, Gerty establishes her separateness from celebrated figures of female strength like Télumée and Tituba. In some respects she emerges as a "masculine" woman with her commitment to independence and autonomy, yet she does not embody the negative traits associated with women such as Susanna Endicott. Pineau thus presents Gerty as a stereotypical character but one who, on closer examination, reveals the intricacy of female gender identity in the French Caribbean.

La Grande Drive des esprits is a rich novel highlighting Pineau's move away from stereotypes and her emphasis on the gradual evolution of gender identity. While there are elements of the strong woman and the weak man in her portraits, she consistently points to the deeper layers in her characters. Many of them display a variety of masculine and feminine traits, underlining the fluid nature of gender. Pineau's use of magical realism and satire set against the backdrop of the spiritual occurrences of Haute-Terre presents a humorous yet challenging view of Caribbean gender identity.

In her disturbing and complex 1995 novel *L'Espérance-macadam*, Pineau paints an even more challenging portrait of gender identity in the Caribbean, highlighting the impossibility of confining men and women to fixed gender roles. *L'Espérance-macadam* explores the nature of violence, particularly sexual violence, in a Guadeloupean urban backwater. In an interview with Geneviève Belugue, Pineau declares that her characters display "toute la lourdeur d'un monde hanté par le mal, la souffrance d'êtres impuissants comme anéantis pour toujours par le tragique de l'histoire, de leur histoire" [all the weight of a world haunted by pain, the suffering of powerless individuals overwhelmed forever by the tragedy of history, their history].[14] This burdensome historical legacy, reverberating on both the political and the personal levels, carves out a fictional space that is noteworthy for its absence of outstanding individuals. Pineau asserts that many of her male characters fall into the categories of "[b]uveurs, joueurs, lâches, hypocrites, falots, fanfarons" [drinkers, gamblers, cowards, hypocrites, colourless or boastful men],[15] while Kathleen Gyssels affirms that the book is "surchargé de filles maltraitées qui ne réussissent pas à devenir des femmes victorieuses ou des mères résistantes" [overloaded with mistreated girls who do not succeed in becoming victorious women or resistant mothers].[16] Pineau's approach to gender reveals a series of characters who are both strong and weak, feminine and masculine. Moreover, with characters like Rosan who appear overwhelmingly negative, Pineau includes explanations of their behavior that defy a categorical interpretation of right or wrong. She thus provides a controversial view of gender that attests to the changing nature of male-female relationships in the French Caribbean.

The central character and sometime narrator of the novel, Eliette, is a woman who undergoes a great personal transformation in the course of the story. At the outset of the narrative she establishes her desire not to involve herself in the affairs of others, preferring instead to shelter herself from potential pain: "The only thing Eliette sought after was the peace of her cabin . . . Eyes and ears shut, she struggled to keep the sorrow of others at bay" (2). By rejecting involvement in relationships, Eliette sets herself apart from the positive effects of community presented in many fictional works by Caribbean women writers. However, the opening pages of the novel also announce Eliette's embarkation upon a journey of inner growth that provides an original perspective on the theme of the strong woman in Caribbean literature.

Reflecting on her experiences before the life-changing Sunday that provokes her personal metamorphosis, Eliette alerts the reader to the importance of the highly destructive cyclone of 1928 that wreaks havoc in her life. While harmony with the elements is depicted as a feminine, empowering trait in many works of French Caribbean literature, Pineau's portrayal of the natural world in *L'Espérance-macadam* highlights its destructive potential. Eliette underlines the significance of this event by reiterating the words of her mother, Séraphine, who would tell her how the cyclone had dismembered Guadeloupe and thrown a beam right into the eight-year-old Eliette's belly. After surviving this horrific event, Séraphine descends into madness and it is not until the end of the novel that the reader discovers Eliette was the victim of incest by her father the night before that fateful natural catastrophe. Séraphine's reaction could be compared in some ways to Marie Celat's refuge in mental illness after the death of her sons, in *La Case du commandeur*. A frightening "manifestation of men's power over the powerless,"[17] the sexual abuse of Séraphine's child proves too much for her to cope with and she reacts by completely withdrawing from society. In one sense her reaction could be viewed as an adamant rejection of patriarchy's power structures—by refusing to participate in this oppressive social system Séraphine asserts her resounding opposition. In another sense, however, she physically and emotionally abandons Eliette by her inability to support her through one of the most painful events of her life. The lack of a solid maternal influence in Eliette's upbringing greatly affects her evolution into a woman and she displays an uncertainty of character that is more often identified with men. Suffering from the absence of a female role model, Eliette does not display the openness toward relationships that is commonly produced by the mother-daughter bonding process. By failing to grow up in the matrifocal family that characterizes many Caribbean households, she fits more into object-relations theorists' model of male behavioral psychology.

Nina Hellerstein argues that the structure of *L'Espérance-macadam* can be encapsulated in the image of the circle, with the circular and closed nature of incest finding expression in the circular organization of the novel.[18] Valérie Loichot affirms this geometric conception of incest, declaring that, "from a structural standpoint, incest prevents any linear, tree-like family shape, because the branches go back to their origin, thereby enclosing family relations in a circle."[19] Pineau reveals in the character of Eliette that a consequence of this abusive behavior is the loss of female subjectivity. Consistent with the image of the woman silenced by patriarchy, Eliette loses her voice for three years as a way to protect herself from further pain: "keeping the secret with sealed lips to avoid any more pain, prevent the pain from welling back up in the body. The poisonous secret" (210). A recurring symbol in Pineau's work, female voicelessness appears in the character of Célestina in *La Grande Drive des esprits* and also in *L'Espérance-macadam*'s Angela, another victim of incest. While only losing her voice for a short period of time, Angela nonetheless experiences this same phenomenon of powerlessness through a man's exploitation of his position: "She wanted to cry out again, but she'd lost her voice. She wanted to struggle too, but the beast had already forced open the gate, staved it in, pillaged" (153). Although a feeling of connection takes a long time to develop, the bond that ultimately grows between Eliette and Angela through their common experience of incest constitutes a form of female solidarity. A testament to Eliette's own transformation that allows her finally to reach out to others, this empowering friendship becomes a source of healing for the old woman and the young girl.

In relation to the young and damaged Eliette, Pineau reveals that her stepfather, Joab, is the one who helps her to regain her voice after three years of silence. Portrayed as a nurturing and loving man, Joab is little developed in the novel, yet he imprints an image of positive masculinity on an overwhelmingly negative backdrop. When he first moves to Savane, Joab imagines it as "Paradise on earth" (102), suggesting that the dark place described in the book was once more harmonious with its links to nature. As poor people moved in and made it more urban, Savane lost its innocence and became the place of violence and sordidness that features so graphically in the narrative. Hellerstein suggests that the theme of the Garden of Eden plays a major role in Pineau's work and she compares Joab's conception of a paradise based on love to that of Rosan, Angela's father, whose Eden comes from sexually abusing his daughter. As with Rosette, Rosan's wife, paradise comes to embody an escape from reality, attesting to the moral weakness of their characters in comparison with Joab's.[20] Against the pervasive sorrow of life in Savane, Joab consistently perceives opportunities for optimism, representing a ray of hope for the future. Reflecting on the damaging passage of a cyclone through Guadeloupe while she is an adult, for example, Eliette imagines that Joab "would have smiled and applauded Savane, his paradise, the fraternity and friendship that folks demonstrated" (188). While he plays a minor role in the narrative, his influence over Eliette remains vital throughout her development, offering her a stable navigation point at difficult times in her life. Like Yao's formative presence in Tituba's upbringing, Joab's enduring faith helps to strengthen Eliette's character, even if it takes many years for her to realize her own power. In his association with the feminine characteristics of nurturing, affinity with nature and openness to relationships, Joab emerges as a "feminine" man and one of the few positive male characters in the novel.

In a powerful affirmation of her refusal to stereotype characters as either "good" or "bad," Pineau selects the incestuous Rosan as the one who provokes Eliette's profound transformation of character. The unforgettable Sunday that Eliette locates as the turning point in her new approach to her past and present life is the day Rosan is arrested by the police for his sexual abuse of Angela: "That's how, without really meaning to, I met the depth of Rosan's eyes. It was worse than a red-hot iron" (12). Not only does Rosan's behavior cause Eliette to question her detached stand in life, but it also leads to Angela's eviction from her home by her mother. Angela thus becomes a kind of surrogate daughter for Eliette, a domestic arrangement that allows the wounds of both women to heal. Pineau's choice of Rosan as the positive catalyst for Eliette's personal journey underlines the impossibility of simple binary oppositions at work in the creation of her characters. Eliette's emergence at the end of the novel as a confident and hopeful woman demonstrates her ultimate strength of character with her commitment to change. She thus appears as a courageous Caribbean woman without the stereotypical characteristics of the *femme matador*.

Through the character of Rosan, Pineau explores the phenomenon of incest that some French Caribbean authors touch upon in their work but do not treat in detail—for example, Maryse Condé in *Les Derniers Rois mages* or Simone Schwarz-Bart in *Pluie et vent sur Télumée Miracle*. According to Kathleen Gyssels, Pineau's open discussion of sexual violence against women in *L'Espérance-macadam* denounces "la 'sujétion éternelle' de l'Antillaise" [the "eternal subjection" of the Caribbean woman],[21] shining the spotlight on male abuse of power. Pineau draws attention to the frequency of this damaging occurrence in Caribbean society with Rosan's declaration to Angela that such behavior is common among many of the fathers in Savane who search for "light between the legs of their children" (161). Maryse Condé affirms this ugly aspect of French Caribbean life, stating that we "have lived with the illusion that these things don't happen in our societies . . . [but now] the truth is crystal clear."[22] Pineau's raw examination of a subject traditionally considered taboo gives a voice to the victims of sexual violence and offers a tentative explanation for why this miserable conduct may arise. While Pineau unrelentingly portrays the horror of Rosan's sexual preying on his daughter, she also provides details of his background that partially contribute to an understanding of his actions. She thus offers a confrontational view of her male protagonist as a perpetrator and victim of abuse.

Nina Hellerstein asserts that "l'inceste témoigne d'un profond malaise identitaire masculin, qui résulte de l'incapacité d'assumer son propre être" [incest bears witness to a deep malaise in masculine identity which results in the inability to assume one's own being].[23] Affirming that the roots of incestuous assault are to be found in the feelings of anger, insecurity and frustration frequently displayed by sexual aggressors, Sandra

Butler goes on to detail society's role in producing these men who find solutions in the rape of their child: society has "taught them to define themselves as a consequence of their gender. When all else in their lives fails,
they have been led to believe that the exercise of the power of their geni-
tals will assure them of their ultimate competence and power."[24] Pineau's
portrayal of Rosan reinforces this image of the fragility of the incestuous
father's identity, his moral weakness evident in his compensation for his
inner lack through the oppression of his defenseless daughter. Jacques
André maintains a Caribbean specificity to the phenomenon of incest,
tracing its source to the gender roles absorbed by Caribbean children. In
his view, Caribbean men become "le dépositaire privilégié des signes de
la sexualité" [privileged depositary of the signs of sexuality][25] which encourages an attitude of sexually conquering and abandoning women.
Moreover, with the lack of recognition of fathers in Caribbean society, André argues that men are denied intimate bonding with their children because the mother acts as "un médiateur incontournable" [an inescapable
mediator].[26] This dual influence of images of a promiscuous sexuality and
an inability to be directly involved in the lives of their children creates in
some Caribbean men a distorted approach to relationships. In one aspect,
then, society contributes to the creation of sexual aggressors.

Rosan's attitude toward his incestuous behavior reflects a conviction
commonly held by people who commit crimes, who assert that they were
unable to help themselves. André observes that criminals do not employ
words of culpability, but, rather, those of persecution, often evoking an external force that pushes them into performing certain actions.[27] Rosan
himself states that he "couldn't stop himself. There was a machine inside
of him, diabolical mechanism that always pushed him into Angela's
room" (180). By refusing to take responsibility for his conduct, Rosan is
able to continue his abuse of Angela with no feeling of guilt. His feeling
of fulfilment that arises through sexual contact with his daughter represents yet another example of Maryse Condé's assertion that Caribbean
men have found solace in patterns of irresponsibility. Rosan shows himself to be incapable of dealing with his feelings of inadequacy, presenting
an image of a morally weak man.

Pineau includes a discussion in the novel of Rosan's upbringing that offers a deeper explanation of his motives and underlines the difficulty of
labelling him as a wholly negative character. As she states in a 2001 interview, "derrière Rosan il y a toute une histoire. Il est en charge de cette histoire; il en est aussi la victime" [behind Rosan there is a whole history. He
is in charge of this history; he is also the victim of it].[28] Detailing Rosan's
childhood in which he is abandoned by his parents and disliked and severely beaten by his grandmother, Pineau draws attention to the role of
the mother in producing an incestuous man. She highlights through the

character of Rosan the effects on male identity of the mother figure's failure to provide her children with a loving and stable home life, revealing that his insecure sense of identity emerges in large part as a result of his mother's and grandmother's neglect in bringing him up: "That man never had no loving, no one ever gave him so much as a pinch of it" (80). She also depicts Rosan's intense hatred of his deserting father who provides a negative yet effective role model for the young child. Rosan's adult emulation of his father's incest is an illustration of the way in which children may unconsciously absorb the example of their parents.

Pineau's graphic descriptions of Rosan's sexual abuse of Angela cannot but shock and move the reader. However, she refuses to allow this harsh portrait of Rosan to stand on its own, presenting contrasting images of him as a devoted husband and father determined to make up for the lack of love he received as a child. For example, he is the man who gathers up the body of a baby thrown from a bridge by its mother. Pineau's characterization of Rosan emphasizes in the most dramatic manner her move away from stereotypes. By offering a compassionate and humane view of her incestuous character she avoids categorizing him as a monstrous example of male violence.

Pineau paints a complex portrait of Rosette, Angela's mother, in relation to her discovery of Rosan's abusive activities. When Rosan is about to penetrate his daughter, Angela experiences an intense desire for the protective qualities of her mother, but deep inside her "a voice called her Judas, so she kept the call locked in her throat" (153). Pineau's evocation of the word "Judas" refers to an earlier incident in the novel in which Rosette accuses her daughter of betrayal. Angela's inability to confide in her mother results in a feeling of powerlessness caused by fear, Angela becoming yet another silent victim of male sexual abuse. Through her inability to protect her daughter, Rosette becomes an implicit collaborator in this heinous crime. Sandra Butler describes two common interpretations of the mothers' role in the occurrence of incestuous assault: in the first instance they are described as abandoning and in the second as colluding. "If a mother is 'passive,' she fails by not having provided her child with the strength to resist incestuous overtures. If she is 'aggressive,' she fails by having caused her husband to feel emasculated and therefore in need of turning to someone else for his emotional and sexual needs."[29] Rosette's insecurities prevent her from facing the realities of life and she proves unable to assimilate the ugly picture of her husband as sexual aggressor into her idealized conception of her family.

Pineau also emphasizes the way in which Caribbean women "mother" their husbands into irresponsible patterns of behavior, stating that Rosette "le protège, elle ne veut pas qu'il souffre" [protects him, she doesn't want him to suffer].[30] Rosette's lack of rebellion against her husband's crime is consistent with Pineau's assertion that many Caribbean women passively accept and indeed foster male abuse: "Femmes toujours prêtes à couvrir la faute du mâle, à pardonner les outrages, à accepter coups et insultes. Femmes prenant l'homme comme un grand enfant, répondant à tous ses caprices, acceptant tous ses abus" [Women always ready to cover the fault of the man, to pardon the outrages, to accept the blows and insults. Women taking the man like a big child, responding to all his whims, accepting all his abuses].[31] The result of Rosette's personal weakness and her desire to shield Rosan from criticism is that she emotionally and physically abandons her daughter. By abdicating her basic maternal responsibility of protecting one's child from harm, Rosette behaves in a way that is comparable to Rosan's mother's departure from her parental role. While Rosette does not physically abuse Angela, her emotional absence appears as neglectful as Rosan's mother's abuse of her son. Pineau thus offers a powerful indictment of the maternal with her graphic depictions of the effect of maternal absence on children's lives.

As with Rosan, Pineau provides an explanation of Rosette's character that softens her appearance as a morally weak woman and defies her categorization into a stereotype. Pineau underlines Rosette's fearful approach to life's hardships by depicting her character's constant need to imagine her existence in fairytale-like terms. When she learns of Rosan's incestuous activities, for example, she is unable to conceptualize this event which strays so far from her vision of "a fairy-tale happy family" (119). As life becomes more unbearable, Rosette involves herself in a group of Rastafarians living in the hills who offer her a more idealized version of the world. Rosette forms a close attachment to Edith whilst in this community, the latter acting as a mother figure to Rosette who was banished from her home by her own mother after pursuing a relationship with Rosan against her mother's wishes. Provoking reflection on her lack of parenting as a young adult, Rosette's childlike attachment to Edith highlights once again the powerful influence of the mother figure. "Her mama had run her out, but she shouldn't cry about that anymore, 'No woman no cry'" (117–18). Rosette's desperate attempts to overcome the sadness of her mother's abandonment by immersing herself in this alternative lifestyle demonstrate the deep scars that exist within Rosette. By sketching a genealogy of neglect in motherhood that proliferates from Rosette's mother down to Angela, Pineau emphasizes the way in which a lack of maternal love in one's upbringing may breed tragic consequences in adulthood.

Pineau renders her portrait of Rosette even more poignant with her portrayal of her character's genuine bewitchment by her own fairytales. When Angela begins menstruation, for example, Rosette teaches her about the importance of preserving her virginity, reassuring her that one day "she'd find an honest man, someone like her father Rosan (53). Already the victim of incest, Angela occupies a vastly different filial space from the one imagined by her mother. Pineau's characterization of Rosette emphasizes the limitations of a woman who is unable to face up to life's tragedies, forming a striking contrast to the image of the *femme matador*. Pineau also draws attention to the dangerous repercussions of living with one's head buried in the sand by showing the innocent Angela as the one who pays the price for her mother's weakness. While Rosette clearly chooses loyalty to her husband over loyalty to her daughter, Pineau depicts her as a woman morally crippled by her own suffering. Her compassionate portrait of Rosette's background provides a nonstereotypical vision of a Caribbean woman and mother of an assaulted child.

The character of Angela offers an alternative vision of female gender identity for she is one of the two primary victims of male abuse in the novel, yet she also emerges as one of the potential figures of strength. Until the time when Rosette drives her out of home and into Eliette's care, Angela appears as an example of silent female suffering. She is unable to share her pain with anyone, not even her mother, and she passively accepts Rosan's sexual advances out of a feeling of powerlessness. Ironically, Angela represents an angel for both her parents—Rosette referring to her in this way when she is pregnant with her and Rosan when she is born—and yet both come to tragically betray her. Despite this state of weakness however, Pineau details a quiet strength of spirit in Angela, expressed, for example, in her passionate political beliefs:

> Rosette had always heard Angela speak of what they were doing to the river as a crime. In the room that Rosan had built with his own two hands, Angela filled her little sister Rita's head with her enraged ranting about the river having become a garbage dump because of the people in Savane, murderers who polluted out of spite or even just for pleasure. (51–52)

This evocative passage demonstrates Angela's independence of thought and the force of her convictions, whilst also acting as a metaphor for Rosan's abuse of his daughter. Angela becomes like the river, the innocent victim of a man who pollutes her for his own pleasure while the people of Savane close their eyes. Pineau's employment of the word "furiously" to describe Angela's reaction to such contamination foreshadows the strength of character that bursts forth from this young victim of incest. While the image of this river that is almost dried up constitutes a powerful symbol of the erasure of the feminine by the masculine in Savane, Pineau emphasizes the redemptive power of her female characters. One of the greatest examples of female courage to arise in *L'Espérance-macadam* is in the character of Angela.

Although Angela is only a child when she attempts to tell her mother about Rosan, Pineau underlines her young character's resilient spirit in her reaction to Rosette's refusal to believe her story. Displaying an overwhelmingly physical response to this denial of her subjectivity by her mother, Angela sends chairs and vases flying in her determined endeavour to convince Rosette of the truth. This all-encompassing action harnessing both body and mind reflects her absolute refusal to be overcome by injustice. At one point there is a danger Angela will become like Rosette, choosing fantasy over reality, when Rosan informs Angela that her young sister Rita is his next victim: "Bob [Marley]'s voice came floating across the courtyard again. Running one hand over her forehead, Angela shut out the memory of Rosan looking for Rita's budding breasts" (161). With the reggae music representing a subtle temptation to bury her head in the sand like her mother, Angela ultimately rejects this solution, finding the inner strength to reveal the truth about Rosan.

Pineau's depiction of the relationship between Angela and Rita demonstrates the fortifying qualities of female solidarity, a bond that proves unbreakable between the two sisters. Angela offers Rita the unconditional maternal love and protection that Rosette denies her eldest child. Moreover, she gains a certain power through her success in preserving her young sister's innocence. Through her depiction of Angela's refuge in Eliette's home at the end of the book Pineau reassures the reader that Angela will recover from her trauma. The two women form their own intimate community that will allow each of them to face the tragedy of the past and move forward into the future. Pineau thus refuses to confine Angela and Eliette to the status of disempowered victims, focusing instead on the hope they draw from each other.

In sharp contrast to Pineau's nuanced conception of many of her protagonists, she also portrays images of extreme male violence in characters such as Régis. An incorrigible oppressor of the vulnerable, Régis derives great pleasure from his inhuman conduct toward others. When he sets up home with his partner, Hortense, for example, he treats her as if she is an animal "that you push into a cage for a life of servility" (60). While Hortense appears blindly romantic in her hopes for a relationship full of "caresses, considerations and sweet words, flowers, sherbets, and green water coconuts" (61) with Governor Régis, she ultimately pays dearly for her lack of judgment. After taking a lover to compensate for Régis' ongoing neglect of her, he responds by killing Hortense and cutting her up into small pieces. Not wanting to be shamed in the eyes of the people of Savane by appearing as a betrayed husband, Régis does not hesitate to inflict suffering upon others in his obsessive need for control. Unlike Rosan, there is no explanation of Régis' background and no pardoning of his crime. He is an extreme example of the way in which a man's moral weakness cripple him to such an extent that he can find expression only in distorted responses. Pineau's inclusion of this aggressive and wholly negative male character offers a devastating picture of female oppression in the Caribbean. While she generally tempers her portrayal of her characters, Pineau's exaggerated depiction of Régis highlights the dangerous potential of male patterns of irresponsibility. It is also a heartrending testament to the Caribbean women who have suffered at the hands of acute masculine violence.

Against the harsh backdrop of life in Savane, Pineau portrays an unlikely voice of hope in the character of Hermancia, a mentally handicapped woman. Appreciating the simple pleasures of a beautiful day or the rare generosity of a Savane resident, Hermancia derives strength through her glorious singing. While much of the novel centers on the series of violent crimes that distinguish Savane's morally polluted environment, Hermancia's music offers an ephemeral connection with spirituality and beauty: "When her song rose, an innocent sun greeting the ordinary day, people stopped to catch a wisp of her story cradled on a wing of wind. The air grew less heavy" (36). The restorative and resistant qualities of song that are explored in characters such as Télumée and Victoire in *Pluie et vent sur Télumée Miracle* come to provide a brief prospect of universal hope in an overwhelmingly desolate novel. Pineau thus links Hermancia to a line of courageous women who face the hardships of life by focusing on the positive elements. In one sense, she embodies a distinctly female strength.

Pineau renders this vision of Hermancia problematic, however, by selecting a simple woman as her positive female figure, thereby underlining Hermancia's inability to understand everything that happens to her. Her innocent and vulnerable nature is nowhere more evident that in Pineau's portrayal of her weekly sexual penetration by seven men in a butcher shop:

> She smiled with her two mouths, and they penetrated her in a never ending renewal of ecstasy. No, they didn't strike her. Didn't force any doors. And they were satiated when they left her, with something hard and sweet inside of them like a piece of polished courbaril wood where their names were engraved amongst the list of the chosen few. After the service, they washed her with ritual solemnity, in a basin scrubbed specially for the purpose. Then, satisfied, they went back to their everyday men's lives, to their cabins filled with kids, to their toothless, fat, and disillusioned wives whom they straddled when night came, still partaking, in dream, of the smiling lips of the half-wit's body. (38)

Pineau's controversial emphasis of the positive aspects of what is essentially an act of rape focuses attention on the nuances of Caribbean gender identity. Pineau subtly invokes the behavior of the stereotypical Caribbean male by depicting the seven men involved in a casual sexual affair before contentedly returning home to their long-suffering wives and children. Furthermore, far from heartlessly abusing Hermancia, these men display a remarkable tenderness toward her. The simple gesture of washing Hermancia in a tub scraped clean from the carcasses of the day symbolizes both the poignancy and the ugliness that is contained in this scene. Nonetheless, Pineau's judgment seems to tend toward the sordid with her description of Hermancia's pregnancy and the spiral of tragedy that characterizes the life of her daughter, Glawdys.

After giving birth alone, Hermancia abandons Glawdys in a breadbasket, unable to cope with the responsibilities of being a mother when her own mental state is barely more than that of a child's. Taken in by Eloïse, the downtrodden mother of a dysfunctional family, Glawdys is kept locked up inside in a scene reminiscent of Cinderella's treatment by her stepmother. While she is removed from this domestic cruelty at the age of six or seven by Social Security, her living conditions do not radically improve and Glawdys returns to Savane ten years later grey from head to toe. Pineau expresses the ultimate tragedy of Glawdys' existence in her depiction of her throwing her own baby to her death from a bridge. Pineau emphasizes the relationship between Glawdys' heartbreaking action and the scars of history, asserting that her character "renouvelait . . . le geste du premier voyage. Tout est lié" [repeats . . . the gesture of the first voyage. Everything is linked].[32] With her evocation of the Middle Passage and the wrenching of African slaves from their homeland, Pineau highlights the continuing presence of the past in the Caribbean.

Growing up as an orphan, Glawdys becomes a symbol of the slaves' orphaning by Mother Africa, displaying the lack that arises through one's unknown parentage. Her inability to assume her role as a mother, in the same way as Hermancia was unable to take on her maternal responsibilities, underlines the damaging effects of history on female identity. In contrast to many French Caribbean writers who stress the repercussions of slavery on male selfhood, Pineau portrays an equally powerful portrait of its consequences for women. Affirming the multiplicity of female identity, then, she avoids stereotyping her female characters into courageous and resilient *femmes matador*.

Eliette's first husband, Renélien, is a memorable example of the fluidity of gender in Pineau's works with his exhibition of both masculine and feminine qualities. On the one hand, Renélien comes across as a heartless wife-beater who had "run his first wife off with a rousing series of kicks in the backside one day when he caught her, mouth between two doors, busily yakking with a neighbor while his dinner . . . was burning on the hot plate" (102). While it would be easy to link Renélien to a chauvinistic attitude with such treatment of his wife, Pineau evokes another, more feminine side to his character. Despite this unfortunate episode Renélien is concerned to distinguish himself from an image of macho masculinity by swearing that violence is not part of his nature and that he would cut off his hand if ever he was to behave like that again. When he becomes involved with Eliette, Renélien is finally able to express his gentleness and compassion, emotions which flood back to her on the fateful Sunday of Rosan's arrest. Intimately associated with the feminine trait of nurturing, Renélien's sexual advances toward his beloved gently smooth out her damaged body, providing her with pleasure where previously this act had caused her to relive her incestuous attack. Amid his delicate caresses, Renélien asks Eliette to promise that if he died tomorrow she would never remarry. This request for eternal fidelity, linked to the masculine desire for possession over women, contrasts with the feminine ambience of romance and love that he creates in this scene. In his synthesis of both masculine and feminine characteristics clearly Renélien resists gender stereotyping. Pineau again stresses the difficulty of applying one-dimensional definitions to the complexities of gender identity.

La Grande Drive des esprits and *L'Espérance-macadam*, despite their narrative differences, explore the common theme of the move away from stereotypes. Both novels include stereotypical characters such as the "swaggering" Caribbean man and the *femme matador*, yet Pineau rejects a superficial portrayal of these familiar figures in French Caribbean literature, satirizing and overturning them in order to provide a more complex vision of gender. One finds, for example, the pious yet promiscuous Sosthène in *La Grande Drive des esprits* and the fearful yet ultimately hopeful Eliette in *L'Espérance-macadam*. She also offers portraits of the fluidity of gender with her depiction of "feminine" men such as Joab and the coexistence of masculine and feminine in a character like Renélien. While these novels acknowledge the enduring role of history in creating Caribbean gender roles, they also pave the way toward the future in which the relationships between men and women are no longer confined to rigid stereotypes. Pineau's books thus offer a powerful statement about the gradually evolving nature of Caribbean gender identity.

NOTES

1. Housing project; low-cost, high-rise housing.
2. Lucía M. Suárez, "Gisèle Pineau: Writing the Dimensions of Migration," *World Literature Today* 75, nos. 3–4 (2001): 10.
3. See, for example, J. Michael Dash, "Afterword," in Gisèle Pineau, *The Drifting of Spirits* (London: Quartet Books. 1999), 238.

4. Kathleen Gyssels, "L'Exil selon Pineau, récit de vie et autobiographie," in Suzanne Crosta (ed.), *Récits de vie de l'Afrique et des Antilles: Enracinement, errance, exil* (Fort-de-France: GRELCA, 1998), 170.

5. Geneviève Belugue, "Entre l'ombre et lumière, l'écriture engagée de Gisèle Pineau," *Notre Librairie* 138–39 (1999): 88.

6. Gisèle Pineau, "Ecrire en tant que noire," in Maryse Condé and Madeleine Cottenet-Hage (eds.), *Penser la créolité* (Paris: Karthala, 1995), 292.

7. Pineau, "Ecrire," 291.

8. Maryse Condé, *La Parole des femmes: Essai sur des romancières des Antilles de langue française* (Paris: L'Harmattan, 1993), 36.

9. Pineau, "Ecrire," 292.

10. Nancy Chodorow, *The Reproduction of Mothering: Psychoanalysis and the Sociology of Gender* (Berkeley: University of California Press, 1978), 213.

11. See Simonne Henry Valmore, *Dieux en exil* (Paris: Gallimard, 1988), 50.

12. Joëlle Vitiello, "Le Corps de l'île dans les écrits de Gisèle Pineau" in Suzanne Rinne and Joëlle Vitiello (eds.), *Elles écrivent des Antilles* (Paris: L'Harmattan, 1997), 249–50.

13. Aimé Césaire, *Cahier d'un retour au pays natal* [1939] (Paris: Présence Africaine, 1983), 18.

14. Belugue, "Entre l'ombre et lumière," 88.

15. Pineau, "Ecrire," 293.

16. Gyssels, "L'Exil selon Pineau," 178.

17. Jane Ussher, *Women's Madness: Misogyny or Mental Illness?* (Amherst: University of Massachusetts Press, 1991), 33.

18. Nina Hellerstein, "Violence, mythe et destin dans l'univers antillais de Gisèle Pineau," *Littéréalité* 10, no. 1 (1998): 49.

19. Valérie Loichot, "Negations and Subversions of Paternal Authorities in Glissant's Fictional Works (*Le Quatrième Siècle, La Case du commandeur, Tout-monde*)," in Eva Paulino Bueno, Terry Caesar and William Hummel (eds.), *Naming the Father: Legacies, Genealogies and Explorations of Fatherhood in Modern and Contemporary Literature* (Lanham, Md.: Lexington Books, 2000), 106.

20. Hellerstein, "Violence, mythe et destin," 49.

21. Gyssels, "L'Exil selon Pineau," 176.

22. Françoise Pfaff, *Conversations with Maryse Condé* (Lincoln: University of Nebraska Press, 1996), 135.

23. Hellerstein, "Violence, mythe et destin," 48.

24. Sandra Butler, *Conspiracy of Silence: The Trauma of Incest* (New York: Bantam, 1979), 58.

25. Jacques André, *L'Inceste focal dans la famille noire antillaise* (Paris: Presses Universitaires de France, 1987), 70.

26. André, *L'Inceste focal*, 123.

27. André, *L'Inceste focal*, 339.

28 Pineau, interview by Bonnie Thomas.

29. Butler, *Conspiracy of Silence*, 104.

30. Pineau, interview by Bonnie Thomas.

31. Pineau, "Ecrire," 293.

32. Belugue, "Entre l'ombre et lumière," 89.

Conclusion

An Analysis of French Caribbean Gender Identity

Slavery and the plantation system left a wound on the French Caribbean psyche. References to their cruel legacies abound in the literature of the region. Such referentiality suffuses the work of Edouard Glissant, Patrick Chamoiseau and Raphaël Confiant—authors whose protagonists remain tied to the past and are overwhelmingly defined by the malign drama of slavery and plantation life. Their narratives' personae embody the thesis that the French Caribbean cannot, should not, divorce itself from the past. Confiant, for one, is well aware that the protagonists in his novels have little to do with present-day reality, but are instead manifestations of a tragic history. "I can't write novels that are set in the present," he has confessed, "it's not possible. No, for me, my imagining stops in 1960."[1] This inflection of past and present illuminates a specifically Caribbean dichotomy between fiction and reality structuring the novels studied in this volume. Glissant, Chamoiseau and Confiant create fiction largely based on the past; Schwarz-Bart, Condé and Pineau are more interested in the present. Maryse Condé stands apart from the others, affirming her interest in the future rather than the dead past. She has affirmed that "I occupy a place apart in French Caribbean literature. That means I refuse to explain everything by the past."[2] Yet the legacies of slavery pervade her work, as well.

Slavery is like a Caribbean Holocaust, haunting the slaves' descendants up to the twenty-first century. Finally recognizing this murderous past, the French government adopted the Christiane Taubira law in May 2001 that acknowledges slavery as a crime against humanity. Lionel Jospin and Christian Paul, minister for the French overseas departments, created a committee for the memory of slavery that is chaired by Maryse Condé.

However, debates around slavery remain unresolved and caused contro-
versy in France and Martinique as recently as 2005 and 2006. Article 4 of
the constitution, which declares the "positive role" of colonization,
sparked public outrage in France and the Caribbean. Demonstrations in
Martinique were so violent that the minister for the interior, Nicolas
Sarkozy, had to cancel his proposed trip there in December 2005. Such
public outcry forced Jacques Chirac to abolish the controversial article 4.
He also announced 10 May as an annual day of remembrance for the victims of slavery. These impassioned responses indicate that slavery and its
relationship to history and memory is an issue of fundamental importance in present-day society.

Condé's involvement in the committee for the memory of slavery
demonstrates an attachment to the past, but also her desire for reconciliation with history. Part of the committee's brief, for example, is to create
an annual commemoration date and to award a prize for the best cultural
work relating to slavery. This refusal not to be obsessed by past crimes
seems more characteristic of French Caribbean women writers than men.
Condé, Schwarz-Bart and Pineau accept the need to move beyond slavery while Glissant, Chamoiseau and Confiant are stuck in an endless re-
hearsal of the past. These contrasting attitudes to history animate the authors' presentation of gender in their novels. The writers' relationship to
the Caribbean proverb "man is a breadfruit and woman is a chestnut" is
revealing about the way each has appropriated the past for their own
purposes. It also demonstrates two ways of reacting to slavery: remaining defined and confined by it, or acknowledging it and moving toward
the future.

Maryse Condé, the most forward-looking of the writers in this volume,
defines herself as a nomadic author. She is free to write about who and
what she wants.[3] Rejecting all labels, Condé sets her novels in a wide variety of countries, cultures and epochs. While some of her books are influenced by the past, others are oriented firmly toward the future. This
balanced attitude recurs in her portraits of gender and she has stated on
many occasions that French Caribbean society is changing. For example,
in 2001 she asserted that "I think that today in Guadeloupe relationships
between men and women are completely different and are in a state of
flux."[4] Condé argues, furthermore, that economic constraints mean that
men can no longer afford to keep a number of mistresses, particularly
when it is usually the women who work. She observes in her own environment that men are starting to help more and that the image of the man
as an unhelpful layabout no longer rings true. She also warns against the
"clichés of the French Caribbean woman: the *femme matador*, the *poteau mitan*, etc.," which, she argues, "arose because women were forced to take
on extra responsibilities in the face of male absence, not because they are

intrinsically stronger."[5] Condé's explicit use of irony and satire in her presentation of stereotypes in her novels underlines her cynicism about rhetoric which explains everything by the past. While novels like *Moi, Tituba, sorcière . . . noire de Salem* and *Les Derniers Rois mages* are situated very much in the Caribbean past, her ironic tone discourages the blind acceptance of historic gender types.

In a 2005 interview, Condé distinguishes between two phases in her writing career: her "Caribbean" phase dating from her first novel *Hérémakhonon*, published in 1976, and her "global" phase initiated by *Desirada* in 1997. According to Condé, her "Caribbean" novels were born of a time when she was still finding her voice, still locating herself in her culture and her past. The French words *voix* (voice) and *voie* (way), pronounced identically, effectively encapsulate her personal journey at this time. From the publication of *Desirada*, however, Condé began writing "in Maryse Condé."[6] With the discovery of her literary voice, Condé claims a complete freedom for herself unbound by language, genre or context. Her 2003 novel, *Histoire de la femme cannibale*, for example, is set in South Africa, a country of which she has little direct experience.

Condé's trajectory as a writer illuminates a progression in her relationship to the past. She accepts that individuals change, societies change and that it is important to look toward the future. Condé locates 1995 as a significant turning point for French Caribbean writers. In her view this date reflects the coming of age of French Caribbean literature. It is a time when the world was witnessing unprecedented globalization, when the French Caribbean could no longer confine itself to its own limited borders. There are now more French Caribbean people living outside the Caribbean than on the islands. The past decade has become a liberating moment for writers, with their works unbound by national and cultural borders. Passports no longer define identity, Condé argues. Instead she paints herself as a global citizen. This is Condé's way of facing the past and moving ahead. Her supple portraits of gender also link to this more fluid understanding of the past. If she wants to be stereotypical she can; if she wants to challenge stereotypes she can. All her work is observed with an ironic eye and it is all portrayed "in Maryse Condé." Condé has thrown off the shackles of the past and emerged intact. Her stance is one of the most positive examples of French Caribbean people coming to terms with historical trauma.

Patrick Chamoiseau and Raphaël Confiant are the polar opposites of Maryse Condé. For them, French colonization and slavery can never be forgotten or "got over." Rather, they have engendered cultural and mental disorders that can be remedied only by political independence. Tragically, however, both Chamoiseau and Confiant acknowledge that independence is almost impossible, thereby condemning themselves to an unhealthy obsession with the past. Confiant, for example, poignantly depicts a longing for a lifestyle eroded by French cultural dominance. "What we describe in our novels is no longer valid," he laments, "it doesn't exist anymore. It's finished, it's over."[7] Confiant's satirical adherence to rigid stereotypes and Chamoiseau's romanticized vision of women attest to their unease with contemporary conceptions of identity. While Chamoiseau appears more able to navigate the increasingly fluid nature of gender in his fictional characters, Confiant is haunted by the disappearance of the way of life he knew as a youngster. The memory of the past here imposes a kind of post-traumatic stress disorder. Chamoiseau and Confiant are stuck in an endless repetition of past traumas.

> Chamoiseau and I play the tragic role by saying that we are the first French Caribbean generation to become old at forty, because a generation normally becomes old at seventy. In other words, when you are seventy or eighty years old you realize that the world you grew up in has disappeared. But for us when we were thirty or forty years old the plantation world of our childhood completely collapsed. . . . We are the last generation, Chamoiseau and I and others, Pépin and so forth, to be able to remember plantation life. We are the last from fifty or sixty years ago. When we were ten, twelve or thirteen it started to collapse and when we were twenty-five or thirty it was completely dead. So Chamoiseau has this magnificent saying: "we were old at forty."[8]

This tragic stance demonstrates Chamoiseau and Confiant's inability to move beyond past wounds. Both writers use French Caribbean history as a constant point of reference. While their stories are undoubtedly rich, their preoccupation with the past limits their vision of contemporary reality. Confiant has admitted that his gendered portraits of butterfly-like men and stoic women are not characteristic of twenty-first-century Martinique. "That's an image of the male-female relationship that collapsed about forty years ago," he stresses, "because forty years ago there was a brutal *francisation* [Frenchification] of our society."[9] Chamoiseau, however, asserts that it "is always necessary to go back to the slave period"[10] to understand French Caribbean gender identity. While there is always interaction between text and context, these writers' presentations of gender are stunted and have a tendency to fall into stereotyping and nostalgia. Their closed approach to current realities forms a striking contrast to Maryse Condé's openness toward the future.

Simone Schwarz-Bart and Edouard Glissant, while completely different in their literary style, belong together within the generation that consolidated the process of cultural self-discovery initiated by Aimé Césaire. Their stories demonstrate two approaches to the French Caribbean's traumatic past. Glissant's fictional, nonfictional and poetic works demonstrate his wholehearted belief that the past offers the key to unlocking present-day reality. However, his increasingly opaque style means that his books are inaccessible to many readers. This abstract approach to literature is reflected in the limited space he accords to gender. It is tempting to observe that gender is not a major concern for Glissant. *La Case du commandeur* is one of the few novels in which it is possible to theorize his conception of male-female relationships, although he constantly subordinates gender to his theoretical concerns. Glissant's stance reveals an ongoing frustration with the French Caribbean's approach to the past. He is convinced that Martinique and Guadeloupe need to reverse the effects of centuries of French domination, but also acknowledges that this move is unlikely. Like Chamoiseau and Confiant, Glissant remains trapped in the past, limiting his ability to connect with contemporary reality.

Unlike Glissant, Schwarz-Bart wishes only to "tell it like it is." She describes a world that is colored by history, but is not paralyzed by it. Her overwhelmingly optimistic characters underline the power of the human spirit to overcome adversity. Her novels remain a permanent testament to the possibilities of the future. Schwarz-Bart's adherence to an older generation means that slavery is not a distant memory. Man Cia's stories of the caged chickens at the market in *Pluie et vent sur Télumée Miracle*, for example, reveal a living past that must not be allowed to continue. "If you want to see a slave," she tells Télumée, "you've only got to go down to the market at Pointe-à-Pitre and look at the poultry in the cages, tied up, and at the terror in their eyes."[11] Man Cia's stirring words bring to life this traumatic history and remind Télumée to appreciate the freedoms in her life. The positive attitude of the novel's characters embodies a way forward that rejects an endless repetition of past traumas. Schwarz-Bart's figures are fully aware of slavery and its continuing socioeconomic effects on their lives. Characters like Reine Sans Nom and Télumée choose to look determinedly forward. Rather than being oppressed by the past, they transform trauma into a courage that allows them to find peace and happiness. *Pluie et vent sur Télumée Miracle* stands out as one of the most optimistic examples of French Caribbean literature. In this book it is the resilient women who hold the key to the future.

Gisèle Pineau, who is the youngest writer discussed in this book, occupies a place mid-point between Condé's determined gaze toward the future and the male writers' immersion in the past. Pineau acknowledges that the relationship between men and women is changing, but she frequently reverts to "that time of slavery" as an explanation for the persistence of gender inequalities. Speaking of Caribbean men, she declares that

there is a trend toward playing mother, they're at home, they do the washing up, they do what lots of men around the planet do. But there is something wrong there, something bothers the women and they often say: "but what is

he always doing in my way? Why is he always there?" It's very disturbing . . .
[we] reproduce the behaviors of our mothers and grandmothers.[12]

Pineau's use of the past as a frame of reference pervades her novels on both a social and a personal level and also features in her nonfictional work. In *L'Espérance-macadam*, for example, she refuses to condemn Rosan as a child rapist, citing instead the difficult childhood he experienced and his own painful history. "Behind Rosan, Angela's father, there is a whole history. He is responsible for this history, but he is also its victim."[13] Like Condé, Pineau is a writer who consistently advocates literary and intellectual freedom, but she displays an unwillingness to erase the memories of the past. Her literary project could be conceived from a psychological point of view as dealing openly with past pain, but remaining forever colored by it. She does not obsess about the past as Chamoiseau and Confiant do, but she is not willing to forget it either.

Pineau's engagement with gender stereotypes in her novels reflects both her allegiance to the past and her steadfast refusal to be confined by it. While her works sometimes feature stereotypical characters like Sosthène in *La Grande Drive des esprits*, she refuses to accept anything at face value. Therefore one can draw parallels with the "swaggering" Caribbean men of the past, but also appreciate that the portrait is satirical and humorous. In some ways Pineau is self-contradictory in her relationship to history: on the one hand, her characters are the least stereotypical in the books studied in this volume; on the other, her interviews reveal an ongoing attachment to explaining everything by the past. Her dilemma highlights the continuing difficulties of coming to terms with a painful event from one's history. Should it be perpetually written and rewritten? Should there be a process of reconciliation? Apology? Moving on? French Caribbean writers demonstrate different ways of resolving these questions, ranging from a resolutely forward-looking position to a constant pull back to the past. In this study the female writers are more prepared to face the future; the men prefer to look back. It is clear from all these reactions that the French Caribbean past has all the power of a post-traumatic stress disorder.

These contrasting approaches to the past are reflected in the writers' conceptions of gender. Some consistently invoke the stereotypical "breadfruit" and "chestnuts" from the past; others depict a hybrid fruit. All of the authors studied portray characters that are consistent with the *femme matador* or the philandering Caribbean man, affirming the enduring legacy of history. These portraits highlight the complexity of gender identity in the French Caribbean context, where, for example, the stereotype of the *femme matador* represents a particular Caribbean fusion of femininity and strength, despite the more conventional identification of strength with masculinity. With the abundance of strong women and weak men in these novels, the female characters emerge overall as positive and the male characters as negative. The writers' engagements with these stereotypical portraits of gender differ considerably. The novels also reveal the mixing and merging of masculine and feminine qualities, producing a wonderful proliferation of hybrid fruits to which the way of the future belongs.

The varied works of these contemporary French Caribbean writers provide a fascinating insight into gender identity in this society. The dramatic history of the islands that sparked so many ambiguities in the development of French Caribbean identity continues to constitute an important backdrop to these novelists' writings. Evident in the contrasting gendered portraits examined in this volume, the hybrid identities that formed as a result of slavery, colonization and immigration problematize and nuance the concept of a French Caribbean subjectivity. French Caribbean gender identity emerges in these works as an exciting and evolving state of affairs—identities that are in a process of negotiation between the powerful bonds of the past and a pull toward the future. Transgressions of gender stereotypes in the novels demonstrate a move beyond the trauma of the past through its understanding. This drama is played out between the authors themselves and their fictional visions highlight the role of historical memory in making sense of one's past, carving a place for oneself in the present and unlocking the possibilities of the future.

NOTES

1. Raphaël Confiant, interview by Bonnie Thomas, Martinique, 28 June 2001.
2. Maryse Condé, interview by Bonnie Thomas, Guadeloupe, 27 June 2001.
3. Maryse Condé, unpublished interview by Bonnie Thomas, Perth, 14 July 2005.
4. Condé, interview by Bonnie Thomas.
5. Condé, unpublished interview by Bonnie Thomas.
6. Condé, unpublished interview by Bonnie Thomas.
7. Confiant, interview by Bonnie Thomas.
8. Confiant, interview by Bonnie Thomas.
9. Confiant, interview by Bonnie Thomas.
10. Patrick Chamoiseau, interview by Bonnie Thomas, Martinique, 24 June 2001.
11. Simone Schwarz-Bart, *The Bridge of Beyond* (London: Victor Gollancz Ltd., a division of The Orion Publishing Group, 1982), 37.
12. Gisèle Pineau, unpublished interview by Bonnie Thomas, Paris, 12 July 2001.
13. Pineau, unpublished interview by Bonnie Thomas.

Appendix A

──⌒

Interview with Patrick Chamoiseau (extracts)

*Tribunal, Fort-de-France,
Martinique, 26 June 2001*

BT: In *Texaco* you manage to reconstruct the point of view of a woman through the character of Marie-Sophie. Why did you choose to present the life of Texaco from a female perspective?

PC: First of all, because that's the reality. When I went to Texaco, when I started to make enquiries, people told me that the first inhabitant of Texaco, therefore the person who established the area, was a woman called Madame Sico. So she was there, I went to see her, she told me everything that I recounted in my novel. There was therefore no need to ask the question, it was a woman. If a man had established it, I would have put in a man. But in this case, it was a woman.

BT: How would the story have changed if a man had been the narrator?

PC: It's nearly impossible that it would be a man to the extent that in French Caribbean history the status of men was unique. By that I mean that men are not connected to the earth, they are not connected to their huts or their houses. The men were quite mobile, quite peripheral as far as the family was concerned. Therefore I have difficulty seeing men try to build a suburb or put down roots in the soil. That's women's business. Therefore it's completely plausible, normal and historical that women founded Texaco. That didn't surprise me at all. There is almost no example of men organizing the establishment of a particular place . . . it's not possible. But it's necessary nonetheless to qualify this. When they are part of a couple . . . the French Caribbean family is a matrifocal family consisting of the mother and children. That comes from slavery and the man was always quite peripheral. I would say men are quite on the surface of things. The establishment of gardens, huts, children, everything that relates to creating life, was women's work. But there were nonetheless some couples that functioned normally. There is the rule and there are multiple exceptions. And there are rural couples who tame the earth or realize . . . a bit like in *Texaco* where we have the person, I can't remember her name, who leaves with Esternome and they cultivate the earth. We also have that sort of arrangement. But when the man becomes a builder he always has a woman beside him. He is never alone, whereas a woman alone can always build.

BT: Do inequalities exist between men and women in the French Caribbean and how are they manifested?

PC: All the basic inequalities that we know about between men and women exist here. In short, inequalities or the division of labor. We can call it what we like. There are the traditional inequalities and there are also inequalities peculiar to us. It is always necessary to go back to the slave period. This is really the formative period for us. "Negritude" arose from the period of slavery, from the holds of the slave ships, to claim a sense of identity that would be purely African. From Glissant we know that the voyage in the slave ship's hold between Africa and the Americas was a totally destructive experience. From then on, the African identity floated around with other identities, Amerindian, European and all that, and that was a terrible combination. The other aspect is that slavery is the negation of everything that is human. In slavery, everything is reduced to nothing. And during the slave period, women didn't have the same status as men. It is from there that the separation began. For example, an African couple is taken together on to the slave ships. The man finds himself in chains while the woman is kept in shackles at the front of the ship. When she has a child the child stays with her, and so on. So there was separation. So there was a difference in the treatment of men and women from the time of the slave ships. Secondly, there was a custom on board the ships. The sailors grabbed the women. There was what they called *la pariade*. So there were lots of mixed-blood children who were born soon after the ship's arrival. But that created a major separation, that is, the women were more likely to receive preferential treatment from the colonizers and masters. And this closer relationship to the colonizers and masters continued into the plantations. I mean, the female slave was the object of pleasure for the master and there were no limits . . . and that is why families weren't able to put themselves back together. You can't be the husband or the lover of someone who doesn't belong to you, who is at the master's disposal. The principle of paternity works in the same way. You can't be a father if the father's place is symbolically occupied, or occupied in a terrible fashion, by the image of the master. So men always found themselves a bit apart, which immediately gave rise to a kind of suspicion between men and women. That means that the lives of men and women were almost on parallel trajectories. Which doesn't mean to say that there weren't black women runaway slaves who existed, fought, etc. But the difference in treatment was terrible, so that created further difference. The other element is that during slavery there was no differentiation between the sexes. This is paradoxical. Women and men did practically the same tasks. Even if women cut the grass and men cut the cane, we can practically consider that it was two . . . the men were treated like women and the women were treated like men. The psychologists who study these things say that there was a phenomenon of castration. For men this increased the distance between themselves and women. The French Caribbean female is thus conditioned by this kind of specific treatment, this closeness to the master and this survival strategy organized around the children. You notice that women used the relationships they had with the masters in a particular way to obtain freedom for their children, to allow their children to escape slavery, to escape materially, to obtain emancipation and so on but also to escape in an ontological sense by becoming whiter by having mixed blood or lighter-skinned children. That allowed children to escape the servile condition because it was completely synonymous with being black, which was the dreadful characteristic of slavery in the Americas. In ancient times, slavery represented a legal status. One became a slave because it was a situation one could change. Slavery in the Americas was ontological. To be black was to be a slave. You cannot escape a condition like that. So the women tried to push their children out of this situation by a sort of 'whitening' process. So that created between men and women the sort of distance that is very difficult to bridge. This means that the woman has always been the leader of the family, the builder, the homemaker, the one who thinks, who works, who pushes the children, who sends the children to school, who sacrifices herself for them. In other words, the French Caribbean mother is a kind of omnipotent and omnipresent mother. That is why almost all my novels are about women. In each one there are women who are there and men who are a bit on the side.

BT: In comparison with African men, for example, do these men see themselves as head of the family?

PC: This is very particular to us because here we are in a Creole country. Historically the slaves had the chance to sell the produce from their gardens. In fact they had small gardens of their own. There were the big sugarcane fields but they always had their own little gardens where they grew produce that helped them survive and they would go and sell some of it on Sundays. And it was the women who used to sell. The men didn't go. Commerce is women's business. There is also the African tradition that containers for the produce, the bowls and baskets, belonged to the women. It was the women who were responsible for that. But actually the head of the family was always the woman. She was always the head of the family, but this was not a position of status. First of all, the family is matrifocal. There is not a constituted couple, there is a woman and her children. A woman, her grandmother, her daughter, her sisters. In short there can be three generations of women and children living together. And then around them there is a series of cohabitants who come and go periodically. That is the basic structure. But nevertheless, as this is a Creole country, we have all kinds of structures, because on one side there is the familial structure of the masters. The master has a nuclear family structure—dad and mum. We have seen what happened with the Amerindians. So we have the Amerindian familial model, we have the Hindu immigrants who have a patrilinear structure with a very strong father and the woman who is to one side, and so on. So all kinds of structures exist. But we can effectively have cases where, like the mulattos, there was a nuclear family—the father, mother, the father who is head of the family and the mother who is in the background organizing the house. All these arrangements existed. We have the matrifocal model with the woman at the center and then all kinds of behavior resulting from different personalities. Even when there is a nuclear structure with a clearly identified father, a mother, husband and wife, the culture of this family remains matrifocal. That is, the fundamental decisions are always made, initiated, carried out, and organized more or less directly by the woman.

BT: Since most of your novels are set in the city, do you think nature has a role to play in the Caribbean story?

PC: Of course. They are urban societies with a rural story. That is clear. The Creole culture and language are rural entities. All of humanity is largely rural. All of humanity's thinking is linked to rural functioning. We have scarcely started to lose our fondness for the mechanisms of rural thinking. *Texaco* is a rural way of living in the city, in a community, etc. So the foundation of this society is largely rural. Therefore nature is very present, very, very present. You see that it is omnipresent, it is very powerful. Nature hasn't yet become a cultural object. That is beginning to happen in Western societies. Why isn't it a cultural object? Because we are right in the middle of it and it's very powerful. For example, when you go on the streets you see that verandas and balconies overlook the road, while behind them there is an absolutely magnificent landscape. People face the streets. Nature isn't a problem, it's not an object of contemplation. The street is the object of contemplation, the people who are passing by, their relationships with each other, the traffic. All the traditional cabins are oriented toward the street with their backs to the landscape. It's only now that nature is starting to become a cultural object for the elite so villas are starting to be oriented toward the view. On the other hand, the *békés* have always had this idea of nature not as a cultural object but as an object of charm. So you have the idea of the garden; you will see the *békés'* houses are very beautiful with lovely gardens . . . But nature is still very, very present.

BT: *Eloge de la Créolité* emphasised the variety of races that exist in the French Caribbean and in your books you have presented a mixture of races. Do you think that it's possible to have cultural unity with so many different races and is this possible for the majority of the population?

PC: Yes. I think that the principal contemporary challenge is to try to conceive of diverse unity. There is a certain poverty in trying to make humanity one. Personally, I make a distinction between unity and one-dimensionality. One-dimensionality would tend to be monolithic, to crush everything and make it into a single object. However as I see it, when you look at humanity, at the human condition, there is nonetheless a human presence, a human unity despite the extraordinary diversity of cultures and races. This human unity can only manifest itself in diversity. To try and view the human condition outside of this diversity is to return to a standardizing or slightly impoverished universality. We prefer the notion of diversal rather than universal, diversality rather than universality, because the universal in fact has always been aligned to some degree with western values. What became universal in fact was what the West had considered as the canon of the beautiful, the true, and so on. Whereas the idea of diversality allows us to keep company with human diversity by saying that it is precisely in this diversity that unity is found. And unity can only be contemplated in an exaltation of diversity and that the more this diversity is active, integrated, valorized, the more unity will be realized in a profound way. And that is what we have trouble thinking. Even here people will say: "we are not a people, a real people, we are bastards, what is this country?" They don't think they exist because they take the traditional standard of a people, a nation and an identity and apply it to a situation that is completely new. When we look at most human societies, we notice that these societies are multilingual, multicultural, multiracial and that despite that, it will be necessary to find the link, the flexibility, the social cement. And that will be achieved through a story that makes this link between unity and diversity and doesn't separate them.

BT: Could you explain the concept of creolization?

PC: What we call creolization is the accelerated, massive coming together of several peoples, several languages, etc. It is not unique, all civilizations have been civilizations of contact and metissage. But what happened in the Americas is that the metissage was done in a brutal manner, it was a kind of shock, over scarcely two centuries. It was a huge task for a completely different population in the appalling conditions of slavery, racism and colonialism to find a way of living. So that is creolization. Only creolization doesn't come together smoothly. That is, that it doesn't form a kind of harmonious metissage, societies that were well-mixed where everyone would appreciate each other. They are areas of conflict and when we look at the kinds of creolization in America, Australia, everywhere, we notice that each community, each anthropological mass, cultivates a fantasy of purity. For example, in Martinique, the *békés* who are the descendants of the white colonizers still think that they are European. They intermarry, keep to themselves in order to stay white, white and European. But when they are faced with real white Europeans, they are conscious of all the differences that exist between them and this white European. They are much closer to us than to white Europeans, but they have this imagined culture of Europeanness, of their origin, their superiority, their whiteness. The same applies to the blacks. When we look at the discourse of Negritude, it was the same. They said to themselves: "what have we become here?" They will reclaim a Negro essence in Africa; "we're blacks, we're Negroes and my identity is black, I'm an African." It's a bit like what the African Americans in the US say. So we notice that Creole societies are conflicting, antagonistic societies but at the same time complementary and joined together because even if they cultivate the fantasy of purity, of a pure source, nevertheless in reality, in the culture, there is a creolization, a mixing. So, the one is in the other and the other is in the one. So, in my case, as someone of Negro and African extraction, I am much closer to any white writer from the Caribbean, closer to García Marquéz and Alejo Carpentier than to an African writer who has the same skin color as me. That is the phenomenon of creolization. This is what is going to make big human communities. For example, if we take the example of literature, we would not be able to put together anthologies based on language. I am closer to any English-speaking, Spanish-speaking or Portuguese-speaking writer from the Americas than to a French person, to a French writer. It's not language that makes a community, it's not race, we will no longer be able to put together Negro or African anthologies or anthologies based on race or anthologies based on a nation or anthologies based on language. What makes the human community is the structure of their story. For us, for example, what forms our story? The Amerindian genocide, the New World, the shock of the slave trade, slavery and then this absolutely terrible creolization that creates a conflicting, antagonistic, complementary space. As soon as we speak of creolization we have complex processes, that is, contrary things are linked, opposing things become complementary, conflicting spaces become spaces joined together, based on something broken. We need to try and think about it like this. That is why wherever there is creolization we will have modalities. We see it in the United States and effectively they are communities completely at war, but what happens when we take a black American? There is nothing more "yankee" than a black American, nothing more "yankee" with his American flag. Even if he calls himself an African American, goes to war against white power and so on, the structure of his story is American. Whether it is Michael Jordan or any other American, they are all American. They will go to Africa, they will behave like a yankee, they will order their steaks wrapped in plastic, all the while declaring that they are African. But they are not aware of the structure of their story. This means that in the modern world human families are linked in a completely random way by the structure of their story. It won't be nation or homeland or language or skin color that will create human communities.

Appendix B

⌐⌐

Interview with Maryse Condé (extracts)

Montebello, Guadeloupe, 27 June 2001

BT: Do you think that the ideas derived from the feminist movement are relevant to the condition of women in the French Caribbean?

MC: Yes, firstly, because women have a different perception of themselves as a result of being mothers, and of their relationship to a man, whom they consider rather like one of their children. So, if in Western terminology a woman is oppressed by a man, in French Caribbean culture it is not seen as oppression. Perhaps it is seen as a somewhat excessive demand. But the woman does it with good humor. Obviously this can't be idealized. There is some macho behavior which is a little excessive. But on the whole male-female relationships require another way of being described in European discourse.

BT: What do you think of the image of the French Caribbean woman as head of the family?

MC: I think there is a rather mythical image which intellectuals have spread . . . woman as a sort of central support ["poteau-mitan"] of everything in life. I think that's a little exaggerated. If you read a sociologist like Fritz Gracchus, he has another much more complex picture of the woman in society. He thinks that very often the French Caribbean woman is in fact a "carrier" for alienation, for admiration and for a certain type of Westernization. He thinks that very often the woman has played a negative role in the establishment of French Caribbean society. The book is called *Les Lieux de la mère dans les sociétés afro-américaines*. In my opinion we must not idealize the woman or make of her a sort of pillar of the family. Yes, she was that at a certain time after slavery when the men left and when only women remained on the plantations. She had to assume a number of roles. Yes, but in the end this was not always totally positive. I also think about the irresponsibility of men, which is also a fact. There are many men who are irresponsible and who have abandoned their male duties. But all that in my opinion must be used with a lot of subtlety. Literature and fiction have become attached to what is the most obvious in society. It hasn't presented happy couples—as we say "there's no story in happiness." It has always accented the dysfunctional elements of society and perhaps excessively so. I also think that the image of the man is changing a lot in the French Caribbean. Look at the people around you. For example, there's a young couple renting a house behind mine. I can see that the image of the man is changing. He takes on a lot of responsibility, he shares his time and the work, and so we mustn't any longer talk about the sort of man who doesn't lift a finger. But read Gracchus' book, the title of the book is *Les Lieux de la mère dans les sociétés afro-américaines*.

BT: How do you see the current situation between men and women in the French Caribbean?

MC: First of all I think there has been a big battle for political independence in Guadeloupe, especially Guadeloupe which I know best. Political independence has not been achieved. People are still dreaming about it. But the political battle has united men and women in a new Guadeloupe, in an independent Guadeloupe. A certain type of masculine behavior will not be tolerated. So in struggling together men and women have grown closer. This is a bit like what happened in countries like Algeria during the independence struggle. People have grown closer. Perhaps after victory has been won women will go back to their corner and men will take center stage. Fortunately or unfortunately in Guadeloupe the battle for liberation is not yet over. I don't know why . . . but the political battle has brought men and women closer. For example, if you look at lists of politicians you will see the names of many women. It is no accident that the president of the regional councils of Guadeloupe is Madame Michaux Chevry, a woman with a lot of political experience and extraordinary personal magnetism. Many women have achieved roles, men's roles . . . but in everyday life there is always this problem of polygamy. It is well known Guadeloupean men are not faithful, they have a wife and they have mistresses. But even that is beginning to become less common for purely materialistic reasons. Society is so financially stretched that men can no longer afford to keep a number of mistresses. Most of the time it's the women who work and the men who are unemployed so even this relationship is a little upside down. So I think that today in Guadeloupe relationships between men and women are completely different and are in a state of flux.

BT: Do you think the attitude of women that you described in *La Parole des femmes*, which justifies rather than condemns men's behavior, continues to exist in the French Caribbean?

MC: *La Parole des femmes* is already at least ten, twelve or even fifteen years old. Yes, there still exists a sort of tolerance toward masculine excesses. Women have a sort of belief that men are always men and you can't change them. There's also a tendency for women to think of a man as a little like one of their children. So he's a bit of a pest, he's demanding, so she forgives him. Undoubtedly there is still some of that in society but I would say less and less. Women are beginning to claim their place and this is becoming more and more evident.

BT: In your opinion can we continue to explain male behavior by the metaphorical castration of men on the slave ships?

MC: You know that I occupy a place apart in French Caribbean literature. That means I refuse to explain everything by the past. I think that we have been on this island for four and a half centuries now and that we have developed ways of living and social customs which don't always need to be understood with reference to slavery. I know that Chamoiseau, Glissant, that group of writers, have their eyes fixed on the past, but I don't. I want to look ahead. I think that the plantation system has brought about a sort of promiscuity between men and women. When slavery ended and they were freed, men refused to work. They went off and settled in town while women stayed on the plantations. In my opinion these are much more important reasons than the traumas resulting from being torn from Africa. But we've more or less come out of it nevertheless. We have built something with this trauma, we have created societies which . . . nor should we compare French Caribbean society to European society, which is a mistake because people consider ours a sick society, or to African society because that's a mistake too. Ours is a society which was born in the context of the plantations, freedom from slavery and the abolition of certain rights . . . The slaves' excessive desire for freedom I explain by the present state of the islands and not at all by the past. This is a debate we often have. They have been writing in the past for a long time—I try to write in the present. My last book is called *La Belle Créole*, that's Guadeloupe today. What counts—strikes, power cuts, a union movement gone mad, endless political demands? You have to look around you today and not always back to yesterday. This is a debate we have.

BT: Does the representation of men and women in novels written by men differ from that in novels written by women?

MC: To tell you the truth I don't read many male writers. The only writer that I read a lot is Edouard Glissant. Edouard Glissant places himself, and you have read his books, above the male-female divide, although he has a love, an admiration which I find a bit mythical and a bit idealized, for the character of the runaway slave who is the focus of many of his books. Nevertheless he tries to avoid falling into using clichés and the ideas of other people. So I don't know what men say about women. In the end that doesn't interest me.

BT: Do you see a difference between the attitude adopted by black American women to fight against the problems of race and sexual inequality and French Caribbean women? What are the solutions which French Caribbean women are finding and do they want to find solutions?

MC: I think there is a huge difference. In the United States for example it is very difficult to reach a kind of agreement with one's colleagues, with African-American people who work at Columbia. This is firstly because the relationship which we have with white people is not the same. African Americans find that we are too open to white people, that we're not aggressive enough, that we've lost our way in the struggle. There is also the fact that we have always been in the majority in our islands. I agree that we used to be oppressed by France, but France is 7000 kilometers and eight hours by plane away. In the final analysis the French are a long way away. We have disagreements with the *béké* but the *béké* are Guadeloupeans, they live there, they are natives so it's a little bit like a civil war, a war between enemies who are brothers. So we have a lot less of that aggression based on race than the Americans have. They criticize us, we're not "black" enough for them. And I also think that French Caribbean men don't have the same male chauvinism as African-American men. Here, as I have said, this male chauvinism works a bit like emotional blackmail. A man comes home at midnight, wakes up his wife at midnight to get her to prepare him a meal but with a lot of sweet words, which makes her get up willingly. So there's no brutality . . . well there is . . . it's not generalized, there is a brutality, a sort of violent oppression. So I think that for all these reasons . . . and then there has been a problem between African Americans and French Caribbean people for years, since the beginning of the twentieth century with Marcus Garvey and all that. There's always been a type of chasm and now there are economic problems as well. African Americans with quota systems think that, and this is true elsewhere as well, that many businesses, organizations, banks, universities, whatever you like, fill the quota with French Caribbean people. They are so racist that they prefer to do business with French Caribbean people than with Americans like them which gives Americans the impression that French Caribbean people play a role a bit like strike breakers in a business, which is not true. But that's the impression they have. For example at Columbia where I am the department where I work prefers to employ a French Caribbean woman rather than an African-American woman. So in this struggle, in this relationship we are rather badly thought of. You're always having to explain that you're not there with a hidden agenda, that we're going in the same direction but it's not obvious. You should see a film called *Little Senegal* which explains the problems and tensions between African Americans and French Caribbean people, not just with women but in general.

BT: In *Traversée de la mangrove* you have included a portrait of several Indian women. Are Indian women in the French Caribbean more integrated into society or are they still separate? What sort of inequalities still exist between Indian women and men?

MC: I would say that Indians are integrated but there is a difference which is very difficult to explain. For example the Indians speak Creole. Their curry dish has become the national dish in Guadeloupe. They have several deputies so you could say they are integrated. And they *are* integrated but the difference relates to the fact that we know that their Indian heritage is not the African heritage. that they have brought something different, they have made a feature of their temples and their festivals. In fact when there is a carnival they have a separate parade, they have another type of music and rhythm and everything. They're integrated but they try to be a little bit different. It's rather complex.

BT: People could say that there is a multicultural society in the French Caribbean but when people ask specific questions about the culture the reply only relates to the African heritage.

MC: Yes, what you say is true but it is something we are resisting. We realize the Indians have been excluded from society. There is a movement to include them and at the same time, it's extraordinary, the movement to include them encourages them to claim their difference so that each year there is a festival of "Indianness." They bring Indians straight from India, there are gatherings to practice mantras and to teach the young ones dancing so in the end I think it's a bit like in the States. If we do this carefully we are all part of one society but in different ways. In the States you have a whole range of "microcosms": Haitian Americans, African Americans, Greek Americans, Italian Americans and so on. It's as though they are all mixed up but there's a common ground too. But it's true that the discourse has excluded the Indians for too long. We have to make sure we don't continue doing it.

BT: Are there inequalities between Indian men and women?

MC: I'm not really sure but I think it must be the same as for French Caribbean people of African origin. They have integrated the values of the society so well, the way of life, language and everything that I would have thought it wouldn't be very different.

BT: Why do you place your novels in different countries?

MC: Well, it's because I travel a lot and I find that the novel is a form of communication. We try to reach the other, that doesn't mean that we have to lock ourselves into a territory of I don't know how many square kilometers and stay there. We are in a period of globalization, people travel. There are a lot more French Caribbean people who live outside the Caribbean than those who live in it. There is a whole colony of French Caribbean people in Canada, there is a whole colony of Haitians in New York, so now there are more and more Guadeloupeans and Martinicans who live in the United States. We had several censuses several months ago and we were astonished. We found French Caribbean people in the most unexpected places—in Virginia, in California. The world is exploding, there are no more little borders or little islands closed in on themselves. I can't stand this kind of intellectual chauvinism. Of course I know that I am French Caribbean, but I can be French Caribbean everywhere, in New York, in Paris, in London, wherever. I think the duty of the writer is to follow the changes in the world and not shut oneself up in one place. So my next novel, the one which I'm working on at the moment, is set in Cape Town because I went to Cape Town with my husband last year. This town made a real impression on me and I went back this year to try to understand it better. It is a town of extraordinary beauty but one where human relationships are unbelievably ugly. It is a town which has rejected Africans, which has exiled them into ghettos on the edge of everything that is civilized. Ultimately, how could a place which could be a paradise, which is so beautiful, so enlivening for the spirit, become in fact a place of exclusion, almost of torture. So in the end I think that I really want to talk about that. I don't always want to talk about Guadeloupe, it's charming but nonetheless very limited.

BT: Do you think that even if the color of one's skin is different we can have similar experiences?

MC: You know that I spent twelve years in Africa amongst people whose skin was identical to my own and for twelve years I felt totally foreign. I mean, if you don't share people's culture and their culture doesn't stem from the race they come from or have anything to do with their ethnic group, in the end you have nothing in common. So I realized that race has no meaning and that really you need to look beyond color, beyond insular origins, beyond ethnic origins, to find the people who are more able to understand you, to be close to you. Obviously that takes a lot of time. But it's a task that is worth doing. But generally French Caribbean writers are very inward-looking; their island is the matrix.

BT: Is this inward-looking attitude toward the island caused by concerns about identification?

MC: At the beginning it was that because the French Caribbean didn't exist. No one thought there could be a literature in the French Caribbean or people whose futures were worth taking an interest in. Maybe it's a defensive reaction. I think now that this time has passed, we can speak of ourselves differently . . .

BT: Apart from yourself, are there other people who think like that?

MC: I'm the only one, but that doesn't bother me at all. On the contrary, I like being different from others. I think that all French Caribbean writers say more or less the same thing.

BT: Will the fact of looking beyond the island come through independence from France?

MC: At the beginning of my life I was pro-independence, but we've been talking about independence for forty years now and it hasn't happened. So now I've given up on it a bit and I think along the lines that what is, is, that we can bring about cultural independence at least. From a cultural point of view we can create cultural products which are both particular to us as well as different.

Appendix C

~

Interview with Raphaël Confiant (extracts)

Université des Antilles-Guyane, Martinique, 28 June 2001

BT: Do inequalities between men and women exist in the French Caribbean and do French Caribbean novels reflect these inequalities?

RC: Yes, there are inequalities between men and women, but it's not an inequality which can be understood in the same terms as in the West. Why? Because it's necessary to realize that during slavery, I won't say that men were more oppressed than women, but it was the men who worked, it was the men who worked in the canefields and the women who always had the chance of escaping by having a mixed-blood child with a white man. White men had lots of black women as wives or mistresses and so on. It must be said that black women had a slightly better status than black men during slavery. After the abolition of slavery black men, who hadn't known any family during slavery, didn't have any family, had only the behavioral model of their masters. And the masters' behavioral model was quasi polygamous since they had their official white wives and then a whole lot of colored women and lots of children, lots of mixed-blood children. So, the blacks imitated this behavior, they had a woman at home and they had a whole lot of women on the side. And inevitably, bit by bit, the slightly favored status of black women during slavery became the status of white women. That is, woman as object, woman exploited and so on, but French Caribbean women nonetheless never had this inferior status that we find in African societies or even in Europe because women here have often taken on the family single-handed because there was no father during slavery. It was the mother who brought up the children so she is used to bringing up the children on her own. So even after slavery

177

she has continued to play the role of both father and mother when the men weren't around. This means that if there is inequality you have to understand it within its historical parameters. I mean it is not "classical inequality" such as you find in Europe, the United States, etc.

BT: Could you explain the image of the man who constantly changes partner which one often finds in French Caribbean literature?

RC: Men don't have a fixed home. I mean it's the woman who is at the center. The man who visits several women doesn't have a center. Often he lives with his mother, he doesn't have a fixed home, he goes around from one woman to another. He doesn't have a center whereas the women are the center. They have a house, a cabin, a place and so on . . . So it's not contradictory in the end because the man is like a butterfly. There is even a French word, "papillonner" [to flit about], to describe this. He flits about, but the woman doesn't flit about because she receives men at her house. She doesn't go to the men, they come to her. But that's an image of the male-female relationship that collapsed about forty years ago because forty years ago there was a brutal "Frenchification" [*francisation*] of our society. We have completely adopted the French monogamous model and so what we describe in our novels is no longer valid. It doesn't exist anymore. It's finished, it's over. In fact, it does exist, but in the popular levels of society, amongst the ordinary people, but generally we follow a more European model. That is, lots of people get married compared to forty years ago. They are holding onto a certain bourgeois respectability and what is more, our women have adopted the French feminist discourse over the past thirty years. So because they have adopted the French feminist discourse they criticize us a lot, they hold their heads high, they try to impose their ideas on us and so it's true that if we look superficially, we notice in Martinique, for example, that there is no female mayor, there is no female deputy, no female senator. Women are really ill-represented politically. But I often ask whether political representation is real power because this same male politician who is elected is at the mercy of his wife at home, etc. What is more, we have seen in Guadeloupe something that made everyone laugh . . . A mayor had been sacked because he had embezzled some money and he said to himself: "I'm not going to lose the mayor's office." He had his wife elected. And he told his wife: "listen, when my sentence and the loss of my civic rights is over, you will give the job back to me." She said "yes" and when the period ended she refused . . . and so there were elections and there were two lists, "Mr. and Mrs. X" . . . and in the end they both missed out on the office of Mayor. But that shows nonetheless that women refuse to act as objects. In the past that wouldn't have happened, the woman would have completely given in. So all these tales that you read in French Caribbean literature describe something which hasn't really been true for the last thirty years. The plantation society collapsed at the end of the '60s. At the end of the 1960s the sugar cane industry collapsed. The sugar and rum factories closed in massive numbers and so people immigrated to Fort-de-France, country people, and at the same time we moved from the status of colony to that of a department of France. So France was faced with this economic disaster and they had to deal with it. France distributed aid, subsidies and so on so that we could carry on. France educated people, everyone had a TV, a radio and there was massive cultural 'Frenchification" from the end of the 1960s. From the very beginning of this very strong "Frenchification" people identified with the male-female behavior that existed in France—not completely but in large part. To give a very simple example, I was born on the threshold of two civilizations. For three centuries we were governed by the plantation. I was born in the 1950s and when I was a child and even an adolescent you never saw a couple walking hand in hand or a man kissing a woman on the mouth as you see in Europe or the US. For us that is scandalous. And even today in Fort-de-France you don't see people walking hand in hand or kissing and so on. It is not a part of our culture. But young students of 20 or 25 do it because it's normal. And each time I see this behavior I'm shocked. That is not my world, because they watch TV—*Baywatch*, *Dallas*, soapies, and that's all. We're completely hooked on France. And this map (of the Caribbean and South America) that I've put up on my wall is to reassure me that I'm in America, one hour away from Venezuela. But if you ask anybody "who is the president of Venezuela?" they won't know.

BT: What are the implications of being part of Europe but so close to America?

RC: Geography doesn't play any role today, especially with the Internet and television. For example, when you put your Visa card in the ATM when you need some money, the control center is in Lyons. When I put in my Visa card and I type in my PIN it is checked in Lyons within a fraction of a second. So distance has been completely abolished and that is dangerous for our culture. And then since everything is French here, and European, people don't know the Caribbean or the United States. It's so easy to go to France and I've tried this out on myself. When I go to France I pack my bags on the morning of my flight even though it's an eight-hour flight. But when I go the United States I'm stressed out for a week beforehand, worrying about where my passport is and so on. And afterwards I say "I'm mad." It's a two-hour flight but it's extraordinary because in my head it's not a two-hour flight. The United States seem so far away whereas France . . . I leave at 7am. I throw a few things in a bag and then I leave. I know that when I arrive I won't have any problems . . . I show my passport, I go through, nobody is going to bother me. Whereas when I go to the United States I'm a foreigner, etc. So it's not about geographical proximity. Today, unfortunately, our culture is being threatened because of the French education system that dominates Martinique. All the houses have televisions, French television stations and so forth. There are a lot of French Caribbean people who live in France and a lot of French people who live here, which overshadows the Creole culture in a tragic way if I can put it like that.

BT: Is there a movement to reinvigorate the Creole culture?

RC: We've been fighting for twenty years, especially here at the university, but also outside it, to standardize the language, to give it a place in schools, in the media, but we are doing it at a time when the younger generation has changed its mother tongue. Creole has become our second language. They all speak Creole, but it has changed. In other words, French has become our first language and so perhaps it is too late. Perhaps it is like in Corsica, in Brittany, where they have really left things too late. We have created a recognizable spelling system, we have dictionaries, grammar books, books, novels, and there are two TV channels and one radio station which broadcast the news in Creole. So it is being seen as increasingly important. But France is very Jacobin. It has never accepted dialects, other languages and so on. It only makes concessions when it knows they are no threat. So, for example, Corsican and Breton is hardly spoken so France doesn't care, it lets it go . . . but when they were spoken they wouldn't back down because France has a Jacobin conception of languages. As for us, we've been protected by distance because distance was an important factor in the eighteenth and nineteenth centuries and in the first half of the twentieth century. From the 1960s, '70s, when distance was no longer important, the erosion began and that's where the Creole culture and language are threatened. That's clear. At least we're trying to fight, trying to save what we can, not only to save it, but to bring our culture and our language into the modern age, to put it on the Internet, to do things with it. But we're not at all sure of the outcome. I'm very pessimistic because three-quarters of French Caribbean people remain hostile to Creole culture. Yes, it's not like in Corsica or Brittany where people are passionately attached to their culture. And if people are not attached to Creole culture, they don't care. They want to be French. For example, even in this university, our French Caribbean colleagues in other areas don't exactly despise us in the Creole areas but they look down on us. There's a kind of poster which was put up in the Arts building yesterday where students denounced a Caribbean teacher who teaches English because a student spoke to him in Creole and he said: "Sir, we're not in Haiti here, we're in France so speak French." They got into an argument and went to the dean and there was a huge scandal. But this teacher was only expressing what 90 percent of the Caribbean teachers on this campus think of Creole and Creole culture. English teachers, German teachers, philosophy teachers, linguistics teachers, whatever, they don't give a damn. We're activists so we think we're having a big effect and that activism is winning, but actually . . .

BT: There seems to be a discrepancy between the independence movement and the majority of the population which doesn't have much regard for Creole culture.

RC: Yes because we're trapped. We're trapped by the fact that France couldn't take on black Africa or Algeria because there were too many people, there was an indigenous culture that was too old and so they had to leave. But, first of all, the French Caribbean doesn't have a very old atavistic culture, it's a culture that is three centuries old like the United States. Secondly, we're very small with a very small population. So we cost practically nothing for France. It's 0.0002 percent of the budget and as for the European budget, let's not even talk about it. It's 0.000002 percent of the budget and so it costs nothing for France to construct roads, to do everything they do. It's all useless with these huge traffic jams. In fact, it's extraordinary, everyone has a car, it's completely crazy. It costs them nothing because they tell themselves that all the products here are French anyway, when you go to the supermarket there are French products so even if it costs them, they're French products and so the money comes back again. It gives France a foothold in America. So when the Air France planes land they don't have to pay anything, it gives them a base, and French Guiana is a rocket launching pad. We're trapped by the fact that France can easily take on the maintenance of its territories here. It costs France nothing. And France says to itself "I'm not going to make the same mistakes as in black Africa or Algeria, I'm going to give them a good standard of living so they won't revolt and that way it won't cost us too much." So when you say to people: "we must revolt and become independent," people will ask why because France doesn't oppress us, doesn't do anything to us, we can do what we want, the independence fighters can express themselves, we have the best standard of living in the whole of the Caribbean and Latin America. No one in the street will ask you for money, there are no beggars in the street and no lepers. If you arrive in the island just next door, five minutes by plane from here, you will be surrounded by people at the airport asking for money, poverty-stricken people, in Venezuela, everywhere. So people think it over, they think that maybe they would like to be independent like the other Caribbean or South American people, but the cost is too high. But what is the price of not being independent? In the end, the price is total "Frenchification" be-

cause France does nothing to encourage the Caribbean culture, everything we get is by fighting for it. But what we get are only crumbs. There
is a televised news program in Creole for twenty minutes each day, but
television broadcasts all day, so that means there is twenty-three hours
and forty minutes of French, which is symbolic. They provide things
which are going to appease us a bit, those who are nationalists, but I tell
you that the problem now is that objectively we are completely trapped
because we're too small. If we were a country of four, five, ten million
people we would have cost a bit too much. But 400,000 inhabitants is
nothing, it's not even equal to a large town in France. Even if it costs them,
at least they know that they are there, under the French flag, and there's
no problem. So in the streets there are no police officers, the police force is
French Caribbean in fact, as well as the state security police (CRS), the
cops, everyone. People don't get the impression they are being dominated
by a foreign power. But when there was "classical colonization" in Algeria and Africa, for example, the police officers were white Frenchmen, the
policemen and everyone. But here the "colonization" is completely disguised. When you go to court there are French Caribbean judges and
when you go to university most of the lecturers are Caribbean. So where
does the domination come from? But it's there because when you turn on
the television it's TF1, Antenne 2, the programs are French programs, the
same as in Bordeaux and Marseilles. At the same time there are advantages because we have a good standard of living, a culture, a passport that
allows us to go all over the world. On the other hand it's bad because it's
completely destroying our culture. So we're trapped, that's what I mean
by trapped. In other words, either we choose to protect our culture in
which case there is a price to pay, economic, etc., which is very high, or we
choose to stay in the system but the price of that is the destruction of our
culture. So we're trapped. What is the choice? When you ask people to
choose they choose the easy option: to stay in the system. To give you a
linguistic example, when I was a child there was no television; I saw television for the first time when I was fifteen. We didn't know French slang
words; at that time the slang words were "bagnole" (wheels), "gonzesse"
(chick), etc. I didn't know them, I knew classical French. But my son
knows all the urban slang "la meuf" (chick), "le keuf" (cop), etc. He tells
me: "I saw that on TV." They're directly plugged into French reality,
which was not the case with me. They talk like people from the suburbs,
they have the same taste, rap, etc. Here we try to be as French as possible
because you need to know that after the abolition of slavery and during
slavery black people weren't men, they were animals. When they got
French nationality, French citizenship, they didn't stop wanting to be
French, to learn French. And this symbolizes a return to the past for everything that is Creole culture. They don't even think that Creole culture can

be modern; even if it comes from the plantation it can be modernized. For them it's a step back. For example, it's a scandal in country schools if the children speak French badly. They apply a French law which says that English must be taught in primary schools and Creole is excluded. So already the child doesn't speak the primary language, French, well and then to learn a third language, English, all serves to exclude Creole. People are very francophone so that doesn't pose any problems. But as soon as you leave Lamentin or Fort-de-France or Schoelcher and you go into the villages, it's Creole that people mainly speak. And in the countryside it's Creole more than anything. It's because of that that I say it's threatened. For us, defending Creole is tied to a national feeling; for us, if Creole culture disappeared . . . all political struggle would lose interest for me. What is the point of fighting for independence if the country is completely "Frenchified"? The interest is in having an original culture. The only difference between a French person and a Martinican is in fact the Creole language and culture. If there was a referendum to ask Martinicans if they want to be independent like the other islands, 90 percent would say no. That's the trap I was talking about before . . .

BT: Can we apply European feminism to the French Caribbean woman?

RC: As Henri Val said, French culture has established itself here in a huge way but it hasn't managed to make Creole culture disappear, so men and women here have retained a sort of double personality. Women are Creole when it suits them and French when it suits them. They're French when it comes to demanding equal rights and Creole when it comes to other things. But we men do that too . . . We're completely ambivalent. Who is more opposed to Creole? It's women. Women say to themselves: "I want my child to succeed at school, but if I let him/her speak Creole, when the whole system is in French" . . . They're not totally wrong to be anti-Creole. The system doesn't give opportunities to those who speak Creole. All women here ban their children from speaking Creole, which is something fathers don't do because they are not involved with the children's upbringing. So all those who apply the system of "Frenchification" are women . . . It's true that we're macho, that Martinican literature is a bit macho. We've even been accused of being antihomosexual because we never talk about homosexuals in our novels . . . But why am I going to talk about homosexuals, there is no homosexual movement here . . . I'm not going to write about the life of homosexuals when in reality I never encounter it. It doesn't exist socially, it doesn't have any relevance. So to please the politically correct I'm going to put women, whatever; no, it's because I describe reality and it is like that. Of course, it is in the process of changing and it's for that reason that Chamoiseau and I can't write novels that are set in the present, it's not possible. No, for me, my imagining stops in 1960. I can't write about anything that comes after that. So people tell me "you write novels about the past, and that's not interesting. Write about today." Often I meet readers who tell me that. But what do they want me to write about? The life of a lawyer or a teacher who gets in the car in the morning, spends two hours in traffic jams, gets to work, does some French work and watches TV at home, French TV. I haven't got anything to say about that. So it's true that our novels are always set . . . in 1960, 1965 at the latest. But after that, I can't imagine the modern day. And Chamoiseau and I play the tragic role by saying that we are the first French Caribbean generation to become old at forty. Because a generation normally becomes old at seventy. In other words, when you are seventy or eighty years old you realize that the world you grew up in has disappeared. But for us when we were thirty or forty years old the plantation world of our childhood completely collapsed. And so at thirty or forty years old we could still imagine it. We are the last generation, Chamoiseau and I and others, Pépin and so forth, to be able to imagine plantation life. We are the last from fifty or sixty years ago. When we were ten, twelve or thirteen it started to collapse and when we were twenty-five or thirty it was completely dead. So Chamoiseau has this magnificent saying "we were old at forty" and it's for that reason that we can't speak . . . we are old.

Bibliography

PRIMARY TEXTS

Patrick Chamoiseau

Chronique des sept misères. Paris: Gallimard, 1986.
Solibo Magnifique. Paris: Gallimard, 1988.
Texaco. Paris: Gallimard, 1992.
Texaco. Trans. Rose-Myriam Réjouis and Val Vinokurov. New York: Vintage International, 1998.
Solibo Magnificent. Trans. Rose-Myriam Réjouis and Val Vinokurov. New York: Vintage International, 1999.

Maryse Condé

Moi, Tituba, sorcière . . . noire de Salem. Paris: Mercure de France, 1986.
Les Derniers Rois mages. Paris: Mercure de France, 1992.
I, Tituba, Black Witch of Salem. Trans. Richard Philcox. New York: Ballantine Books, 1994.
The Last of the African Kings. Trans. Richard Philcox. Lincoln: University of Nebraska Press, 1997.

Raphaël Confiant

Eau de Café. Paris: Grasset, 1991.
Ravines du devant-jour. Paris: Gallimard, 1993.
Eau de Café. Trans. James Ferguson. New York: Faber & Faber, 1999.

Edouard Glissant

La Lézarde. Paris: Seuil, 1958.
Le Quatrième Siècle. Paris: Seuil, 1964.
La Case du commandeur. Paris: Gallimard, 1997.
The Fourth Century. Trans. Betsy Wing. Lincoln: University of Nebraska Press, 2001.

Gisèle Pineau

La Grande Drive des esprits. Paris: Stock, 1993.
L'Espérance-macadam. Paris: Le Serpent à Plumes, 1995.
The Drifting of Spirits. Trans. J. Michael Dash. London: Quartet Books, 1999.
Macadam Dreams. Trans. C. Dickson. Lincoln: University of Nebraska Press, 2003.

Simone Schwarz-Bart

Pluie et vent sur Télumée Miracle. Paris: Seuil, 1972.
Ti-Jean l'horizon. Paris: Seuil, 1979.
The Bridge of Beyond. Trans. Barbara Bray. London: Victor Gollancz Ltd., a division of The Orion Publishing Group, 1982.

SECONDARY TEXTS

Alibar, France, and Pierette Lembeye-Boy. *Le Couteau seul: La condition féminine aux Antilles. Vol. I: Enfance et adolescence*. Paris: Editions Caribéennes, 1981.
——. *Le Couteau seul: La condition féminine aux Antilles*. Vol. II: *Vies de femmes*. Paris: Editions Caribéennes, 1982.
André, Jacques. *Caraïbales: Études sur la littérature antillaise*. Paris: Editions Caribéennes, 1981.
——. *L'Inceste focal dans la famille noire antillaise*. Paris: Presses Universitaires de France, 1987.
Anim-Addo, Joan. "Introduction." In Joan Anim-Addo (ed.), *Framing the Word: Gender and Genre in Caribbean Women's Writing*. London: Whiting & Birch, 1996.
—— (ed.). *Framing the Word: Gender and Genre in Caribbean Women's Writing*. London: Whiting & Birch, 1996.
Antoine, Régis. *Rayonnants écrivains de la Caraïbe*. Paris: Maisonneuve & Larose, 1998.
Araujo, Nara (ed.). *L'Oeuvre de Maryse Condé: À propos d'une écrivaine politiquement incorrecte*. Paris: L'Harmattan, 1996.
Arnold, A. James. "The Erotics of Colonialism in Contemporary French West Indian Literature." *New West Indian Guide/Nieuwe West-Indische Gids* 68, nos. 1–2 (1994).
—— (ed.). *A History of Literature in the Caribbean*, Volume One: *Hispanic and Francophone Regions*. Philadelphia: John Benjamins, 1994.
——. "The Gendering of *créolité*." In Maryse Condé and Madeleine Cottenet-Hage (eds.). *Penser la créolité*. Paris: Karthala, 1995.

———. "From the Problematic Maroon to a Woman-Centred Creole Project in the Literature of the French West Indies." In Doris Y. Kadish, (ed.), *Slavery in the Caribbean Francophone World: Distant Voices, Forgotten Acts, Forged Identities.* Athens: University of Georgia Press, 2000.

———. "Frantz Fanon, Lafcadio Hearn et la supercherie de 'Mayotte Capécia.'" *Revue de Littérature Comparée* 76 (2002).

———. "Francophone Postcolonial Studies: The Field: Regional vs. Global Models." *Francophone Postcolonial Studies* 1, no. 2 (2003).

Aub-Buscher, Gertrud, and Beverley Ormerod Noakes (eds.). *The Francophone Caribbean Today: Literature, Language Culture.* Kingston: University of the West Indies Press, 2003.

Barriteau, Eudine. "The Construction of a Postmodernist Feminist Theory for Caribbean Social Science Research." *Social and Economic Studies* 41, no. 2 (1992).

———. "Theorizing Gender Systems in the Project of Modernity in the Twentieth-Century Caribbean." *Feminist Review* 59 (1998).

Beauvue-Fougeyrollas, Claudie. *Les Femmes antillaises.* Paris: L'Harmattan, 1979.

Bebel-Gisler, Dany. *Léonora, l'histoire enfouie de la Guadeloupe.* Paris: Seghers, 1985.

Belugue, Geneviève. "Entre ombre et lumière, l'écriture engagée de Gisèle Pineau." *Notre Librairie* 138–39 (1999).

Benjamin, Jessica. *The Bonds of Love: Psychoanalysis, Feminism, and the Problem of Domination.* London: Virago Press, 1990.

Bernabé, Jean, Patrick Chamoiseau and Raphaël Confiant. *Eloge de la Créolité.* Paris: Gallimard, 1989.

Bloch, Ruth H. "A Culturalist Critique of Trends in Feminist Theory." In Nikki R. Keddie (ed.), *Debating Gender, Debating Sexuality.* New York: New York University Press, 1996.

Bonnet, Véronique. "Gisèle Pineau: L'âme prêtée à l'écriture." *Notre Librairie* 138–39 (1999).

Bouchard, Monique. *Une lecture de Pluie et vent sur Télumée Miracle de Simone Schwarz-Bart.* Paris: L'Harmattan, 1990.

Bowlby, John. *Childcare and the Growth of Love.* Harmondsworth: Penguin, 1965.

———. *Attachment and Loss.* New York: Basic Books, 1980.

Britton, Celia M. "Discours and histoire, Magical and Political Discourse in Edouard Glissant's *Le Quatrième Siècle.*" *French Cultural Studies* 5, no. 2[14] (1994).

———. "Opacity and Transparence: Conceptions of History and Cultural Difference in the Work of Edouard Glissant." *French Studies* 49, no. 3 (1995).

———. *Edouard Glissant and Postcolonial Theory: Strategies of Language and Resistance.* Charlottesville: University of Virginia Press, 1999.

Brodber, Erna. *Perceptions of Caribbean Women: Towards a Documentation of Stereotypes.* Cave Hill, Barbados: Institute of Social and Economic Research, University of the West Indies, 1982.

Buchbinder, David. *Masculinities and Identities.* Melbourne: Melbourne University Press, 1994.

Bueno, Eva Paulino, Terry Caesar, and William Hummel (eds.). *Naming the Father: Legacies, Genealogies and Explorations of Fatherhood in Modern and Contemporary Literature.* Lanham, Md.: Lexington Books, 2000.

Burton, Richard D. E. "Comment peut-on être martiniquais? The Recent Work of Edouard Glissant." *Modern Language Review* 79, no. 2 (1984).

——— . "Debrouya pa peche, or Il y a toujours moyen de moyenner: Patterns of Opposition in the Fiction of Patrick Chamoiseau." *Callaloo* 16, no. 2 (1993).

——— . *Le Roman marron: Études sur la littérature martiniquaise contemporaine.* Paris: L'Harmattan, 1997.

——— , and Fred Reno (eds.). *French and West Indian: Martinique, Guadeloupe and French Guiana Today.* London: Macmillan, 1995.

Bush, Barbara. *Slave Women in Caribbean Society 1650–1838.* Bloomington: Indiana University Press, 1990.

Butler, Judith. *Gender Trouble: Feminism and the Subversion of Identity.* New York: Routledge, 1990.

Butler, Sandra. *Conspiracy of Silence: The Trauma of Incest.* New York: Bantam, 1979.

Caldwell, Roy Chandler. "*Créolité* and Postcoloniality in Raphaël Confiant's *L'Allée des soupirs.*" *The French Review*, 73 no. 2 (1999).

Camus, Albert. *L'Etranger.* London: Methuen, 1960.

Capécia, Mayotte. *Je suis martiniquaise.* Paris: Corrêa, 1948.

Césaire, Aimé. *Cahier d'un retour au pays natal.* Paris: Présence Africaine, 1983.

——— . *The Collected Poetry.* Trans. Clayton Eshelman and Annette Smith. Berkeley: University of California Press, 1983.

Chamoiseau, Patrick. "Interview avec Odile Broussillon et Michèle Desbordes." *Notes Bibliographiques Caraïbes* 48 (1988).

——— . Interview by Bonnie Thomas. Martinique, 26 June 2001.

——— , and Raphaël Confiant. *Lettres créoles: Tracées antillaises et continentales de la littérature: Haïti, Guadeloupe, Martinique, Guyane 1655–1975.* Paris: Gallimard, 1999.

Chevannes, Barry. *Learning to Be a Man: Culture, Socialization and Gender Identity in Five Caribbean Communities.* Kingston: University of the West Indies Press, 2001.

Childs, Peter, and Patrick Williams. *An Introduction to Post-Colonial Theory.* Hempstead: Prentice Hall/Harvester Wheatsheaf, 1997.

Chivallon, Christine. "*Texaco* ou l'éloge de la 'spatialité.'" *Notre Librairie* 127 (1996).

Chodorow, Nancy. *The Reproduction of Mothering: Psychoanalysis and the Sociology of Gender.* Berkeley: University of California Press, 1978.

——— . *Feminism and Psychoanalytic Theory.* Cambridge: Polity Press, 1989.

Clark, Vèvè A. "'Je me suis réconciliée avec mon île': Une interview de Maryse Condé." *Callaloo* 12, no. 1 (1989).

Clarke, Edith. *My Mother Who Fathered Me.* London: George Allen & Unwin, 1957.

Clément, Catherine, and Hélène Cixous. *La Jeune Née.* Paris: Union Générale d'Editions, 1975.

Collins, Patricia Hill. *Black Feminist Thought.* London: Routledge, 1990.

Condé, Maryse. *La Parole des femmes: Essai sur des romancières des Antilles de langue française.* Paris: L'Harmattan, 1979.

——— (ed.). *L'Héritage de Caliban.* Paris: Jasor, 1992.

——— . "The Role of the Writer." *World Literature Today* 67, no. 4 (1993).

——— . Interview by Bonnie Thomas. Guadeloupe, 27 June 2001.

——— . Interview by Bonnie Thomas. Perth, 14 July 2005.

——— , and Madeleine Cottenet-Hage (eds.). *Penser la créolité.* Paris: Karthala, 1995.

Confiant, Raphaël. "Préface." In Effe Géache, *Une nuit d'orgie à Saint-Pierre Martinique*. Paris: Arléa, 1992.

———. "Questions pratiques d'écriture créole." In Ralph Ludwig (ed.), *Ecrire la 'parole de nuit': La Nouvelle Littérature antillaise*. Paris: Gallimard, 1994.

———. Interview by Bonnie Thomas. Martinique, 28 June 2001.

Corzani, Jack. *La Littérature des Antilles-Guyanes françaises*. 6 vols. Fort-de-France: Desormeaux, 1978.

Cottenet-Hage, Madeleine and Lydie Moudileno (eds.). *Maryse Condé: Une nomade inconvenante*. Guadeloupe: Ibis Rouge, 2002.

Coulthard, G. R. *Race and Colour in Caribbean Literature*. Oxford: Oxford University Press, 1962.

Cranny-Francis, Anne. *The Body in the Text*. Melbourne: Melbourne University Press, 1995.

Crosta, Suzanne. "Corps, écriture et idéologie dans *Les Derniers Rois mages* de Maryse Condé." In Suzanne Rinne and Joëlle Vitiello (eds.), *Elles écrivent des Antilles*. Paris: L'Harmattan, 1997.

———. "Exil, migration, écriture: une entrevue avec Maryse Condé." In Suzanne Crosta (ed.), *Récits de vie de l'Afrique et des Antilles: enracinement, errance, exil*. Fort-de-France: GRELCA, 1998.

——— (ed.). *Récits de vie de l'Afrique et des Antilles: Enracinement, errance, exil*. Fort-de-France: GRELCA, 1998.

Cudjoe, Selwyn (ed.). *Caribbean Women Writers: Essays from the First International Conference*. Wellesley, Mass.: Calaloux, 1990.

Dagenais, Huguette. "L'Envers du mythe: La situation des femmes en Guadeloupe." *Nouvelles Questions Féministes* 9–10 (*Antillaises* special edition, ed. Arlette Gautier) (1985).

———. "Women in Guadeloupe: The Paradoxes of Reality." In Janet H. Momsen (ed.), *Women and Change in the Caribbean: A Pan-Caribbean Perspective*. Kingston: Ian Randle/ Bloomington: Indiana University Press/ London: James Currey, 1993.

Dash, J. Michael. "In Search of the Lost Body: Re-defining the Subject in Caribbean Literature." *Kunapipi* 11, no. 1 (1989).

———. "Writing the Body: Edouard Glissant's Poetics of Re-membering." *World Literature Today* 63, no. 4 (1989).

———. "Introduction." In A. James Arnold (ed.), *A History of Literature in the Caribbean*. Volume One: *Hispanic and Francophone Regions*. Philadelphia: John Benjamins, 1994.

———. *Edouard Glissant*. Cambridge: Cambridge University Press, 1995.

———. "Afterword." In Gisèle Pineau, *The Drifting of Spirits*, trans. J. Michael Dash. London: Quartet Books, 1999.

Davies, Carole Boyce and Elaine Savory Fido. "Introduction: Women and Literature in the Caribbean: An Overview." In Carole Boyce Davies and Elaine Savory Fido (eds.), *Out of the Kumbla: Caribbean Women and Literature*. Trenton, N.J.: African World Press, 1990.

——— (eds.). *Out of the Kumbla: Caribbean Women and Literature*. Trenton, N.J.: African World Press, 1990.

Dayan, Joan. "Codes of Law and Bodies of Color." In Maryse Condé and Madeleine Cottenet-Hage (eds.), *Penser la créolité*. Paris: Karthala, 1995.

Debien, Gabriel. *Les Esclaves aux Antilles françaises, XVIIe–XVIIIe siècles*. Basse-Terre: Société d'Histoire de la Guadeloupe/ Fort-de-France: Société d'Histoire de la Martinique, 1974.

Deleuze, Gilles, and Felix Guattari. *Mille plateaux*. Paris: Minuit, 1980.

Delvaux, Martine. *Femmes psychiatrisées, femmes rebelles*. Le Plessis-Robinson: Institut Synthélabo, 1998.

Dinnerstein, Dorothy. *The Mermaid and the Minotaur: Sexual Arrangements and Human Malaise*. New York: Harper & Row, 1976.

Duffey, Carolyn. "Tituba and Hester in the Intertextual Jail Cell: New World Feminisms in Maryse Condé's *Moi, Tituba, sorcière . . . noire de Salem*." *Women in French Studies* 4 (1996).

DuFour, M.-J. "Gisèle Pineau: La fin des tabous." *Le Figaro*, 20 May 1998.

——— . "Gisèle Pineau: Infirmière et romancière." *Le Progrès*, 26 October 1998.

Dukats, Mara L. "A Narrative of Violated Maternity: *Moi, Tituba, sorcière . . . noire de Salem*." *World Literature Today* 67, no. 4 (1993).

DuRivage, Françoise. "Texaco: From the Hills to the Mangrove Swamps." *Thamyris* 6, no. 1 (1999).

Edmondson, Belinda (ed.). *Caribbean Romances: The Politics of Regional Representation*. Charlottesville: University of Virginia Press, 1999.

Ellis, Pat (ed.). *Women of the Caribbean*. London: Zed Books, 1986.

Emberley, Julia V. *Thresholds of Difference: Feminist Critique, Native Women's Writings, Postcolonial Theory*. Toronto: University of Toronto Press, 1993.

Ette, Ottmar, and Ralph Ludwig. "En guise d'introduction: points de vue sur l'évolution de la littérature antillaise: entretien avec les écrivains martiniquais Patrick Chamoiseau et Raphaël Confiant." *Lendemains* 67 (1992).

Faithful, Francesca Velayoudom. "La Femme antillaise." *Présence Africaine* 153 (1996).

Fanon, Frantz. *Peau noire, masques blancs*. Paris: Seuil, 1952.

Flax, Jane. "Postmodernism and Gender Relations in Feminist Theory." *Signs* 12, no. 4 (1987).

Fonkoua, Romuald-Blaise. "Edouard Glissant et le langage: Du langage du cri à la raison du langage." *Notre Librairie* 127 (1996).

Fuss, Diana. *Essentially Speaking: Feminism, Nature and Difference*. New York: Routledge, 1989.

Gates, Henry Louis Jr. *Black Literature and Literary Theory*. New York: Methuen, 1984.

——— . *Reading Black, Reading Feminist: A Critical Anthology*. New York: Meridian, 1990.

Gautier, Arlette. "Les Esclaves femmes aux Antilles françaises, 1635–1848." *Réflexions Historiques* 10, no. 3 (1983).

——— . *Les Soeurs de solitude: La Condition féminine dans l'esclavage aux Antilles du 17e au 19e siècles*. Paris: Editions Caribéennes, 1985.

——— . "Sous l'esclavage, le patriarcat." *Nouvelles Questions Féministes* 9–10 (*Antillaises* special edition, ed. Arlette Gautier) (1985).

Gifford, Paul, and Johnnie Gratton (eds.). *Subject Matters: Subject and Self in French Literature from Descartes to the Present*. Amsterdam: Rodopi, 2000.

Gisler, Antoine. *L'Esclavage aux Antilles françaises, XVIIe–XIXe siècles*. Fribourg: Editions Universitaires, 1965.

Glaser, Marlies, and Marion Pausch (eds.). *Caribbean Writers: Between Orality and Writing*. Amsterdam: Rodopi, 1994.

Glissant, Edouard. *Soleil de la conscience*. Paris: Seuil, 1956.

——— . *Le Discours antillais*. Paris: Seuil, 1981.

——— . "Entretien avec le CARÉ." *CARÉ* 10 (1983).

——— . *Caribbean Discourse: Selected Essays*. Trans. J. Michael Dash. Charlottesville: University of Virginia Press, 1989.

——— . *Poétique de la relation*. Paris: Gallimard, 1990.

——— . *Poetics of Relation*. Trans. Betsy Wing. Ann Arbor: University of Michigan Press, 1997.

Goolcharan-Kumeta, Wendy. *My Mother, My Country: Reconstructing the Female Self in Guadeloupean Women's Writing*. Bern: Peter Lang, 2003.

Gracchus, Fritz. "L'Antillais et la question du père." *CARÉ* 4 (1979).

——— . *Les Lieux de la mère dans les sociétés afro-américaines*. Paris: Editions Caribéennes, 1986.

Greene, Sue N. "Report on the Second International Conference of Caribbean Women Writers." *Callaloo* 13, no. 3 (1990).

——— . "Report on the Third International Caribbean Women's Writer's Conference." *Callaloo* 15, no. 1 (1992).

Grosz, Elizabeth. *Jacques Lacan: A Feminist Introduction*. St. Leonards: Allen & Unwin, 1990.

Guérin, Daniel. *Les Antilles décolonisées*. Paris: Présence Africaine, 1956.

Gyssels, Kathleen. "Du titre au roman: *Texaco* de Patrick Chamoiseau." *Roman 20–50* 20 (1995).

——— . "Feminine Identity and Closed Space in the Caribbean Novel: The Works of Simone Schwarz-Bart, André Schwarz-Bart and Beryl Gilroy." *Canadian Revue of Caribbean Literature* 22, nos. 3–4 (1995).

——— . "Dans la toile d'araignée: Conversations entre maître et esclave dans *Pluie et vent sur Télumée Miracle*." In Suzanne Rinne and Joëlle Vitiello (eds.), *Elles écrivent des Antilles*. Paris: L'Harmattan, 1997.

——— . "L'Exil selon Pineau, récit de vie et autobiographie." In Suzanne Crosta (ed.), *Récits de vie de l'Afrique et des Antilles: Enracinement, errance, exil*. Fort-de-France: GRELCA, 1998.

——— . "La Difficile inscription de/dans l'(H)*histoire*: Le corpus schwarz-bartien." In Thomas Bremer and Ulrich Fleischmann (eds.), *History and Histories in the Caribbean*. Frankfurt: Vervuert/ Madrid: Iberoamericana, 2001.

Haigh, Sam (ed.). *An Introduction to Caribbean Francophone Writing*. New York: Berg, 1999.

——— . *Mapping a Tradition: Francophone Women's Writing from Guadeloupe*. London: Maney Publishing, 2000.

Hallward, Peter. "Edouard Glissant between the Singular and the Specific." *Yale Journal of Criticism* 11, no. 2 (1998).

Hawkins, Peter, and Annette Lavers. *Protée noire: Essais sur la littérature francophone de l'Afrique noire et des Antilles*. Paris: L'Harmattan, 1992.

Hazaël-Massieux, Marie-Christine. "À propos de *Chronique des sept misères*: Une littérature en français régional pour les Antilles." *Antilla* 11 (décembre 1988–janvier 1989).

———. "Chamoiseau, cet écrivain qui écrit le créole directement en français." *Portulan* (2000).

Hellerstein, Nina. "Violence, mythe et destin dans l'univers antillais de Gisèle Pineau." *Littéréalité* 10, no. 1 (1998).

Helm, Yolande (ed.). *L'Eau: Source d'une écriture dans les littératures féminines francophones.* New York: Peter Lang, 1995.

Helm, Yolande. "Prolégomènes." In Yolande Helm (ed.), *L'Eau: Source d'une écriture dans les littératures féminines francophones.* New York: Peter Lang, 1995.

Hennessy, Alistair (ed.). *Intellectuals in the Twentieth-Century Caribbean.* Volume II, *Unity in Variety: The Hispanic and Francophone Caribbean.* London: Macmillan, 1992.

Henry-Valmore, Simonne. *Dieux en exil.* Paris: Gallimard, 1988.

———. "La Place n'était pas vide . . . de la psychanalyse aux Antilles: Mythes et réalités." *Oeuvres et Critiques* 19, no. 2 (1994).

Herman, Judith Lewis. *Father-Daughter Incest.* Cambridge, Mass.: Harvard University Press, 1981.

Herndon, Gerise. "Gender Construction and Neocolonialism." *World Literature Today* 67, no. 4 (1993).

Hewitt, Leah D. "Condé's Critical Seesaw." *Callaloo* 18, no. 3 (1995).

———. "Rencontres explosives: Les intersections culturelles de Maryse Condé." In Nara Araujo (ed.), *L'Oeuvre de Maryse Condé: À propos d'une écrivaine politiquement incorrecte.* Paris: L'Harmattan, 1996.

Higman, Barry. *Slave Population and Economy in Jamaica, 1807–1834.* Cambridge: Cambridge University Press, 1976.

Hilaire, Marie-Michelle. *Martinique: Familles, enfants et société.* Saint-Estève: Nouvelles du Sud, 1997.

hooks, bell. *Talking Back: Thinking Feminist, Thinking Black.* Boston: South End Press, 1989.

Hrdy, Sarah Blaffer. *The Woman That Never Evolved.* Cambridge, Mass.: Harvard University Press, 1981.

Irigaray, Luce. *This Sex Which Is Not One.* Ithaca, N.Y.: Cornell University Press, 1985.

Jacobs, Michael. *Sigmund Freud.* London: Sage Publications, 1992.

Kadish, Doris Y. (ed.). *Slavery in the Caribbean Francophone World: Distant Voices, Forgotten Acts, Forged Identities.* Athens: University of Georgia Press, 2000.

Kadish, Doris Y. "Guadeloupean Women Remember Slavery." *The French Review* 77, no. 6 (2004).

Keddie, Nikki R. (ed.). *Debating Gender, Debating Sexuality.* New York: New York University Press, 1996.

Kemedjio, Cilas. "De *Ville cruelle* de Mongo Beti à *Texaco* de Patrick Chamoiseau: Fortification, ethnicité et globalisation dans la ville postcoloniale." *Esprit Créateur* 41, no. 3 (2001).

Kesteloot, Lilyan. *Aimé Césaire.* Paris: Seghers, 1962.

Knight, Vere W. "Edouard Glissant: The Novel as History Rewritten." *Black Images* 3, no. 1 (1974).

Kom, Ambroise. "Négritude." In Peter France (ed.), *New Oxford Companion to Literature in French.* Oxford: Clarendon Press, 1995.

Landry, Donna, and Gerald MacLean (eds.). *The Spivak Reader*. New York: Routledge, 1996.

Larrier, Renée. "'Crier/écrire/cahier': Anagrammatic Configurations of Voice in Francophone Caribbean Narratives." *The French Review* 69 (1995).

Le-Fol, Sebastien. "Gisèle Pineau: La fin des tabous." *Le Figaro*, 20 mai 1998.

Leiris, Michel. *Contacts de civilisations en Martinique et en Guadeloupe*. Paris: UNESCO, 1955.

Lesel, Livia. *Le Père oblitéré: Chronique antillaise d'une illusion*. Paris: L'Harmattan, 1995.

Loichot, Valérie. "La Créolité à l'oeuvre dans *Ravines du devant-jour* de Raphaël Confiant." *The French Review* 71, no. 4 (1998).

———. "Negations and Subversions of Paternal Authorities in Glissant's Fictional Works (*Le Quatrième Siècle, La Case du commandeur, Tout-monde*)." In Eva Paulino Bueno, Terry Caesar, and William Hummel (eds.), *Naming the Father: Explorations of Fatherhood in Modern and Contemporary Literature*. Lanham, Md.: Lexington Books, 2000.

Ludwig, Ralph (ed.). *Ecrire la 'parole de nuit': la nouvelle littérature antillaise*. Paris: Gallimard, 1994.

Makward, Christiane. *Mayotte Capécia ou l'aliénation selon Fanon*. Paris: Karthala, 1999.

———. "Presque un siècle de différence amoureuse: Simone Schwarz-Bart (1972), Gisèle Pineau (1996)." *Nottingham French Studies* 40, no. 1 (2001).

Manzor-Coats, Lillian. "Of Witches and Other Things: Maryse Condé's Challenges to Feminist Discourse." *World Literature Today* 67, no. 4 (1993).

McClintock, Anne. *Imperial Leather: Race, Gender and Sexuality in the Colonial Contest*. New York: Routledge, 1995.

McCusker, Maeve. "De la problématique du territoire à la problématique du lieu: Un entretien avec Patrick Chamoiseau." *The French Review* 73, no. 4 (2000).

Mekel, Alexyna. "Interview with Maryse Condé." *Caribbean Contact* (1989).

Milne, Lorna. "From *Créolité* to *Diversalité*: The Postcolonial Subject in Patrick Chamoiseau's *Texaco*." In Paul Gifford and Johnnie Gratton (eds.), *Subject Matters: Subject and Self in French Literature from Descartes to the Present*. Amsterdam: Rodopi, 2000.

Milne, Lorna. "Sex, Gender and the Right to Write: Patrick Chamoiseau and the Erotics of Colonialism." *Paragraph* 24, no. 3 (2001).

Mohammed, Patricia. "Nuancing the Feminist Discourse in the Caribbean." *Social and Economic Studies* 43, no. 3 (1994).

———. "Towards Indigenous Feminist Theorizing in the Caribbean." *Feminist Review* 59 (1998).

Mohanty, Chandra Talpade. "Under Western Eyes: Feminist Scholarship and Colonial Discourses." In Chandra Talpade Mohanty, Ann Russo, and Lourdes Torres (eds.), *Third World Women and the Politics of Feminism*. Bloomington: Indiana University Press, 1991.

———, Ann Russo, and Lourdes Torres (eds.). *Third World Women and the Politics of Feminism*. Bloomington: Indiana University Press, 1991.

Mordecai, Pamela, and Betty Wilson (eds.). *Her True-True Name: An Anthology of Women's Writing from the Caribbean*. Oxford: Heinemann, 1990.

Mortimer, Mildred. "A Sense of Place and Space in Maryse Condé's *Les Derniers Rois mages.*" *World Literature Today* 67, no. 4 (1993).

Moss, Jane. "Postmodernizing the Salem Witchcraze: Maryse Condé's *I, Tituba, Black Witch of Salem.*" *Colby Quarterly* 35, no. 1 (1999).

Moudileno, Lydie. "Portrait of the Artist as a Dreamer: Maryse Condé's *Traversée de la mangrove* and *Les Derniers Rois mages.*" *Callaloo* 18, no. 3 (1995).

Murdoch, H. Adlai. *Creole Identity in the French Caribbean Novel.* Gainesville: University Press of Florida, 2001.

Murray, David A. B. "Homosexuality, Society, and the State: An Ethnography of Sublime Resistance in Martinique." *Identities* 2, no. 3 (1996).

Nasta, Susheila (ed.). *Motherlands: Black Women's Writing from Africa, the Caribbean, and South Asia.* London: Women's Press, 1991.

N'fah-Abbenyi, Juliana Makuchi. *Gender in African Women's Writing: Identity, Sexuality and Difference.* Bloomington: Indiana University Press, 1997.

Ngal, M. a M. *Aimé Césaire: Un homme à la recherche d'une patrie.* Dakar: Les Nouvelles Editions Africaines, 1975.

N'Zengou-Tayo, Marie-José. "Littérature et diglossia: Créer une langue métisse ou la 'chamoisification' du français dans *Texaco* de Patrick Chamoiseau." *Traduction, Terminologie, Rédaction* 9, no. 1 (1996).

O'Callaghan, Evelyn. *Woman Version: Theoretical Approaches to West Indian Fiction by Women.* London: Macmillan Caribbean, 1993.

Ormerod, Beverley. "Beyond Négritude: Some Aspects of the Work of Edouard Glissant." *Savacou* 11–12 (1975).

———. "Discourse and Dispossession: Edouard Glissant's Image of Contemporary Martinique." *Caribbean Quarterly* 27, no. 4 (1981).

———. *An Introduction to the French Caribbean Novel.* London: Heinemann, 1985.

———. "Magical Realism in Contemporary French Caribbean Literature: Ideology or Literary Diversion?" *Australian Journal of French Studies* 34, no. 2 (1997).

———. "The Representation of Women in French Caribbean Fiction." In Sam Haigh (ed.), *An Introduction to Caribbean Francophone Writing.* Oxford: Berg, 1999.

Pageaux, Daniel-Henry. "Raphaël Confiant ou la traversée paradoxale d'une décennie." *Portulan* (1996).

Paravisini-Gebert, Lizabeth and Olga Torres-Seda (eds.). *Caribbean Women Novelists: An Annotated Bibliography.* Westport, Conn.: Greenwood Press, 1993.

Parker, Rozsika. *Torn in Two: The Experience of Maternal Ambivalence.* London: Virago Press, 1995.

Patterson, Orlando. *The Sociology of Slavery.* London: MacGibbon & Kee, 1967.

Pausch, Marion. "'Exprimer la complexité antillaise à l'aide de la tradition orale': Interview avec Patrick Chamoiseau." In Marlies Glaser and Marion Pausch (eds.), *Caribbean Writers: Between Orality and Writing.* Amsterdam: Rodopi, 1994.

Pfaff, Françoise. *Entretiens avec Maryse Condé.* Paris: Karthala, 1993.

———. *Conversations with Maryse Condé.* Lincoln: University of Nebraska Press, 1996.

Pinalie, Pierre. Interview by Bonnie Thomas. Martinique, 28 June 2001.

Pineau, Gisèle. "Écrire en tant que Noire." In Maryse Condé and Madeleine Cottenet-Hage (eds.), *Penser la créolité.* Paris: Karthala, 1995.

——— . Interview by Bonnie Thomas. Paris, 12 July 2001.

——— , and Marie Abraham. *Femmes ies Antilles: Traces et voix*. Paris: Stock, 1998.

Price, Richard, and Sally Price. "Shadowboxing in the Mangrove: The Politics of Identity in Postcolonial Martinique " In Belinda J. Edmondson (ed.), *Caribbean Romances: The Politics of Regional Representation*. Charlottesville: University of Virginia Press, 1999.

Proulx, Patrice J. "Situer le 'moi' féminin dans *Pluie et vent sur Télumée Miracle*." In Suzanne Rinne and Joëlle Vitiello (eds.), *Elles écrivent des Antilles*. Paris: L'Harmattan, 1997.

Reiter, Reyna (ed.). *Toward an Anthropology of Women*. New York: Monthly Review Press, 1975.

Rinne, Suzanne, and Joëlle Vitiello (eds.). *Elles écrivent des Antilles*. Paris: L'Harmattan, 1997.

Rosello, Mireille. *Littérature et identité créole aux Antilles*. Paris: Karthala, 1992.

——— . "*Les Derniers Rois mages* et *La Traversée de la mangrove*: Insularité ou insularisation?" In Suzanne Rinne, and Joëlle Vitiello (eds.), *Elles écrivent des Antilles*. Paris: L'Harmattan, 1997.

Rubin, Gayle. "The Traffic in Women: Notes on the 'Political Economy' of Sex." In Reyna Reiter (ed.), *Toward an Anthropology of Women*. New York: Monthly Review Press, 1975.

Scarboro, Ann Armstrong. "Afterword." In Maryse Condé, *I, Tituba, Black Witch of Salem*. New York: Ballantine Books, 1994.

Scharfman, Ronnie. "Mirroring and Mothering in Simone Schwarz-Bart's *Pluie et vent sur Télumée Miracle* and Jean Rhys' *Wide Sargasso Sea*." *Yale French Studies* 62 (1981).

Schnepel, Ellen M. "The Other Tongue, The Other Voice: Language and Gender in the French Caribbean." *Ethnic Groups* 10, no. 4 (1993).

Senior, Olive. *Working Miracles: Women's Lives in the English-Speaking Caribbean*. Cave Hill, Barbados: Institute of Social and Economic Research, University of the West Indies; London: James Currey; Bloomington: Indiana University Press, 1991.

Seringe, Philippe. *Les Symboles: Dans l'art, dans les religions et dans la vie de tous les jours*. Genève: Helios, 1985.

Sheridan, Richard. *The Development of the Plantations to 1750: An Era of West Indian Prosperity 1750–1775*. Kingston: Caribbean Universities Press, 1970.

Sinclair, J. M. (ed.). *Collins English Dictionary*. Sydney: HarperCollins, 2001.

Smith, Raymond T. *Kinship and Class in the West Indies: A Genealogical Study of Jamaica and Guyana*. Cambridge: Cambridge University Press, 1988.

Sourieau, Marie-Agnès. "Patrick Chamoiseau, *Solibo Magnifique*: From the Escheat of Speech to the Emergence of a Language." *Callaloo* 15, no. 1 (1992).

——— . "Un entretien avec Maryse Condé: L'identité culturelle." *The French Review* 72, no. 6 (1999).

Spear, Thomas C. "Les Perles de la parlure de Raphaël Confiant." In Maryse Condé (ed.), *L'Héritage de Caliban*. Paris: Jasor, 1992.

——— . "Jouissances carnavalesques: Représentation de la sexualité." In Maryse Condé and Madeleine Cottenet-Hage (eds.), *Penser la créolité*. Paris: Karthala, 1995.

Suárez, Lucía M. "Gisèle Pineau: Writing the Dimensions of Migration." *World Literature Today* 75, nos. 3–4 (2001).

Summers, Anne. *Damned Whores and God's Police*. Ringwood, Victoria: Penguin, 1994.

Taleb-Khyer, Mohamed B. "An Interview with Maryse Condé and Rita Dove." *Callaloo* 14, no. 2 (1991).

Taylor, Lucien. "Mediating Martinique: The 'Paradoxical Trajectory' of Raphaël Confiant." In George E. Marcus (ed.), *Cultural Producers in Perilous States*. Chicago: University of Chicago Press, 1997.

——— . "Créolité Bites: A Conversation with Patrick Chamoiseau, Raphaël Confiant and Jean Bernabé." *Transition* 7, no. 2 (1998).

Tong, Rosemarie. *Feminist Thought: A Comprehensive Introduction*. London: Routledge, 1994.

Toumson, Héliane, and Roger Toumson. "Interview avec Simone et André Schwarz-Bart: Sur les pas de Fanotte." In *Textes, études et documents* 2 (1979).

Toumson, Roger. "La Littérature antillaise d'expression française." *Présence Africaine* 121–22 (1982).

Toureh, Fanta. *L'Imaginaire dans l'oeuvre de Simone Schwarz-Bart*. Paris: L'Harmattan, 1986.

Ussher, Jane. *Women's Madness: Misogyny or Mental Illness?* Amherst: University of Massachusetts Press, 1991.

Vitiello, Joëlle. "Le Corps de l'île dans les écrits de Gisèle Pineau." In Suzanne Rinne and Joëlle Vitiello (eds.), *Elles écrivent des Antilles*. Paris: L'Harmattan, 1997.

Walker, Alice. *In Search of Our Mothers' Gardens: Womanist Prose*. London: The Women's Press, 1987.

Walvin, James. *Black Ivory: A History of British Slavery*. London: HarperCollins, 1992.

Whitford, Margaret (ed.). *The Irigaray Reader*. Cambridge: Blackwell, 1991.

Wieringa, Saskia (ed.). *Subversive Women: Women's Movements in Africa, Asia, Latin America and the Caribbean*. London: Atlantic Highlands, 1995.

Williams, Patrick, and Laura Chrisman (eds.). *Discourse and Post-colonial Theory: A Reader*. Hemel Hempstead: Harvester Wheatsheaf, 1993.

Wilson, Elizabeth. "Sorcières, sorcières: *Moi, Tituba, sorcière . . . noire de Salem*, révision et interrogation." In Nara Araujo (ed.), *L'Oeuvre de Maryse Condé: À propos d'une écrivaine politiquement incorrecte*. Paris: L'Harmattan, 1996.

Woolf, Virginia. *A Room of One's Own*. London: Grafton, 1977.

Index

About the Author

Bonnie Thomas completed her PhD on contemporary French Caribbean literature in 2003 at the University of Western Australia. She immediately took up a position in French Studies at Macquarie University in Sydney, before returning to the University of Western Australia in 2004 as a lecturer in French and francophone literature. Bonnie has a passion for teaching and learning and in 2002 was a Teaching Intern and in 2005 a Teaching Fellow at the University of Western Australia. She is also the recipient of awards for teaching excellence and has published articles on teaching French at the university level. Bonnie has published widely on French Caribbean identity issues and is currently working on her second book project, which focuses on history, memory and resilience in contemporary French Caribbean literature. She has also been involved in organizing international conferences at the University of Western Australia, including the 2005 Australian Society of French Studies conference at which Maryse Condé and Richard Philcox were the keynote speakers.